Production and Decision Theory under Uncertainty

Production and Decision Theory under Uncertainty

KARL AIGINGER

Basil Blackwell

©Karl Aiginger, 1987

First published 1987

Basil Blackwell Ltd
108 Cowley Road, Oxford, OX4 1JF, UK

Basil Blackwell Inc.
432 Park Avenue South, Suite 1503
New York, NY 10016, USA

All rights reserved. Except for the quotation of short passages for the purposes of criticism and review, no part of this publication may be reproduced, stored in a retrieval system, or transmitted, in any form or by any means, electronic, mechanical, photocopying, recording or otherwise, without the prior permission of the publisher.

Except in the United States of America, this book is sold subject to the condition that it shall not, by way of trade or otherwise, be lent, re-sold, hired out, or otherwise circulated without the publisher's prior consent in any form of binding or cover other than that in which it is published and without a similar condition including this condition being imposed on the subsequent purchaser.

British Library Cataloguing in Publication Data
Aiginger, Karl
 Production and decision theory under
 uncertainty. – (Uncertainty and
 expectations in economics).
 1. Production management – Mathematical
 models 2. Decision making – Mathematical
 models 3. Mathematical optimization
 I. Title II. Series
 658.5'036'0724   TS155

ISBN 0-631-14792-6

Library of Congress Cataloging-in-Publication Data
Aiginger, Karl.
 Production and decision theory under uncertainty.

 Bibliography: p.
 Includes index.
 1. Production functions (Economic theory)
 2. Decision making. 3. Uncertainty. I. Title.
 HB241.A52   1987   338.5   87-23854
 ISBN 0-631-14792-6

Typeset by Dobbie Typesetting Service, Plymouth, Devon
Printed in Great Britain by T.J. Press (Padstow) Ltd, Padstow, Cornwall

To ELSA, TOM and PHIL

Contents

List of tables	x
Part I Introduction	1
1 The impact of uncertainty – a theoretical topic of great relevance for real-world behaviour	**3**
1.1 The aim of the book: confrontation of theories with empirical evidence	3
1.2 Structure	5
1.3 The innovative content of the treatise	9
1.4 Some concepts used	11
Part II Theoretical part	13
2 Interpreting reported expectations as optimal decisions (actions) under uncertainty	**15**
2.1 The empirical phenomenon of biased reported expectations	17
2.2 Biasedness and rationality	18
2.3 Interpreting reported expectations as optimal forecasts under uncertainty	21
2.4 Where to go from here	25
3 Expected utility maximization and its alternatives	**28**
4 General propositions on the influence of uncertainty on optimal decisions	**34**
5 The theory of the firm under uncertainty (one-period models for optimal output or price decisions)	**41**
5.1 Introduction	41
5.2 Competition	42
5.3 Monopoly	49
5.4 Uncertainty about productivity (production uncertainty)	61
5.5 Conclusions	64
6 Inventory models under uncertainty	**67**
6.1 The relation between inventory theory and the theory of the firm	67
6.2 The newsboy model	68

6.3	Approximation of the dynamic effects resulting from goodwill costs and holding costs (Mills 1962)	69
6.4	Dynamic models using the dynamic programming method	70
6.5	The crucial role of backlogging	73
6.6	An extension to non-linear models	75
6.7	Traditional prejudices of mainstream literature on the influence of uncertainty on the optimal inventory level	77
6.8	Limitations of the models presented so far – references to further literature	79

7 The impact of uncertainty on the optimal choice of inputs   **82**

7.1	Introduction	82
7.2	Static models	83
7.3	Dynamic investment models under uncertainty	88

8 *Ex post* flexibility of production decisions   **93**

9 Summing up the results of the theoretical models   **97**

9.1	Evaluation of the overall results	97
9.2	'Petty' *v.* 'severe uncertainty': elements of an alternative dichotomization	103
9.3	Inventory models	107

10 Decision theory and empirical evidence   **108**

Part III Empirical information on the relevance of the models and on the range of critical parameters   **113**

11 Empirical evidence on the function of inventories (and order backlogs) under uncertainty   **115**

11.1	The evidence required	115
11.2	Why do firms carry inventories?	116
11.3	Macroeconomic inventory functions	119
11.4	Survey information on the role of inventories	123
11.5	Empirical information on profits *v.* costs and goodwill *v.* inventory-holding costs	123
11.6	Testable implications of the inventory model	125
11.7	Determinants of order backlogs – are backlogs negative orders?	126
11.8	Test for finished-good inventories in the US, Germany and Austria	128
11.9	The evidence we got	132

12 Empirical evidence on whether prices are an action variable, a random variable or a relatively 'stable' exogenous variable   **134**

12.1	The question to be answered	134
12.2	Pricing in the light of surveys and econometrics	135

12.3	Empirical evidence of cost behaviour patterns	142
12.4	The feasibility of short-term price and quantity reactions to demand shocks	147
12.5	Measures for price rigidity *ex post* and *ex ante*	151
12.6	Competition and price flexibility	155
12.7	Summing up the evidence on the role of prices in industries	156

13 Towards a realistic description of the decision process in modern industrial society   **159**

13.1	Overview of the chapter	159
13.2	Asymmetries in the flexibility of the production factors	159
13.3	Are entrepreneurs risk-averse?	163
13.4	On the type and mode of uncertainty	163
13.5	Industrial behaviour under uncertainty	165

Part IV Conclusions   **169**

14 The main findings of the book   **171**

Appendix 1	Schedule of repeatedly used symbols	179
Appendix 2	Business surveys as sources of information	181
Appendix 3	Rational expectations and policy ineffectiveness	184
Appendix 4	Categorization of the literature with regard to backlogging	188
Appendix 5	Survey of firms' strategies under uncertainty	196

References	199
Index	212

List of Tables

Table		Page
2.1	Mean and unbiasedness of thirty-nine series of reported expectations	16
2.2	Expected and actual production (sales, exports, investment) in the Japanese manufacturing industry	18
2.3	Expected and realized changes (annualized) for inflation and industrial production (1961–85) in the US	18
2.4	Synopsis of alternative concepts of 'expectations'	20
9.1	Summary of the theoretical models	98
9.2	Petty *v.* severe uncertainty	106
11.1	Stock-adjustment models with alternative assumptions about desired stocks	121
11.2	Inventory assessment and capacity utilization in peaks and troughs in EEC countries	122
11.3	The ratio of cash flow to value added in six countries	124
11.4	Inventories (finished goods) and order backlog in % of annual sales	130
11.5	Volume and 'voluntarity' of raw-material and finished-good inventories in German manufacturing (February 1983)	131
12.1	Regression estimates for price behaviour in Austrian manufacturing – the importance of costs, demand and international prices	138
12.2	Linear demand systems for determination of quantities, prices and inventories	141
12.3	Empirical cost curves with fixed capacities	143
12.4	Survey results on unit cost curve in the USA (Eitemann & Guthrie 1952) and Austria (1981)	144
12.5	Response to a demand shock	145
12.6	Volatility of prices and quantities in the Austrian manufacturing industry	149
12.7	Forecasting performance for prices and production in industrial sectors in West Germany 1965–83 (coefficients of correlation)	150
12.8	Differences in the responses to demand shocks for differences in the degree of competition	152

Table	Page
13.1 The asymmetry of plan revisions	161
13.2 Number and average of revisions of investment plans on the firm level	162
13.3 Cost differences by errors of same size and different sign (1100 firms, Austria)	162
A4.1 Survey on inventory models with special regard to the BL case	189
A4.2 Overall record of twenty-seven inventory models	193

Part I

Introduction

1 The Impact of Uncertainty – A Theoretical Topic of Great Relevance for Real-world Behaviour

1.1 THE AIM OF THE BOOK: CONFRONTATION OF THEORIES WITH EMPIRICAL EVIDENCE

The book addresses two questions. The first is: Under what conditions can optimally formed reported expectations of firms (like sales or investment anticipations) deviate from realizations (like actual sales or investment) even in the long run (on average)? The phenomenon of – usually downward – biased reported expectations is well documented in empirical surveys on inflation, export sales or investment 'expectations', for consumers, firms and sometimes even for macroeconomic forecasting institutions.[1] The Rational Expectations' Hypothesis as developed by Muth (1961), dominating macroeconomic literature in the specialized version of 'expectations as conditional expected values' suggests that the equality of the means of expectations and realizations should be the very lowest benchmark for rationality. We try to find under what circumstances 'economically rational' expectations should deviate consistently from realized values or from expected values.

The second question is: Is there a systematic difference between optimal decision under certainty and uncertainty, and especially do these differences show some general structure, for example does uncertainty bias the optimal value in the upward or the downward direction? We focus mainly on the optimal production decision, with less intensity on the price and input decisions. Since it is hopeless to assume that optimal decision will change under uncertainty in one direction under all logical circumstances and for all variables, we will first try to structure the theoretical models in a way that shows us what features of the models matter, then we will try to find out what can be told empirically about the crucial variables for modern industrialized countries.

This attempt to structure theoretical models and assess their relevance empirically is probably a rather singular feature of the present book. Most

4   *Introduction*

theoretical books on uncertainty stop many steps short of empirical assessment, and some restrict empirical evidence to experiments (e.g Kahneman & Tversky 1979). On the other hand, most empirical work (for example macroeconomic models but also empirical work by business economists) stops far short of addressing questions of uncertain environment in any explicit way (the unexplained part may be considered to stem from uncertainty but it may also be due to incomplete specification, etc.). The attempt to bridge the gap between theory and actual behaviour may seem unsatisfactory from both points of view. Its justification lies probably in the increasing importance of uncertainty for our economies since the mid-1970s, following the first oil crisis, but also due to political development.

Aiming at a realistic assessment and arriving at some dichotomies between the compelling logic of neoclassic equilibrium theory (or that of prevalent theoretical thought in general) and empirical facts of presumably suboptimal behaviour, we shall in Part II either bypass the question of the course of action actually followed or we may in fact decide in favour of the second course. But this second course need not necessarily be irrational: as a rule it can be rationalized by making certain assumptions on market form, rigidities, cost of collecting information, etc. The danger of arguing *ad hoc* or being accused of *ex post* rationalizing must be faced.

Here are some examples of deliberately dwelling on such dichotomies:

- In the competition model it is solely the model of price uncertainty that is theoretically unassailable, yet the model of quantity uncertainty (where firms have to choose a production level before quantity demanded becomes known, see 5.2.4) is not *a priori* discarded. It can be interpreted as a competition model of short-term price rigidity, as a competition model under short-term fixed market share, as a description of oligopolistic behaviour, or of markets under price regulation, as a fixed price model under stochastic rationing or as a 'specific' reaction, particularly under considerable uncertainty. This model is presented in Part II and the objections are discussed (5.1), in Part III we shall seek information on the empirical relevance of price rigidity – essential for this model – in near competitive markets (11.5).
- In the competition model under price uncertainty, risk aversion decreases optimal output. This distortion disappears if there are future markets for all products (Holthausen 1979). The present study is a partial analysis, rendering the entrepreneurial decision under uncertainty from the entrepreneur's point of view without enquiring into its consequences for market equilibrium or investigating the conditions of attainment of the equilibrium with and without future markets.[2] A possible step from the *ex ante* decision towards a market equilibrium is the *ex post* flexibility of the production decision. This is discussed in chapter 8 (Part II). In Part III, substantiations are sought for flexibility in

output decision on the one hand, and on the other hand some indications on whether it is market equilibria or disequilibria that are the rule in the industrial commodities markets (chapters 10-12).
- Three modes of behaviour are possible in monopoly under uncertainty: price setting, quantity setting, and price and quantity setting before the uncertainty about the demand curve clears. These behaviour patterns could (under certain assumptions) be ranked according to expected utility, and description might be confined to the one promising maximum expected utility. We present all these three behaviour patterns side by side in Part II, letting the empirical material decide on the relevance of the models.
- We consider the situation of a seller on one side of the market, i.e. a so-called partial analysis. It is difficult in an uncertainty model to interrelate the two sides of the market because there is the need endogenously to explain – beside the price – also the stochastic processes at work in the market. Failure to perform the consolidation restricts the persuasiveness of the findings. To be compelling, they need additional untested assumptions to be made – a highly unsatisfactory situation for the theorist.

While deliberately setting limits to the level of theoretical aspirations we also recognize limits to our empirical aims. The empirical findings are derived from market performance, pointing to conceptual differences from individual optimization in the theoretical part. Neglecting reference to the distortive power of possible or actual problems of aggregation the empirical sections aim only at evaluating the various theoretical models' plausibility or at obtaining indications about critical parameters without hope of explaining isolated, empirically interesting problems. Thus, in explaining prices' determination or inventory fluctuations we forgo the introduction of *ad hoc* justifiable auxiliary variables for the maximization of the coefficients of determination. We try to remain within the framework of the explanatory variables used in the theoretical model and to establish if they play their assigned role in practice.

The theoretical models are limited to business planning (although, as mentioned, even expert and consumer forecasts are distorted); the empirical results are mostly derived from data on the Austrian industry, supplemented where available from German, American and Japanese sources.

1.2 STRUCTURE

In the theoretical part (Part II), we discuss models dealing with the impact of uncertainty on the firm's production, price, inventory and input decision. In the first place the concept of reported business expectations as an optimal plan under uncertainty is developed and correlated with the common interpretation of expectation, in particular with the mainstream operationalization of the so-called Rational Expectations' Hypothesis (Muth 1961), as a conditional expected value.

The firms are assumed to be 'Neumann – Morgenstern Utility-Maximizers' (expected utility hypothesis), not because of its supposed closeness to reality but because of its operationality and its strict demands on the rationality of the economic units. That hypothesis will be a stringent standard for the rationality of 'distortions'.

Alternatives to the 'Neumann – Morgenstern utility theory' are dealt with in chapter 3. Among them are the traditional 'safety-first principles' (quite likely often applied as rules-of-thumb in daily practice) as well as the Prospect Theory, derived from the empirically ascertained infringements of the Neumann – Morgenstern axioms, as well as the Regret Theory or Machina's fundamental contribution. More than half a century ago Knight (1933)[3] proposed to distinguish between 'risk' and 'uncertainty'. In risk he held it possible to estimate probabilities (the present study treats the risk case mainly by this distinction) – but not in uncertainty proper. Keynes and the Post-Keynesians are rather concerned with uncertainty (as dealt with at length by Rothschild, 1981) or – as we should say since the term of 'uncertainty' has largely displaced risk in the literature – with uncertainty proper, when largely new or unique constellations are at issue and when in consequence the economic actors can hardly have any knowledge of the probabilities. We propose to show how the concepts of risk and uncertainty proper despite their seemingly basic differences can in fact have mutually fertilizing effects. Uncertainty proper, for example, contributes potential rationality of price rigidity and emphasizes the advantages of flexibility. Among the possible model constructs in a Neumann – Morgenstern universe this book gives comparatively more room than in published literature to models featuring price rigidities or emergency strategies (*ex post* flexibility of quantity). We propose a new dichotomization of uncertainty models in section 9.2, where the applicability of a certain method (Neumann – Morgenstern's Utility-Maximization) is not the decisive criterion, but the structure of the model (what variables are fixed and what are endogenous). We label these alternatives as 'severe' versus 'petty' uncertainty.

Most results of the theoretical models may be interpreted as special cases of one of four general models (chapter 4). Best known in literature is the fact that risk aversion combined with linear technology (Z_{XX} equals zero, Z being the argument of the objective function, X the random variable, suffixes representing partial derivatives) will lead to downwards distortion of the optimal value of the action parameter under uncertainty, $\hat{Y}$, when compared with that in the certainty model, Y^*. We, on the contrary, shall concentrate on the case or risk neutrality – not as though risk aversion were *a priori* to be excluded, but rather because the preponderant attention paid in literature to the risk attitude evokes the impression that uncertainty had no influence on decisions under risk neutrality. In such a case a 'concave technology' (in the sense of $Z_{YXX}<0$) or marginal costs of uncertainty as will result from the chance – increasing with rising y – of unsaleability of output, lead to this distortion. These (second and third) classes of determinants for distortions are not much dealt with in the literature in the generality here presented (though special cases are discussed). The fourth emerges if preliminary decisions can be revised more easily (less costly) upwards than downwards.

Three branches of theories deal with the effect of uncertainty on the entrepreneur's decision (see chapters 5–7); they are distinguished by the action variables, but also by the ruling assumptions concerning random variables and the general setting (e.g. concerning price flexibility).

The theory of firms under uncertainty (chapter 5) deals primarily with one-period decisions concerning optimal price and output but excludes the effect of stocks on that decision. Attention is concentrated on the influence of market structure, cost curves and the specific modelling of the types of uncertainty. Other than mainstream literature, we do not *a priori* exclude the competition model under quantity uncertainty, because among other things, its effects, and in particular the non-clearance of the markets due to price rigidity, could also be typical for a wide range of oligopolistic markets, monopolistic competition or regulated markets. Among the monopoly markets (5.2) we also deal with a type of uncertainty that is neglected in the literature, because of the dominant position held by Leland's (1972) study.

The inventory theory (chapter 6) aims particularly at considering revenues and costs of future periods, thus representing a necessary complement to the theory of firms under uncertainty. We simplify by mostly implying linear costs and fixed prices where alternative market forms or types of uncertainty are left aside. The present study concentrates on determining the optimal stock on hand (stocks after output, before demand), it accepts constant unit revenues and costs as well as identical, independent distributions over demand (i.i.d.).[4]

In contrast to most writings on the subject, we do not focus on availability and the uniqueness of the solution (they are given due to the simplicity of our assumptions) but on the question whether the optimal stock on hand lies above or below expected demand.

We want to show which parameters act on this problem thereby modifying the one-period models. Contrary to the ruling implicit and explicit prejudice that inventory should rise with uncertainty, the opposite seems more plausible.

That prejudice has led to some writers imputing – without specifying the assumption – a special case (the lost-sales case) and in some cases even an error of omission is traceable through study after study, distorting the findings in the direction of the prejudice (see appendix 4).

The literature on optimal choice of production inputs (chapter 7) under uncertainty draws attention to production techniques. The outcome of

8 Introduction

the models depends on the specific production function and on the question: Which factors are to be chosen before and which after the veil of uncertainty has lifted?

A further step to increasing the models' realism lies in being able to modify the production decision after uncertainty has lifted at least in part (or at higher cost). The tendential effect of this *ex post* flexibility is demonstrated by means of two models (chapter 8).

Chapter 9 summarizes the findings of Part II and elaborates those critical parameters and assumptions on which the effect of uncertainty depends. These critical assumptions and parameters will be tested in empirical analyses. A dichotomization of uncertainty models into ones of 'petty uncertainty' and others of 'severe uncertainty' is proposed, in which mainly the availability of *ex post* controls – not the ability to construct a probability function – is the dividing criterion.

Chapter 10 is the bridge between the theoretical part of the book and the empirical. In particular, we characterize the role empirical evidence will play, which is not always that which purists would like to be able to achieve. The evidence does not come from carefully planned experiments but from surveys and time series gathered for other than theoretical purposes. No definite answer on the validity of the models can be expected, but hopefully we get some hints as to which models are more realistic than others.

Part III examines which of the models offered by theory are better able to describe the production process in industry. This is done in part by empirically checking the assumptions of the models and in part by reviewing whether their implications are empirically valid. Thus we examine the empirical determinants of net inventories, the problem of rigidity or flexibility of the action parameter determined in the initial decision.

The influence of durability on the production decision calls for thorough empirical examination because, first, the theoretic models are extremely diverse and secondly because the tendential result depends on the empirically established range of certain parameters. The empirical relevance of backlogging in particular, the relative costs of storing and bottlenecks as well as the relative insignificance of speculative stocks are important for the explanatory power of the models (chapter 11).

Some of the theoretic models assume short-term price rigidity, others stipulate market clearance by *ex post* variable prices. The real rigidity of prices in industry as well as the other implications of equilibrium models and disequilibrium models are scrutinized in chapter 12.

Chapter 13 tests whether the output decision, and the investment decision is equally (at even cost) variable upwards and down. The asymmetry of *ex post* flexibility as well as the possible irreversibility of the investment decision were assessed in the models to be important factors of a potential distortion of decision under uncertainty.

Part IV – which contains only chapter 14 – tries to summarize the important findings and restraints concerning the whole complex under investigation.

The impact of uncertainty 9

Appendix 1 gives a survey of abbreviations repeatedly used in the text; appendix 2 describes and discusses the problems and pitfalls of information gathered by surveys; appendix 3 demonstrates that the famous 'policy impotence result' does not hold with asymmetric losses due to expectational errors; appendix 4 gives an overview on the incorrect treatment of backlogged orders in management science literature; and appendix 5 presents the complete text of a survey frequently cited in the text.

1.3 THE INNOVATIVE CONTENT OF THE TREATISE

It is *not* the objective of this book to add to the countless models of entrepreneurial decision under uncertainty, a few more, distinguished by alternative assumptions concerning an action variable or uncertainty variable (demand, price, efficiency, input availability, etc.). What may be slightly innovative here is the somewhat more distinctly articulated modelling of productivity uncertainty (section 5.3), *ex post* flexibility (chapter 8) and a correction of current notions about revenues from backlogged orders (sections 6.5 and 6.6).

The envisaged innovation is an attempt to structure the numerous models by general types (propositions 1-4), to assign contradictory findings to implicit or explicit assumptions and to work out economic principles that had led to the models' specific outcomes.[5] The regularities, once established, are empirically tested for closeness to reality.

A considerable shift of emphasis *vis-à-vis* mainstream writings will be observed in this volume. Within the general types of models the problem of risk aversion dominates extant literature[6] (proposition 1 or operationalization A in chapter 4), where as the third cross derivative of the argument of objective function (Z) to the action and the uncertainty variable (Z_{YXX}) has as a rule been neglected: proposition 2 (operationalization B) has never, to my knowledge, been developed as a general possibility for distortion in models of firms theory under uncertainty, although – mathematically – it trivially follows from the well-known Rothschild – Stiglitz condition. The mathematically trivial difference between U_{YXX} and Z_{YXX} has an economic consequence, *viz.* the shift of the argument from (subjective) risk behaviour to technological (objective) decision determinants. This shift is meant to prevent the effect of uncertainty from automatically being reduced to risk behaviour about which, incidentally, not much is known (cf. Lippman & McCall 1981). Under risk neutrality, too, uncertainty theory is a large and interesting subject, and there cost and market conditions determine the outcome, thereby making it accessible to empirical enquiry. Of course, the equilibrium theorist has to love risk aversion since it will often assure the existence and the uniqueness of the results; however, in the present partial analysis we resist the temptation.

The second shift of emphasis lies in our moving from equilibrium models (meaning models with *ex post* control bridging the imbalance between planning and realization of the uncertainty variables) to disequilibrium models where, for example, planned output and demand are not equated automatically by some *ex post* control.

The latter are known in literature, but they are marginally dealt with within standard theory.[7] In this study they receive extensive consideration and are the subject of a rather general condition (preposition 3). Uncertainty creates an extra cost component (as compared with certainty) which is labelled as 'marginal costs of uncertainty'. Now marginal revenue is equated to marginal costs plus this extra component, thus leading to 'lower' optimal values under uncertainty.

This condition, too, is obviously implicit in many models, but it is neglected in literature as a general source for biasing the optimal decision downward.

Finally, this study seeks some reconciliation between diverse approaches in economic thought.

Firstly, we attempt to lessen the gap between mathematically oriented standard theory, which treats of uncertainty in the framework of Neumann – Morgenstern Utility Theory (thus basing itself on Knight's 'risk situation'), and the Keynesian view of 'true' uncertainty (wherein the economic actor is unable to evaluate the probabilities, and acts 'quite differently'). We will therefore incorporate some of the 'stylized facts' emphasized in the Keynesian view, such as price rigidity or the flexibility issue into the Neumann – Morgenstern Utility-Maximizer's model construction.

Secondly, we aim to reconcile the Rational Expectations' Hypothesis (Muth 1961) with the Keynesian system and also with the empirical findings from business surveys. This is done by underlining the original more general version of Rational Expectations' Theory, which did not rely on linear objective functions. If the objective function is not linear then a continuing divergence between (point) expectations and realizations is not contradicting the hypothesis. If, however, the objective function is linear, which is the operationalization dominating the application of the hypothesis to economic policy, then we can apply the concept of conditional expected values and any persistent difference between expectations and realization has to be considered as irrational. For our approach it becomes necessary to differentiate between the mathematical concept of the conditional expected values (or density functions) on the one hand and optimally formed decisions (plans, anticipations) which would be called actions in decision theory. It is the specific hypothesis of this study that empirically reported expectations (forecasts, plans) approximate the optimal decision. In contrast to the mathematical concept of the conditional expected value, these economic expectations incorporate risk attitude and consequences of eventual errors on the argument of the objective function. This, although not yet the Keynesian view of expectations, gives leeway for incorporating the determinants of 'expectations' mentioned by Keynes (1937) into decision relevant anticipations (plans, actions).

The impact of uncertainty 11

Thirdly, some conciliation is sought between the tendentially normative theory of firm under uncertainty, which knows price flexibility, the existence of future markets and mainly speculative inventory fluctuations, and the empirical literature, which takes certain price rigidities, involuntary inventory movements and rapid production changes for granted, trying to explain them frequently *ad hoc*. Business surveys and econometric results are used in selecting and constructing the models.

1.4 SOME CONCEPTS USED

The abbreviations used are summarized in appendix 1. The concepts used in general follow the literature but it may be useful here to repeat some of them.

The *decision variable* is that variable by which optimization is done. The *random variable* is the variable whose realization is not known *ex ante* and which is known *ex post* and under certainty (where we will assume it to take the value $X_0 = \mathrm{E}X$. *Ex post flexibility* designates a situation in which the decision variable can be adjusted in a second step after the veil of uncertainty has lifted.

An *ex ante control* is a variable about which we have to decide before the veil of uncertainty is lifted, an *ex post* control can be chosen or is simply adjusted after the event. A *mode* is a situation characterized by the assumption about the *ex ante* control (a p-mode, for example, is behaviour in a model in which we assume that the price has to be set *ex ante*, in the p-q-mode both variables have to be decided *ex ante*).

As *disequilibrium models* we label models wherein production or demand differs or in which input installed and the input used differ. If there are *ex post* controls, part or all of the differences will optimally be bridged, so that there is no unsatisfied demand, unsold product or free capacity.

As *technological concavity* we label a marginal product concave in the decision variable, where the concavity stems from objective reasons (like technology, demand curve, etc.), in contrast to risk attitude.

We contrast the optimal decisions between *certainty* and *uncertainty*. Introduction of uncertainty is one subcase of *increasing uncertainty*. Usually the assumptions necessary for unambiguous results are stricter for the more general class of the problem. Propositions 1, 2 and 4 apply unmodified to the wider class of the problem, for proposition 3 the effect of increasing uncertainty usually depends on whether the optimal value will be in the range of $F(Y) \gtreqless 0.5$. Since we argue that it will usually be in the 'smaller range', the effect of increasing uncertainty and of introduction of uncertainty will again tend in the same direction, though this may not be true under all circumstances.

We deal with *partial* decision models in the sense that one agent maximizes its utility in a certain given environment. Neither the behaviour

12   Introduction

of the other side of the market is changing nor the development of the market itself is modelled. For questions of industry equilibrium see Sheshinsky & Dreze (1976), for general equilibrium under uncertainty see Radner (1982). We model *passive situations* in the sense that firms do not learn actively about their environment and they cannot change the information set. For active or adaptive situations see Hey (1981) or Lippmann & McCall (1981).

Finally I want to thank all persons who helped me through the many periods of uncertainty I passed in writing this book. Among the academics I would like to thank first of all my teacher Erich Streissler of the University of Vienna for his persistently encouraging comment, then my colleagues Michael Winkler, Michael Wüger and Michael Pfaffermayr for help and control when problems threatened to outgrow my finite set of mathematical knowledge.[8]

NOTES

1   Cf. Aiginger 1977, 1979, 1981a,b, 1983.
2   Neglect of future markets can also be justified on the grounds that uncertainty in particular inhibits everyone from committing themselves for too long, and that future markets (for most goods) do not exist (Rothschild 1981, p. 24).
3   First edition: 1921.
4   i.i.d. (identically, independently distributed) means that the same distribution function is assumed for each period, irrespective of any (the most recent) realizations.
5   Thus Leland (1972) claims that the quantity setting the monopolist's production decision does not change through uncertainty; Nickell (1978) arrives at the opposite view without explaining the contradiction to Leland's finding. Hymans (1966) comes to the conclusion that less is produced in the competition model under uncertainty than under certainty, whereas we find it asserted in the bulk of the literature that output is the same in each case.
6   To substantiate the claim that rational expectations should yield on average correct forecasts, as well as that most authors disregard influences on optimal decision under uncertainty that go beyond the risk aversion, we may quote Arrow (1978, p. 159): 'A moderate version of the rational expectations' hypothesis is that the anticipated price equals the expected price. A stronger version is that the economic agent knows that the price is a random variable and uses in his decisions the true distribution. (The stronger hypothesis is significant if the agent is a risk averter, so that his decisions are not determined merely by knowledge of the expected value).' The quotation discloses the neglect of all forms of technological concavity, of disequilibrium costs and asymmetries in *ex post* flexibility. Neglect of the first component is especially astonishing since a general condition concerning the effect of uncertainty (U_{YXX}, cf. equation 3 in chapter 4) has been known since Rothschild & Stiglitz (1971). From this it may be seen that it is not the utility function alone which decides on the optimal action.
7   Cf. the neglect in the excellent summary studies of Hey (1979, 1981) or in the article by Lippmann & McCall (1981).
8   Thanks to to Fred Prager for translating the book, to Dagmar Guttman, Elisabeth Lebar, Traude Novak, Maria Seidl and Getrude Wenz for collecting the data, rearranging the calculations, drawing up the tables and for typing, checking, retyping etc. Manfred Nermuth, Gerhard Orosel, Kurt Rothschild, Gunther Tichy and Georg Winckler supplied me with critical comments in earlier stages of the work.

Part II

Theoretical part

2 Interpreting Reported Expectations as Optimal Decisions (Actions) under Uncertainty

The term 'expectations' is extensively used by firms, politicians and economists. This is done often without specifying the underlying concept of 'expectations'. I will use the term within inverted commas whenever I refer to expectations without making explicit the definition used.

In particular, there seems to be an unbridgeable gap between the 'expectations' reported by firms as sales forecast, as investment anticipations or price forecasts on the one side, and the term 'expectations' used by macroeconomists if they refer to conditional expected values (a concept known as Rational Expectations' Hypothesis). We want to include in the first group of 'expectations' firms' expectations, but also consumers' expectations and experts' forecasts for macroeconomic variables and label them 'reported expectations'; while we will use the term *mathematical expectation* for concepts like expected values or density functions.

We will show in section 2.1 that there are striking divergencies between reported expectations and implications of mathematical concepts, among them that reported expectations are biased as seen from the viewpoint of the most popular operationalization of the Rational Expectations' Hypothesis. The bias is discussed in section 2.2. We will then develop the hypothesis that reported expectations can be considered as (approximations) to *economically rational expectations* which deviate from pure mathematical concepts insofar as they include the consequences of potentially incorrect expectations (2.3). The merits and disadvantages of this concept of economically rational expectations and the role of uncertainty theory to demonstrate that this concept may not only be a feasible but an important one, are discussed in section 2.4.

Table 2.1 Mean and unbiasedness of thirty-nine series of reported expectations testing for the identity (H_0) of expected and actual changes (t-test)

	H_0 rejected 95% (99%)	H_0 non-rejected	Mean of expectations		Among the rejections of H_0	
			lower than the mean of realizations	higher than the mean of realizations	lower	higher
All data	15 (13)	24 (26)	29	10	14	1
Quantitative business surveys	10 (9)	6 (7)	14	2	9	1
Qualitative business surveys	0 (0)	7 (7)	3	4	0	0
Consumer surveys	3 (3)	0 (0)	3	0	3	0
Experts	2 (1)	11 (12)	9	4	2	0

Testing for unbiasedness
H_0: $(k,b)=(0,1)$ in $a_t = k + be_t$; F-test

	H_0 rejected 95% (99%)	H_0 non-rejected
All data	21 (16)	18 (23)
Quantitative business surveys	14 (11)	2 (5)
Qualitative business surveys	2 (1)	5 (6)
Consumer surveys	3 (3)	0 (0)
Experts	2 (1)	11 (12)

Source: Aiginger (1981b)
a, e actual change (e.g. of sales), expected changes.

2.1 THE EMPIRICAL PHENOMENON OF BIASED REPORTED EXPECTATIONS

Data on business and consumer expectations are available for many countries, variables and business sectors. One of the striking results of most empirical investigation is that reported expected changes (of sales, output, inflation) are consistently (for long periods) lower than actual changes. This difference is found for medians as well as for means; it is even present – albeit smaller – in periods of decelerating growth. It may be demonstrated on the aggregate and on the micro level. For an overview on the aggregate level see Aiginger (1979, 1981a,b), on the level of individual answers Figlewsky & Wachtel (1981), Zarnowitz (1981), Nerlove (1986), Zimmermann (1984), Kawasaki & Zimmermann (1984). The underestimation tendency is especially strong for entrepreneurial expectations. Macroeconomic forecasts[1] underestimated real growth in the 1960s, but not in the 1970s (though the really surprising fact is that growth forecasts were not too optimistic in this period of negative shocks). Experts underestimate actual inflation according to the famous 'Livingston survey' for the US, the same seems to be true for Michigan's consumer expectations (for these data of the Consumer Research Institute the final assessment depends on the quantification procedure used), and for Austrian data on expected inflation (Breuss & Wüger 1986). Inflation forecasts by macroeconomic forecasting institutions seem to escape the spell of downward-biased forecasts (Aiginger 1979, Neumann & Buscher 1980, Kirchgässner 1982).

Table 2.1 shows the bias for a sample of thirty-nine variables grouped into quantitative business expectations (about sales, investment, exports), into qualitative business data (about production, order and price trends), consumer expectations and experts' forecast. The average expected change is smaller for twenty-nine variables out of thirty-nine as compared with actual change. In testing for unbiasedness in the usual sense of a zero constant and a unity regression coefficient, twenty-one variables failed to pass the test. Among the subset of the quantitative business expectations unbiasedness had to be rejected for fourteen out of fifteen variables at the 95% level of significance. Table 2.1 replicates results from Aiginger (1981b); the data mainly ended in 1975.

Tables 2.2 and 2.3 present data for Japan and the US which demonstrate that the bias did persist in the period of slow growth since the mid-1970s. For all four variables expected changes in Japan are lower than the actual ones also in the period 1976–85; in two cases the bias is statistically significant even in this short slow growth period 1976–85. For the US, Livingston data show that experts continued to underestimate inflation and industrial output.

18 *Theoretical part*

Table 2.2 Expected and actual production (sales, exports, investment) in the Japanese manufacturing industry

	1963–75		1976–85		1963–85	
	Mean	SD	Mean	SD	Mean	SD
Production						
expected change	2.92	0.83	1.52	0.86	2.33	1.09
actual change	3.54	2.90	1.89	2.24	2.84	2.77
significance of difference	—	**	—	**	—	**
Sales						
expected change	3.06	0.95	1.67	0.93	2.47	1.18
actual change	3.55	2.40	1.92	2.42	2.87	2.59
significance of difference	—	**	—	**	—	**
Exports						
expected change	2.96	2.87	0.77	1.53	2.03	2.61
actual change	5.38	6.43	2.66	3.56	4.24	5.59
significance of difference	**	**	**	**	**	**
Investment						
expected change	0.45	3.56	−5.12	5.44	−1.90	5.23
actual change	2.79	6.93	1.59	7.25	2.28	7.05
significance of difference	*	**	**	**	**	*

SD = standard deviation. *Source:* Bank of Japan.

Table 2.3 Expected and realized changes (annualized) for inflation and industrial production (1961–85) in the US

	Consumer price		Industrial production	
Livingston	mean	SD	mean	SD
6-month forecast	4.34	2.65	2.49	3.99
12-month forecast	4.50	2.56	3.28	2.66
actual change	5.40	3.56	4.16	5.88
Significance of differences for forecast as compared to actual change				
6 month	*		**	
12 month	—		—	

Source: Livingston Survey, USA. *(**) denote 95(99%) level of significance

2.2 BIASEDNESS AND RATIONALITY

Biasedness of reported expectations are in conflict with at least that operationalization of the 'Rational Expectations' Hypothesis' (REH) which dominates macroeconomic literature (and even more economic policy literature).

The basic idea of the REH approach as proposed by Muth (1961) is that information is an economic good, which should be used economically in the process of the formation of expectations, and secondly that expectations depend on the whole structure of the economic system and therefore cannot be independent from economic policy. In the following application of this REH in economic models and especially for evaluating the effects of economic policy in a world of 'rational expectations', the concept was nearly without exception cast into the specialized version of the conditional expected value. This specialized version of the wider (and nearly irrefutable) notion was suggested by examples in the article by Muth himself, though Muth did not forget to stress that he had switched to a special form[2] of the hypothesis implying a quadratic objective function (and allowing a linear expectation operator). This specialized version allowed a whole battery of empirical tests on the 'rationality' of reported expectations, which start from the presumption that errors in the expectations should on average be zero (more exactly, the expected error should be zero, a tendency which in the long run should imply that *ex post* errors level out too).

The fact that Muth wanted to propose a notion of rationality which did not hinge on the linearity of models is evident since he was a member of a research group at the Carnegie Mellon University which had intensively studied the applicability and advantages of certainty equivalents (Holt *et al.* 1960). However, economists making use of his hypothesis clung to the specialized form of the conditional expected value. This concept influenced economic policy in the 1970s in a very profound way leading to the so-called 'Policy Inefficiency Theorem': together with its twin hypothesis that economic agents act in response to differences between expected and realized values, rational expectations guarantee that systematic economic policy (like monetary policy) does not matter. The most prominent articles of this 'rational expectation revolution' are Lucas (1972), Sargent (1976), Sargent & Wallace (1976), and McCallum (1976, 1978, 1979). For overviews on this literature see Mishkin (1983), Sheffrin (1983), or Carter & Maddock (1984). There had been objections against the inefficiency theorem, focusing on the twin hypothesis, on the informational assumptions of the REH, it was shown that overlapping or divergent expectations between individuals, etc., would destroy the strong implications of the REH, but there had been no critique that that same inefficiency result crucially depended on the assumption of linear models. Shiller (1978) conjectured this in a survey without finding the dependence on the linearity extremely restrictive, Lucas (1978) used a concept in which the whole subjective probability function of the agents had to match the objective probability function and theoretical studies tried to find whether a unique solution could be found for non-linear, rational-expectation models. But most applications of the concept for economic policy as well as all tests on the 'rationality' of reported forecasts implicitly or explicitly assumed linearity. We will therefore refer to this specialized version of the hypothesis which moulds 'rational expectations' into the expected

Table 2.4 Synopsis of alternative concepts of 'expectations'

Concept	Definition	Examples
'Expectations'	unspecified concept, implicitly assumed to be the only sensible concept by the individual applicant	e.g. politicians declare investment activity to be hampered by 'expectations' economists want to specify the influence of economic policy on the formation of 'expectations' importance of inflationary 'expectations'
Mathematical expectations	density function of a random variable expected value or conditional expected value (as a one-point approximation, e.g. MAREH, equation 2.1)	density function for demand or sales; most likely demand or sales (where expected demand or sales are independent from consequences)
Economically rational expectations	optimal decision incorporating the expected utility of the decision using a probability assessment, the set of consequences and a utility function (equation 2.3)	sales forecast underlying the production; expected monetary growth (inflation) used for evaluating wage offers, forecast published by forecaster
Psychological (irrational) expectations	subjective assessment (evaluation, mood) whose formation has other than economic reasons	waves of optimism and despair contagious processes according to Jöhr or Pigou the incalculable part of the decision (sudden changes in long-run expectations according to Keynes)

Hypothesis in this book: the reported expectations (plans or forecasts supplied in entrepreneurial surveys, inflation expectations reported in consumer surveys, published macroforecasts) are approximations to economically rational expectations.

conditional value as the 'Mainstream Rational Expectation Hypothesis' (MAREH). It implies that 'one need only apply a very weak form of the Rational Expectations' Hypothesis to infer that inflation cannot be under- or overestimated year after year' (Poole 1976, p. 465). Biased expectation, in the sense of a persistent difference between expected and realized values, as well as biasedness in the sense that regressing actual data on expectations does not yield a zero constant and a unity regression coefficient, is in conflict with the MAREH.

One reaction to the 'bias' of reported expectation is to declare them 'unreliable', invoking 'errors of measurement', 'sampling biases', (McCallum 1976, Lahiri 1976, etc.). This does not seem a good strategy, since there is evidence that reported expectations possess the same or even (in period of structural changes) better forecasting performance than econometric investment function or consumption functions or autoregressive proxies, and they add to the forecasting performance of macroeconomic models.[3] We know that production expectations lead actual production (or at least published data about production), that inflationary expectations outperform autoregressive proxies, etc. Predictive ability, for turning points and cyclical developments on the one hand and sampling errors and irrational biases on the other, is an improbable combination.

2.3 INTERPRETING REPORTED EXPECTATIONS AS OPTIMAL FORECASTS UNDER UNCERTAINTY

The alternative proposed in this book is to interpret reported expectations as optimal forecasts or as actions in the terminology of decision theory, including an evaluation of the consequences (gains or losses) of 'wrong' reported expectations. In its most general version we can use the well-known concept of expected utility maximization, where we interpret the reported expectation to be the decision variable of this maximization. As an intermediate step we propose a concept of Loss-Evaluating Rational Expectations (LEREH), which is a specialized version of expected utility maximization in which the source of the bias of reported expectations is made evident.

The Mainstream Rational Expectation Hypothesis (MAREH) is described by formula 2.1. We know a probability function of the variable x and use the information available up to the end of $t-1$. The use of the conditional expected value as a one-point representation, Ex, of the random variable can be justified by the assumption of a symmetric quadratic loss function in case of errors.

Standard operationalization of the REH (MAREH):

$$\hat{x} = \int_{-\infty}^{\infty} x f(x|I_{-1}) dx = Ex|I_{-1}. \qquad (2.1)$$

22 Theoretical part

Considering the possibility of a more general loss function L (y, x) where losses depend on the action, y, and the random variable, x, yields a concept of 'loss-evaluation expectations'. An optimal choice of y depends now on the property of the loss function. A special case of Loss-Evaluating Expectation is given if the decision variable and random variable coincide (see equation 2.2a). Optimal expectation (for example, the optimal sales forecast $\hat{x}$) now depends on losses accruing from differences in the actual changes and expected changes x^e). If the losses due to a positive difference and a negative difference are identical, we can return to the mainstream version. If larger than actual expected sales yield a smaller loss than the contrary error of the same size it is rational to report (act on) a lower expected value. Economically rational expectation has in this case rationally and persistently to be lower than the mathematical expectation.

Loss -Evaluating Rational Expectations (LEREH) (where y is a decision variable and x a random variable):

$$\hat{Y} \doteqdot \min_{y} \int_{-\infty}^{\infty} L(x,y) \, f(x|I_{-1}) dx = \min_{y} \; EL(x,y). \tag{2.2}$$

Special case where $x = y$:

$$\hat{x} \doteqdot \min_{x^e} \int_{-\infty}^{\infty} L(x, x^e) \, f(x|I_{-1}) \, dx = \min_{x^e} \; EL(x, x^e), \tag{2.2a}$$

where the sign $\doteqdot$ means 'is derived from', $L(x, x^e)$ means loss in case of plan (reported expectation) x^e and the realization x, $L(x,y)$ means loss of the decision y and the realization x, $f(x|I_{-1})$ means density function of x (conditional on I_{-1}).

The most general version of decision-making under uncertainty is to cast the problem into the expected-utility framework. Expected utility depends on the utility function $U(Z)$, the probability function, $f(x)$, and the consequences $Z(y,x)$. Expected utility is maximized, and we interpret the optimal value of the decision variable as that figure aimed at in the firm's planning process and also reported in surveys and forecasts (reported expectations). For example, the optimal sales plan, $\hat{y}$, is chosen in a world of price uncertainty (x = price).

General concept for economically rational expectations (LEREH):

$$\hat{y} = \max_{y} \int_{-\infty}^{\infty} U[Z(x,y)] \, f(x|I_{-1}) dx = \max_{y} \; E \, U[Z(x,y)], \tag{2.3}$$

where $U(Z)$ is utility function and $\hat{y}$ is optimal decision (economically rational expectation).

To interpret reported expectations as approximations to optimal decisions under uncertainty is by no means an innocent concept. One of the main premises of decision theory requires a distinction between 'expectations' and 'consequences'. Expectations as defined by decision theory are a mathematical or statistical concept (for example a density function or as a one-point approximation of its expected value), these expectations have to be independent from individual preferences and consequences. The assumption that reported expectations may be economically rational because they incorporate intentionally the (maybe asymmetric) consequences of wrong 'expectations' is equivalent to interpreting 'expectations' as optimal actions (decisions) in the terminology of decision theory. The concept of mathematical expectations as used in the decision theory and the proposal of this book to interpret reported expectations as deliberately incorporating the consequences of expectational errors should be distinguished carefully to save confusion. We want to label our concept as 'economically rational expectations' to stress that reported expectations diverge from mathematical ones due to economic reasons (cost and demand conditions, shape of utility function, etc.), and not due to irrationality or psychology.

We have to admit that economic theory today nearly without exception identifies 'expectations' with the concept of mathematical expectations.[4] In more technical and more theoretical work expectations are usually modelled as density (probability) functions, in more applied work mainly expected values are used. As mentioned already, models which try to incorporate the impact of expectations on economic policy nearly without exception use that operationalization of the REH concept in the way that 'expectations' are conditional expected values.

This is probably not the kind of 'expectations', which was focused on as economists started to worry about 'expectations'. Pigou (1927) wanted to demonstrate how waves of optimism and pessimism were able to generate business cycles; Keynes (1936) stressed the importance of expectations for the investment process and wanted to refer to the incalculable part of the decision; Jöhr's interpretation of cycles as 'contagious diseases' can hardly be represented by simple mathematical concepts. Muth wanted to develop a broader concept of rationality, but conceded that real-world expectations would diverge from any concept of rationality – explicitly he mentions over- or under-assessment of recent information (Muth 1961, p. 321).

However, neither is it relevant which concept of expectations economic theory used at its beginning, nor which dominates today, but which phenomenon we want to deal with. If we want to describe a situation in which a casual and personally hardly interested person is asked to make a forecast, it seems plausible to accept mathematical concepts of expectations which abstract from consequences of wrong forecasts. But if we want to describe the process in which economic agents derive those decisions on which they have to act personally with high stakes at issue, or the forecast of experts on which their prestige and future incomes will depend, we cannot abstract from the incorporation of (potentially asymmetric) consequences. There is only the alternative to model a one-step decision or a two-step decision process. A one-step decision would purport that the economic agent forms an economically based decision which jointly assesses mathematical expectations and loss considerations. A two-step procedure would involve economic agents first trying to find a mathematical expectation (usually a density function), then in the second step considering the economic consequences of errors before making the decision. The two-step process is the analytically cleaner procedure. But there are not too many indicators that the two steps are separated explicitly in real-world decisions. Economic models with rational expectations do not use a two-step process either (only the first step is modelled), usually firms make only a single forecast for future investment and sales. Surveys do not specify which sales forecast they would like to know in cases where two (or more) forecasts are made. Unbiasedness is considered one of the least important criteria for accuracy of macro forecasts (implying quadratic symmetric losses). Casual evidence therefore supports that firms do not distinguish between 'mathematically expected sales' and 'sales forecast on which employment and production decisions are based', nor do macro forecasters in practice distinguish between things they believe and things they forecast because they are optimal for the economy or for their own prestige. From a normative point of view, agents should use a two-step process, but even then published sales expectations or forecasts will be more likely 'economically rational forecasts' than mathematical expectations.[5]

To sum up, the hypothesis for understanding 'expectations' in this book will be that *reported expectations* (plans or forecasts supplied by firms in surveys, inflation or income expectations reported in consumer surveys, macroeconomic forecasts published by institutions) *are approximations to economically rational expectations*. These economically rational expectations are actions (decisions) in the terminology of decision theory incorporating mathematical expectations, loss and utility considerations. Reported expectations therefore can be modelled with the usual expected utility maximization procedure (see equation 2.3).

An important implication of this hypothesis is that reported expectations may diverge from realizations even in the long run (on average) in the case of asymmetric consequences (for errors of opposite sign but the same size), or more generally in the case of non-linear models. In particular, the downward bias empirically demonstrated in section 2.1. is economically rational if the negative consequences of a 'too-low' value of the decision variable are less *severe* than those of a 'too-high' value.

What could be the reasons for such an asymmetry? The models presented in chapters 3–8 try to find out why biases are not only feasible, but are very likely and usually work in the 'downward' direction. The feasibility alone would not be very surprising, since it is well known in statistical literature that expected values are a fair representation in case of linear models only. Unbiasedness is a valid measure of forecasting performance only in the case of symmetric losses. This again is well known in statistics, though the knowledge had been temporarily forgotten in the 'policy ineffectiveness literature' which based strong conclusions on linearity without evidence (see appendix 3 for an illustration).

2.4 WHERE TO GO FROM HERE

We apply the theory of the firm under uncertainty (chapter 5), inventory theory (chapter 6) and models on input decisions (chapter 7) to find optimal values of output, prices, inventories, etc., under uncertainty. We then compare these optimal values with their counterpart in the world of certainty. In cases where the unique optimal values under certainty do not exist (for example, under competition with linear costs), the optimal decision will be compared with some expected value (for example, with expected demand).

The eventual result that the optimal value under uncertainty is lower than under certainty is related to, but not identical with, the finding that reported expectation (expected sales as reported in a survey) will optimally be lower than actual sales. Strictly speaking the models would imply that the expected and actual value of a decision variable would have to be identical, since what has to be decided *ex ante* cannot be changed *ex post*. Most models separate variables into some which are *ex ante* control variables and cannot be changed *ex post* and some which are *ex post* control variables for which it is not necessary to make an *ex ante* assessment.

The persistent biases of surveys on the aggregate level and the much more volatile relations between plans and actual outcome on the micro level 'indicate'[6] that in practice most variables supposed to be *ex ante* control variables (at least for a part of the firms) like production, investment, employment, can be altered during the period in which uncertainty is gradually lifted. A complete fixedness for example of production would imply – together with sticky prices – extreme imbalances. Therefore it seems to be realistic to assume a certain degree of *ex post* flexibility in the sense of partial and costly *ex post* revisions of the decision variables.

If the *ex post* adjustment of the decision variable is feasible it has to be incorporated into the optimal decision. We develop such models in chapter 8.

In the case of *ex post* flexibility, the relation between biased reported expectations and the impact of uncertainty is quite straightforward. Uncertainty leads to a cautious (low) preliminary choice of the decision variable, later on this can be revised (upwards). Reported values of the decision variable (in a survey or a firm's plan) and later 'realized' values have to be different. For the majority of the models the relation is not so straightforward; maybe from a purist's point of view one could even insist that the impact of uncertainty on the optimal decision and bias are totally unrelated problems. We think, however, that the demonstration that uncertainty leads to lower values for decision variables tends to 'open space' for later upward revisions at least for aggregate data. This is evident for disequilibrium models, where there is no *ex post* control to close the gaps between production and demand.

Our models are intentionally partial models which specify the optimal decision of firms. We can imagine that the market equilibrium[7] is reached in one of the following ways: the first may be that there exist two sectors of firms in the economy, the first being large firms which have to make early commitments (as modelled in the theory of firms) and the second consisting of small firms, which are able to close the discrepancies due to their flexibility. A second way would be that though a variable is an *ex ante* control in principle, fine-tuning of the decision variable (not modelled in theoretical models) is feasible to close a small part of the discrepancy.[8] In either of these cases the reported expectation may differ a little – though in a systematic way – from actual values, in the first case in the aggregate only, in the second for each optimizing firm. The greater and the less ambiguous the impact of uncertainty on the firms, the greater the downward bias will be for a given 'inexactness' of the theoretical model.

In surveys on sales, prices or investments firms are asked for their estimates whether these variables are *ex ante* or *ex post* controls. We know from the theory of firms that different modes may be optimal under uncertainty depending on the cost structure. For example, the monopolist can choose the price and use demand as an *ex post* control, he can choose quantity and use demand as an *ex post* control or he can fix both *ex ante*. Costs will decide (see Lim 1980) which is better for expected profits, the optimal and implied values for the individual variables are not identical under these three modes. Therefore it can and will happen that a given aggregate of reported expectations will be a mixture of reports about decision variables, expectation about the value of an *ex post* control and perhaps sometimes of variables for which fine-tuning of preliminary decisions is possible. If theory predicts that the optimal (preliminary) decision under uncertainty will be lower than under certainty under a lot of circumstances, the aggregate of reported expectations (as formed in an optimal or suboptimal procedure, considered as preliminary or fixed, etc.), will tend to be lower than the later outcome.

NOTES

1 Cf. Mincer & Zarnowitz (1969), Zarnowitz (1981), Aiginger (1983).
2 Cf. Muth (1961), n. 4 on p. 317.

3 Cf. Okun (1960), Friend & Taubmann (1964), Friend & Thomas (1970), Fair (1971), Kuhbier & Sauer (1983).
4 Pertinent literature may at a stretch concede a distinction between mathematical and psychological expectations (see Poole 1976, p. 465). As distinct from that implied insinuation of 'irrational' expectations, the present study considers the deviation of measured expectations from REH economically well founded ('economic' expectations in contrast both to 'mathematical' and 'irrational' expectations).
5 Interestingly enough, protagonists of MAREH argue precisely against empirically measured expectations with the argument that these, contrary to implicit expectations (as for instance resulting from actually pertaining nominal interest, if the latter is interpreted as the sum of a constant real rate of interest and expected inflation) are not the true action relevant expectations, because 'reporting' of expectations in a field survey does not involve consequences. (Cf. Pyle (1972), Pesando (1975), McCallum (1976).) Against this we argue the production, sales and investment expectations are precisely the entrepreneurial plans that are the basis of the real production process as carried out by management, taking into account uncertainty, production technology and market development.
6 We choose the verb 'indicate' because from the discrepancies visible on the aggregated level (and even bigger ones on the micro level) all that can be deduced is that there are either 'involuntary changes of plan' (e.g. caused by breakdowns of machinery) or deliberately introduced revisions. It may also be that production is no *ex ante* control at all.
7 Examples of problems of market equilibrium under uncertainty may be found in the following studies (and the literature quoted there): Sheshinsky & Dreze (1976), Drazen (1980), Hey (1981, p. 181ff.), Radner (1982).
8 Finally it might also be possible that some firms use price *and* output as *ex post* control (in part as a decision variable, partly as a performance target). This would accord with the certainty situation – as shown in the discussion of the outcomes by Oi (1961) (cf. Nelson 1961, Hey 1979, Pleeter & Horowitz 1974). During a period of 'uncertain demand' it is plausible that firms of different size may wait for different periods before committing themselves about their output. Large firms are probably inclined to the concept of *ex ante* control via at least one variable, whereas smaller firms may tend to the situation of *ex post* control by means of all variables.

3 Expected Utility Maximization and its Alternatives

Economic theory of uncertainty is dominated by the assumption that economic agents behave as if they were maximizing expected utility.[1] In this book we follow along this tradition of mainstream theory. The first reason for this is that this flexible and elegant framework allows one to model an enormous variety of situations in a consistent way. The second is that it is much harder to prove the notion 'that agents should behave cautiously under risks' within this framework than under some less elegant alternatives.

Concerning Knight's dichotomization between 'uncertainty' as the situation in which agents do not possess a probability function over the random variable, and 'risk' as the situation where they do, we refer in the following to the latter.[2] Again the formal elegance and the fact that the environment of risk seems to be the stronger test for our hypothesis is the reason for this. In cases of total ignorance minimax rules or the Hurwicz rule are criteria which lead to rather pessimistic decisions.

The same is true for the mean variance criteria which dominate portfolio theory[3] and tend to suggest optimal decision parameters below the respective certainty values. The mean variance criterion, however, is consistent with expected utility maximization at least under restrictive circumstances.[4]

Different versions of 'safety-first principles' minimize the probability of losses,[5] the probability that loss exceeds some critical value or some similar criterion. Arzac (1976) proposes four different criteria (applying them to competition under price uncertainty) and finds that production is less than (or the same as) that under certainty. Some versions of the safety-first principle are consistent with expected utility maximization, implying risk-averse utility functions.

Hey (1980) argues that there is no *a priori* reason why we should define as risk-neutral agents indifferent between a certain prospect and an uncertain one with the same (arithmetic) mean. If we define as risk-neutral an agent indifferent to a prospect with the same geometric mean we get a logarithmic utility function. Agents risk-neutral in this sense should now behave like risk-averse agents in the standard theory.

Kahneman & Tversky (1979) base their critique of the standard theory on empirically revealed preferences between prospects which are inconsistent with expected utility theory in at least three respects. The 'certainty effect' means that people underweight outcomes that are obtained with certainty. This tendency contributes to risk aversion in choices involving sure gains and to risk-seeking in choices involving sure losses. The 'isolation effect' characterizes the behaviour that people generally discard components that are shared by all prospects under consideration. This tendency leads to inconsistent preferences when the same choice is presented in different forms. The 'reflection effect' means that people behave risk-averse in the positive domain but risk-seeking if they have to choose between alternative losses. Kahneman & Tversky develop an alternative theory, called prospect theory, in which value is assigned to gains and losses rather than to final assets, and probabilities are replaced by decision weights (which may not add up to one). This value function is normally concave for gains, commonly concave for losses, and is generally steeper for losses than for gains.

'Regret theory' shares the intention of prospect theory to explain the empirical violations of the expected utility maximization, but purports to do this in a much simpler way (Loomes & Sugdan 1982). In contrast to 'choiceless utility' which is experienced from an income an agent experiences without choice, people experience sensations called regret and rejoicing if they can choose among alternatives. They experience regret if they know with hindsight that they could have chosen a better action for the realized state of nature, and they experience rejoicing if they have made a good choice. Formally, people are maximizing the expected value of a modified utility function depending on the choiceless utility of 'what is' and of sensations of 'what might have been'.[6] As one of the many extensions of regret theory we want to refer to Bell (1983) who calculates a risk premium for decision regret and a wider definition of risk aversion, now combining two components: decreasing value and regret aversion.

Another group of papers were intended to formalize 'that individuals generally avoid situations which offer the potential for substantial gains but which also leave them even slightly vulnerable to losses below some critical value' (Menezess et al. 1980, p. 921). This behaviour labelled 'aversion to downside risk' or to 'below-target returns' is related to prospect theory insofar as it uses a reference point to translate monetary outcome into gains and losses, and that the utility (or value) function is fundamentally different for gains and losses. It is further related to the safety-first criteria and to decision criteria using higher moments (see again Menezess et al. 1980). One distribution has more downside risk than another if it can be obtained from the other by shifting dispersion from the right to the left without changing mean and variance. Downside risk aversion can be compatible with expected utility theory if it is defined as

30 Theoretical part

a presumption about the third derivative of the utility function. In principle, risk-averse and risk-seeking individuals can have utility function with a negative third derivative of their utility function. One of the empirically important rationales for downside risk aversion is the possibility of ruinous losses. Laughunn *et al.* (1980) investigated the risk preferences for below-target returns of 224 managers and reported them to be risk-seeking as long as no ruinous losses were included, but the majority switched to risk aversion for below-target returns after ruinous losses were included. Downside risk aversion tends to bias downwardly optimal decision as compared with certainty – for example, the competitive firm under price uncertainty produces less under uncertainty and downside risk aversion, (see Stewart 1982, p. 146).

Another attack on the descriptive value of expected utility theory stresses the cognitive limits of agents. Since most economic decisions are extremely complicated, simultaneous maximization of all relevant variables exceeds the cognitive limits of the decision maker and people usually restrict their efforts to reach a satisfactory level of targets, maybe in a sequential decision process (Simon 1955, 1978). Radner (1975) has developed a formalization for satisficing behaviour. Shackle (1955) constructed a model where people base their decision on focus values (which describe one favourable and one unfavourable scenario) and on potential surprises; Pye (1978) proposed one in which flexibility and robustness are important.

Instead of violating the premises of expected utility maximization Machina (1982) tried to incorporate the conflicting empirical evidence by generalizing the Neumann-Morgenstern theory. Machina shows that the results of the expected utility hypothesis can be derived if we substitute the independence axiom by a more general one ('smoothness of preferences over alternative probability functions'). Machina's 'generalized expected utility theory' is no more in conflict with the Allais or the Petersburg paradoxa, it is able to explain the coexistence of lotteries and insurances and downside risk aversion.

The great divide of uncertainty theory into models dealing with risk and models dealing with uncertainty proper has been blurred already by the contribution of Simon, Shackle, Kahneman, Tversky and others; further compromises are offered by models with partial information where only rough guesses of the relevant probabilities are available or at least the ranking of the probabilities of the states of nature is available (see DeFinetti 1937, De Groot 1970).

Nevertheless the great divide of decision theory has found its parallel in economic theory. Neoclassical economists rely on expected utility theory modelling the world of uncertainty similar to that of certainty but substituting a known variable by an uncertain one (sometimes simply by the help of an expected value). Keynes and the Post-Keynesians on the one hand purport that economic agents will behave qualitatively different under uncertainty. Economic uncertainty has to be characterized as singular or at least unrepetitive constellation (Rothschild 1981, p. 107), in which agents cannot assess probabilities for the outcomes, sometimes they do not even know the relevant alternatives, or as Keynes put it, 'we simply don't know' (Keynes 1937, p. 113f). As a consequence of uncertainty proper, agents regress to simple rule of thumb or conventions, they behave in a conservative way reacting only to dramatic changes in the environment.[7] Some specific reactions to uncertainty proper are mentioned in the following (Rothschild 1981):

- the importance of liquid assets is increased;
- conservative price-setting and price and wage rigidities become rational even in the absence of monopolistic or oligopolistic markets;
- economic agents will refrain from long-term commitments;
- firms will prefer flexible production techniques; and
- disequilibria will be a widespread phenomenon.

Though we use the technique of expected utility maximization in this book we will try to bridge the divide in economic theory a little. We will respect the arguments of the Post-Keynesians in the selection of the models and in the upshot we will get some results which are Keynesian in spirit.

Proponents of the Keynesian school never tire of stressing that price rigidity will be a rational strategy under uncertainty; we follow this presumption insofar as we give more room to models with price rigidity than other monographs do (for example we do not dismiss the competitive model with demand uncertainty, see section 5.1.5, which is in conflict with the taste of neoclassical economists). We allow a monopoly model without any *ex post* control though under most circumstances expected profit is lower under this mode than under alternatives. We construct a model where the preliminary value of the decision variable can be adjusted *ex post*. The lower the cost of adjustments, the higher are expected profits in this mode.[8] Keynesian arguments suggest that we should not dismiss these models, hence we apply the formal apparatus of expected utility maximization on these as well as on the more neoclassical models.

We are able to show that optimal decision will differ under uncertainty from certainty partly depending on the third derivative of the objective function, partly due to the very existence of uncertainty. In the summary of the findings of the theoretical models (chapter 9) we raise the question whether we should try to structure the results into a group where uncertainty seems to be of less importance and one where it changes optimal result to a greater extent (section 9.2). We will label the first group 'petty uncertainty' since there differences between certainty and uncertainty are relevant only under circumstances about which we do not know much empirically and since the *ex post* control allows one to mitigate the effects of uncertainty. The second group will be labelled 'severe uncertainty' since uncertainty changes optimal decisions independent of specific ranges of a parameter or the curvature of the objective function, and there is no *ex post* control. Though 'severe uncertainty' is related to uncertainty proper and to the Keynesian view, and though 'petty uncertainty' is related to risk and to conventional neoclassical models, in both concepts we apply expected utility maximization. It is the way we construct the model (what we do consider as endogenous, whether there is an *ex post* control, etc.), which differs, not whether probabilities can be assessed or not.[9]

To sum up we can see that there are a lot of problems with the dominant paradigm of decision theory, namely with the expected utility theory.[10] Empirical experiments have revealed behaviour inconsistent with some of the premises of expected utility theory indicating that the theory does not work on the empirical level. They cannot however prove that people should not behave according to expected utility theory from the normative point of view. Alternative theories like prospect theory, regret theory, aversion to downside risk, generalized expected utility theory, etc., have been developed, other authors suggesting that people are not really maximizing or that people cannot assess probabilities. We nevertheless will apply expected utility theory in the following chapters, since most of the alternatives are not operational or convincing in general, while they have merits to explain important specific issues. We furthermore will try to show that many stylized facts which can be seen in the real world (and are used by opponents of expected utility theory as evidence against this theory) can be explained as rational by the means of expected utility theory. It is often the way the world is modelled (the objective function, its constraints, which variables are exogenous, etc,), which matters, not the method used to solve the models.

NOTES

1 For an overview on this theory and its axioms see Luce & Raiffa (1957) or Hey (1979); for a critique see Kahneman & Tversky (1979), Allais & Hagen (1979), Schoemaker (1982).
2 At the same time we assume a probability density function to be continuous, symmetric and differentiable (thus there being a distribution function which, by definition, assumes values between zero and one). The symmetry of the density function is not required for the bulk of the outcomes; it acquires importance where the decision under uncertainty is compared with the expected value of demand (cf. section 5.2.4 and chapter 6); occasionally it facilitates the derivation of the result. Given asymmetrical density functions the results would only make comparison of optimal action with the median of the distribution. Assumption of symmetrical density can be justified by assuming that a firm's demand consists of a relatively large 'certain' and a relatively small 'uncertain' part, and models are only meant to model the latter. For total demand, symmetrical distributions would not be very likely (e.g. because zero, anyway as a rule, would constitute an absolute limit for quantities in demand, and (conversely) very large quantities – though unlikely – would not be impossible).
3 Cf. Markowitz (1952, 1959), Tobin (1958). For higher moments see Allais & Hagen (1979).

Expected utility maximization 33

4 There is compatibility if the utility function is quadratic or when the yields of each and all investment outlets are normally attributed.
5 Roy (1952).
6 See Fishburn (1977), Machina (1982), Loomes & Sugdan (1982).
7 Keynes (1937); for further rules of behaviour derived from Keynes see Falkinger (1983).
8 The degree of flexibility (costs of revision of decision) in the present model is exogenous; one might approach the Post-Keynesian design even more closely by endogenizing decision on the degree of flexibility and internalizing it into the utility maximization.
9 With this reciprocal fertilization of the Keynesian position and Neumann–Morgenstern Utility-Maximization we take a stance similar to Nermuth's (Nermuth 1983, p. 4): 'Effects ascribed to genuine uncertainty, incapable of being analysed according to Keynes, may just as well – if not better – be derived by standard theory.' Contrary to Lucas (1977), who considers the concept of rational expectations under Knight's uncertainty inapplicable: 'In cases of uncertainty, economic reasoning will be of no value.' The 'ingestion' of the Post-Keynesian position by the apparatus of the Neumann–Morgensternian utility-maximization does not deprive the Post-Keynesians of all merit and function. Were it not for their perpetual criticisms, standard theory would be ever more seduced by the elegance and solubility of mathematical constructions instead of making verisimilitude the loadstar of its models, would not let 'imperfections' such as price rigidities, disequilibria and two-phase decision processes enter into its model constructions. See Solow (1984) for a Keynesian who supports a formally consistent way to promote Keynesian ideas.
10 Overviews on the problems of, and alternatives to, expected utility maximization are to be found in the proceedings of the biannual conferences on the 'Foundation of Risk and Utility Theory' (Stigum & Wenstop 1982, Daboni *et al.* 1986).

4 General Propositions on the Influence of Uncertainty on Optimal Decisions

Optimal decisions under uncertainty are calculated – as under certainty – by the maximization of an objective function with respect to the decision variable. We will label the optimal value of the decision variable under uncertainty as $\hat{Y}$, as compared with Y^* in case of certainty. We will develop four classes of models under which we can make unambiguous assessments of the influence of uncertainty on the optimal decision, namely whether the optimal value will be higher, the same as, or lower than under certainty. If a model fits into one of these classes, we can make a statement as to the qualitative influence of uncertainty without calculating the optimality conditions explicitly.

We assume a utility function (4.1) in which utility U depends on the variable Z (which can be understood as profits): Z itself depends on two variables X and Y, (which usually are quantity produced and priced). In the world of certainty X_0 is known and there exists an optimal solution Y^* for the decision variable Y, under which profits are maximized (the second-order condition is assumed to hold).

$$\text{Max } U \, [Z(X_0, Y)] \rightarrow Y^* \text{ (certainty maximum).} \qquad (4.1)$$

Under certainty we assume maximization of expected utility (Neumann–Morgenstern Utility-Maximization). Uncertainty exists about the variable X for which a probability density function $f(X)$ is known, its expected value is assumed to be the same as the fixed value X_0 under certainty (mean preserving introduction of risk).

$$\text{Max E } U \, [Z(X,Y)] \rightarrow \hat{Y} \quad \text{(uncertainty maximum).} \qquad (4.2)$$

The optimal value of the decision variable labelled $\hat{Y}$ under uncertainty can be shown to be smaller (equal, larger) than the optimal value under certainty Y^*, if U_{YXX} is smaller (equal or larger) than zero. (Rothschild & Stiglitz 1971, Diamond & Stiglitz 1974, etc.).

Optimal decisions under uncertainty 35

$$\hat{Y} \lesseqgtr Y^* \quad \text{if } U_{YXX} \lesseqgtr 0. \tag{4.3}$$

Unfortunately this condition is not very useful, since U_{YXX} proves for most problems to be neither unambiguously positive nor negative. It changes its sign in the domain of X for nearly every sensible problem (see Hey 1981 or Kraus 1979).

Under each of two modifications (operationalization A and B) unambiguous results are available. The predominant way in the literature is to assume a linear technology, i.e. $Z_{XX}=0$.[1] This means that though the realization of the random variable X has an influence on Z, the expected value of Z does not depend on the degree of uncertainty.

Under the additional condition that the decision variable under certainty depends positively on the uncertainty variable, $dY^*/dX>0$, we get the result of equation 4.4, that the optimal decision under uncertainty will be lower, (the same, higher) than under uncertainty, if people are risk-averse (neutral, loving).

Operationalization A: $Z_{XX}=0$, $dY^*/dX>0$:

$$U_{ZZ} \lesseqgtr 0 \Rightarrow \hat{Y} \lesseqgtr Y^*. \tag{4.4}$$

Proposition 1: Given that $dY^*/dX>0$, and a linear technology ($Z_{XX}=0$), then risk aversion (neutrality, loving) implies a lower (the same, a higher) optimal value for decision variable under uncertainty.

This result is not only known in literature, it is actually dominating articles on economic behaviour under uncertainty to a degree that it is often forgotten that there may be channels through which uncertainty influences behaviour other than risk attitude, and that the impact of risk attitude depends crucially on the sign of dY^*/dX. The condition $dY^*/dX>0$ may be considered an innocent assumption if output and output prices are the relevant variables, but it cannot be considered as a matter of fact; see for example the relation between output volume and input prices.

The alternative way to get unambiguous results is to assume risk neutrality. The qualitative impact of uncertainty now depends on the sign of Z_{YXX}. If Z_{YXX} is positive, zero or negative, then the optimal decision under uncertainty is as given in equation 4.6.

The proof makes use of the assumption that the second-order condition for maximization under certainty holds ($Z_{YXX}<0$) and of Jensen's inequality for convex or concave functions. We prove the case of $\hat{Y}>Y^*$ defining Z_Y concave in X.[2]

$$Z_Y(X_0, \hat{Y}) > EZ_Y(X, \hat{Y}) = 0. \tag{4.5}$$

The inequality holds for any concave function (and so for Z_Y), the equality stems from the first-order maximization under uncertainty.

It follows that $Z_Y(X_0, \hat{Y})$ is positive, and using $Z_{YY}<0$ this implies that $\hat{Y}$ is smaller than Y^* (where $Z_Y=0$).

The result may also be derived from the Rothschild–Stiglitz condition, but though the derivation is mathematically trivial, it has to my knowledge never been done explicitly.

Operationalization B: $U_{ZZ}=0$
$Z_{YY}<0$ (second-order condition under certainty)

Proposition 2: a linear utility function ($U_{ZZ}=0$) and technological concavity, neutrality, convexity ($Z_{YXX}<0, Z_{YXX}=0, Z_{YXX}>0$) yield the following sufficient condition:

$$Z_{YXX} \lesseqgtr 0 \rightarrow \hat{Y} \lesseqgtr Y^*. \qquad (4.6)$$

The effect of uncertainty does not now depend on the risk attitude, but on elements of $Z(X,Y)$, these may be demand conditions, cost conditions or other elements of the production technology. We want therefore to label this channel as *technological concavity* (linearity, convexity) to stress the difference in attitude to that in proposition 1. Though other influences than risk attitude are not unknown in the literature, the trivial modification of the Rothschild–Stiglitz condition (4.3) to arrive at equation (4.6) has not been performed in the literature and the scattered models showing the relevance of uncertainty in the absence of risk aversion have up to now not been classified according to Z_{YXX}.

The attractiveness of the two operationalizations (A and B) lie in the fact that we can determine the qualitative influence of uncertainty without maximizing expected utility at all. It suffices to calculate Z_{XX} respectively Z_{YXX} for the certainty model.

Unfortunately both operationalizations cannot be used for disequilibrium models.[3] We want to refer to disequilibrium models as models in which production and sales (demand) may differ. Competition with demand uncertainty, monopoly with *ex ante* control of prices and quantity and many inventory models belong in this category. In these cases production and demand differ, thereby creating a cost component under uncertainty which does not exist under certainty. Or in terms of the two operationalizations dY^*/dX respectively Z_{YXX} cannot be calculated since production (Y) and demand (X) are identical under certainty.[4]

We derive a fairly general result for this type of disequilibrium model below. We assume a certainty model (equation 4.7) in which revenue and costs depend on production (the components are separable), and derive the well-known first- and second-order conditions (equations 4.8 and 4.9).

Optimal decisions under uncertainty

Then we assume an uncertainty model in which expected sales depend on the smaller of demand (X) or production (Y) and we get optimality conditions 4.11 and 4.12.

The first-order condition, 4.11, has one additional element as compared to the certainty condition, 4.8, and this component is unambiguously negative. Therefore we get the very strong result, that optimal production will be lower under uncertainty as compared to certainty (4.13).

Certainty model:

$$\pi = r(Y) - c(Y). \qquad (4.7)$$

$$\pi_Y = r'(Y) - c'(Y) = 0. \qquad (4.8)$$

$$\pi_{YY} = r''(Y) - c''(Y) < 0. \qquad (4.9)$$

Uncertainty model:

$$E\pi = \min[r(X), r(Y)] - c(Y). \qquad (4.10)$$

$$\frac{\partial E\pi}{\partial Y} = \underbrace{r'(Y)}_{\substack{\text{marginal} \\ \text{revenue} \\ \text{under} \\ \text{certainty}}} - \underbrace{F(Y) \cdot r'(Y)}_{\substack{\text{marginal costs} \\ \text{of uncertainty}}} - \underbrace{c'(Y)}_{\substack{\text{marginal} \\ \text{costs} \\ \text{under} \\ \text{certainty}}} = 0. \qquad (4.11)$$

$$\frac{\partial^2 E\pi}{\partial Y^2} = r''(Y)[1 - F(Y)] - r'(Y) \cdot f(Y) - c''(Y) < 0. \qquad (4.12)$$

Proposition 3: Given a certainty model of the type 4.7 and an uncertainty disequilibrium model of the type 4.10, uncertainty adds an additional marginal-cost component which is positive (since the distribution function $F(Y)$ as well as $r'(Y)$ are positive), this yields, for this type of model, the unambiguous result of equation 4.13 (recall that $r''(Y)$ is smaller than $c''(Y)$ in the neighbourhood of Y^* by equation 4.9).

$$\hat{Y} < Y^*. \qquad (4.13)$$

The economic rationale for this strong result is that there is an additional cost component under uncertainty, namely potentially unsold production or potentially unsatisfied demand. It is the very existence of this component, and not whether these extra components increase or decrease with the production chosen, which matters. This additional cost added to the usual upward-sloping, marginal-cost curve gives a crossing with the marginal-revenue curve left of the certainty optimum. We will label the new component 'marginal costs of uncertainty'.

Proposition 3 allows the derivation of qualitative results for the competitive model with demand uncertainty (see section 5.2.4), and also for models where demand is negatively related to price or for some cases of uncertainty about productivity (5.4). Components similar to 'marginal costs of uncertainty' are present in the $p-q$ *ex ante* mode for the monopolist and in most inventory models. In all these models the very presence of uncertainty leads to a factor tending to reduce optimal production due to the potential disequilibria. No third derivative is necessary as in proposition 2.

One characteristic of the model has to be mentioned, which may limit its use and which may explain why it has not been investigated more thoroughly in the literature. The exogenous price in both the certainty and in the uncertainty model have to be identical to allow comparisons. This seems to be a reasonable assumption for partial models – such as are used in this book – but may not be the case in more general models.

The fourth factor that could change the optimal production is given if it is possible to make a *preliminary* decision about the decision variable; and then, after that veil of uncertainty is lifted, to revise this decision at some cost. It is easy to understand that if the cost of revising the decision upwards is larger than that of downward revision the preliminary optimal production will rise, in the other case it will fall. Downward irreversibility of gross investment is one related form of asymmetry.

Proposition 4: Suppose it is possible to make a preliminary decision $\hat{Y}$ and revise this upward (downward) at cost c_1 (c_2) then $c_1 \lesseqgtr c_2$ tends to imply $\hat{Y} \lesseqgtr Y^*$.

This source of asymmetry is unattractive from the theoretical point of view: it seems to be almost too trivial. Nevertheless, no general model is available which models the effect of asymmetric *ex post* flexibility in a general way, so we had to use the words 'tend to' in proposition 4. In chapter 8 we develop a linear model in which asymmetric *ex post* adjustments of the optimal are feasible. For non-linear equilibria models the result depends (as shown by Turnovsky 1973) on the interaction of 'normal production costs' and 'emergency cost' (third cross derivative). (For irreversibility of downward investment see section 7.3.2.)

From the practical point of view upward revisions seem often to be much easier (less costly) than downward revisions. Reselling production, getting rid of investment goods, laying off personnel in the short run (especially in business troughs or facing shocks affecting a whole industry), usually proves very difficult.

Let us sum up. We have found four propositions under which general rules forecasts on the impact of uncertainty are available. Risk aversion, technological concavity, disequilibria and asymmetric flexibility with high losses in case of too high values of the decision variable will tend to bias down the optimal value of the decision variable. Risk-loving, technological convexity and higher losses in case of too low values of the decision variable will tend to increase the optimal value under uncertainty.

Three of the four propositions refer to 'objective' factors related to costs, demand curves or other model characteristics, but not to risk attitude. We will call these factors 'technological reasons in the wider sense' to stress that it is not the subjective attitude towards risk (about which the economist does not have much information and even less right to make normative assumptions) which decide in these models. Stressing the objective factors does not mean that we deny that people may be risk-averse in many cases (see section 12.3 for very rough empirical evidence) on risk attitude. There are, however, reasons for this emphasis since

- the literature heavily concentrates on the risk attitude;
- there is little *a priori* information on risk attitudes, and these may change according to wealth and/or the riskiness of a decision; and
- under repeated decisions or choosing among diversified assets, firms should behave as if they were risk-neutral (see for example Nickell 1978, p. 8).[5]

The technological factors on the other hand are independent of subjective attitudes and relevant under repeated decisions. This may be of special importance if we use the results of these models to explain downward-biased expectation. Expected sales biased downward due to risk aversion could be dismissed into the group of errors due to psychological reasons in a sense, expected sales biased downward due to cost, demand and market structure are the greater challenge for the economists as a profession.

NOTES

1 Let it be remembered that these concepts of 'linear' and 'non-linear' technology differ from those used in production theory (where concavity and convexity respectively of the production function are termed 'non-linear' technology).
2 The derivation of equation 4.6 results, for example, directly from the equation for U_{XXY} (quoted by Hey 1981, p. 44), but there a follow-up of this special case, where U is linear in Z, is rejected for being trivial. The one-sided interest of economics in the consequences of risk attitude also becomes apparent when Lippmann & McCall (1981, p. 212) in an article on the state of uncertainty theory feel obliged to point out that other factors besides risk attitude can make uncertainty theory interesting: '... though in many circumstances risk aversion is a fact ..., much economic behaviour is a direct consequence of uncertainty and is independent of risk aversion.'
3 I am grateful to Manfred Nermuth from the University of Bielefeld for the statement that a 'failure' of operationalization must not be understood to mean that uncertainty in this case is not accessible to interpretation.

40 Theoretical part

4 The case that price will drop so low that demand is deliberately not produced, is usually excluded in the literature (cf. Leland 1972, Karlin *et al.* 1962, Hey 1979).
5 See, for example, Nickell (1978, p. 84): 'If there exist firms with identically but independently distributed random profits, then as $n \to \infty$ any risk-averse investor will wish each and every firm to maximize its expected profit.' The existence of large firms or the correlation of profits over a business cycle restricts application of this rule in practice.

5 The Theory of the Firm under Uncertainty (One-period Models for Optimal Output or Price Decisions)

5.1 INTRODUCTION

Even within the framework of expected utility maximization, the number of ways in which the decision of firms can be modelled under uncertainty are abundant and so are the papers written on this subject. One can model different market structures (the 'structure') like monopoly, oligopoly, monopolistic competition or competition proper; we have to conjecture which variable has to be decided upon *ex ante* (the 'mode'); uncertainty can exist about output prices or demand, about productivity or input prices or the availability of one or more factors (the choice of the random variable). Some models contain a variable which can be adjusted (or adjusts automatically) after the veil of uncertainty is lifted to guarantee the identity of production and demand, some models allow disequilibria, some partial adjustments (the 'flexibility' issue). Uncertainty can be modelled in general functional forms, if specific forms are used, we have to decide whether uncertainty occurs in an additive way or in some multiplicative type (the 'type').

Since we can combine many – albeit not all for logical reasons – kinds of 'structures', 'modes', 'types', 'degrees of flexibilities' and random variables, we can imagine how many models can be constructed.

As far as the 'structure' is concerned we will restrict ourselves to the cases of competition and monopoly, though we think that the one of our competitive model with demand uncertainty may be (and in literature is) considered a fair representation of oligopolistic strategy and that the monopoly model can incorporate elements of monopolistic competition. As far as the choice of the decision variable – the 'mode' – is concerned, we concentrate on the output decision; in some cases we deal with output price or both price and output as the decision variables ($p-q$-mode). Input choices are deferred to chapter 7. We will deal with disequilibrium models and partial flexibility in chapter 8. We cannot help dealing with the crucial question of the exact

42 Theoretical part

specification of the uncertainty term – the 'type' issue – since the results are not only sensitive to the question whether the uncertainty variable is added in an additive or multiplicative way, but also because even for the multiplicative type alternative sub-types are available.

We restrict ourselves in this chapter to one-period models (inventory models will be dealt with in chapter 6, dynamic investment models in section 7.3). We will use comparable notations for all models and show that the results can be derived for the majority of the models from one of the four propositions derived in chapter 4. In the literature, the results were arrived at in various and imaginative ways, despite the fact that most papers were written after the Rothschild–Stiglitz condition had been published. We will try to find which empirical facts are consistent with the model and which would contradict its assumptions as well as its forecasts in order to assess the relevance of the models in later parts of the book. We repeat that we use a partial approach since we optimize the decision of one side of the market.

5.2 COMPETITION

5.2.1 Conceptual Problems of Competition under Uncertainty

The competition model under certainty assumes, as we know, that the enterprise accepts the (uniform) market price and at that price can sell any chosen quantity. Profit maximization is attained at that output volume where marginal costs are identical with the (known) market price.

The competition situation under uncertainty poses conceptual problems even if the question of uncertainty as to input decision (or about the production function) is disregarded. The simplest model, most frequently dealt with in the literature, assumes price uncertainty[1] and retains the assumption that any chosen output can be sold. In this case the optimal output (Q ex ante mode) that has to be decided upon *ex ante*. An *ex ante* setting of the price (in uncertainty about the market clearing price) is not compatible with optimizing behaviour: if the selected price lies below the subsequently established market price, possible earnings are forgone, if it lies above, nothing can be sold.

The assumption of quantity uncertainty – uncertainty about demand – appears at first sight to contradict the basic idea of a competition model, because this sets out from the marketability of any output; therefore some authors (e.g. Hey 1979, p. 133) reject demand uncertainty as 'logically incompatible'.[2] Others (e.g. Hymans 1966) accept demand uncertainty in a competition model; most papers in inventory theory assume demand uncertainty under given prices without discussing the mechanism that makes the price exogenous.

The more recent disequilibrium theory describes models identical in structure and outcome with the competition model under demand uncertainty, as fix-price models under stochastic rationing (cf. Malinvaud 1980, p. 29ff, esp. formula 11, Benassy 1982, p. 45ff, and appendix C, Costrell 1983).

The rationale of price rigidity can be manifold. Of the authors who present the model of quantity uncertainty under competition, Hymans (1966) mentions the Cyert and March theory of the 'behavioural firm' that sees in price rigidity an attempt to reduce uncertainty. Hymans follows this up with his own concept of simultaneous price changes in industry overall, individual suppliers have no intention of increasing their market share and disposing of their eventual overproduction. The simultaneous price change of the whole industry is not quick enough to prevent an oversupply of goods making market clearance at short notice impossible. The short-term price rigidity in a competitive market may also stem from institutional causes (price regulation) or from the high cost of changing price (cf. the summary article by Amihud & Mendelson 1983, or the discussion on rational price rigidities in chapter 12 of this study).

Price rigidity in the oligopoly model as a possible mode of behaviour (beside price war) is well documented, it may – even without agreement – be an optimal strategy to preserve attained equilibrium (cf. for example, Scherer 1970, p. 25, where price rigidity is justified on grounds of the fragility of coordination problems and the kinky demand curve). Given rational causes for at least the short-term fixing of prices and market shares in oligopoly, the so-called competition model under demand uncertainty may capture some features of oligopoly behaviour under uncertainty.

However, price rigidities need not be caused by monopolistic or oligopolistic elements, inertia or information costs; they may be reactions to the uncertainty situation. Rothschild (1981, p. 114) says: '... firms' price setting behaviour does not – under uncertainty – conform to the "rules" of the equilibrium model, and that for good "rational" reasons. Prices are not as quickly as possible adapted to the prevailing state of the (positive or negative) surplus demand but are kept arrested over a longer period. This facilitates buyers' and sellers' planning for the shorter-term (uncertain) future. ...' Further reasons for such behaviour are given (cf. Rothschild 1981 or Okun 1980).

The model of section 5.2.4 shall be called for short the 'competition model under demand uncertainty', but its propositions are valid for price rigidity howsoever caused, be it one that can be tolerated in a competition model, that it results from oligopoly behaviour, be it information or transaction cost caused, enforced by price regulation or an optimal reaction to reduce uncertainty.

In the terminology of disequilibrium theory it would be designated a *fix-price model with stochastic rationing*.

44 Theoretical part

In the comparison here undertaken between certainty models and uncertainty models the respective exogenous price p is taken to be identical in both situations. In the partial analysis here presented (more exactly, a market side's partial analysis) this is probably the most obvious assumption. It would seem most realistic for the initial phase of an uncertainty situation (when the old prices are still valid). Generally speaking, in a more general uncertainty model the equilibrium price in the certainty model need not correspond to the equilibrium price under uncertainty.

5.2.2 Competition, Price Uncertainty, q-mode

Sandmo (1971) may be quoted as the classical reference for this model. Contrary to him and in keeping with the structure of our study we shall initially assume risk neutrality.

The producer faces an uncertain output price, but has some notion about the probability distribution of possible prices: $f(p)$. He must determine his output before the actual price is known, and will then accept the market price. He is a profit maximizer (equation 5.1) and chooses his quantity in such a way that marginal costs correspond to the expected value of the price (equation 5.2):

$$E\pi = \int_0^\infty [pq - c(q)] \, f(p) dp, \qquad (5.1)$$

$$\frac{\partial E\pi}{\partial q} = \int_0^\infty [p - c'(q)] \, f(p) dp = Ep - c'(q) = 0, \qquad (5.2)$$

where π is profit, p is unit price, $c(q)$ is cost function, and q is output (here also demand $x = q$).

Assuming that the expected price equals actual price under certainty, $p_0 = E(p)$, then produced quantity is equal under uncertainty and certainty ($\hat{q} = q^*$).

The result may also be derived from the calculation of Z_{YXX}. The maximization of the objective function under certainty (5.3) with respect to $Y(Y=q)$ results in the well-known marginal condition (5.4). The twofold differentiation by $X(X=p)$ shows the technology of this model to be linear.[3]

$$Z = \pi = p \cdot q - c(q) \text{ (objective function under certainty)}, \quad (5.3)$$

$$Z_Y = \pi_q = p - c'(q), \qquad (5.4)$$

$$Z_{YXX} = \pi_{qpp} = 0 \Rightarrow \hat{q} = q^* \text{ (according to proposition 2 in chapter 4)}. \qquad (5.5)$$

The economic substantiation of the outcome lies in the fact that a contingent higher price would increase the profit to the same extent that a lower price would decrease it, consequently expected profits are equal to actual profits under certainty. Expected profits cannot be increased by higher or lower output, therefore action is the same as under certainty.

5.2.3 Non-linear Objective Function

Under non-linear objective function (risk-aversion, risk-loving) maximization of expected utility will result in an outcome that differs from maximization of expected profit. This was demonstrated by Sandmo for risk aversion ($U'(\pi) > 0, U''(\pi) < 0$), and, somewhat modified by Hey (1979, p. 128f), the result is 'mirror-inverted' for risk-loving (equation 5.12ff).

The following equations show the objective function (5.6) and its first (5.7) and second (5.8) derivative. Since total output can be sold, output and quantity sold are identical ($q = s$; where s = quantity sold).

$$EU(\pi) = \int_0^\infty U[pq - c(q)]\, f(p)dp = EU\,[pq - c(q)], \quad (5.6)$$

$$\frac{\partial EU(\pi)}{\partial q} = E\{U'(\pi)\cdot [p - c'(q)]\} = 0, \quad (5.7)$$

$$\frac{\partial^2 EU(\pi)}{\partial q^2} = E\{U''(\pi)\cdot [p - c'(q)]^2 - U'(\pi)c''(q)\} < 0. \quad (5.8)$$

Next, the term with $c'(q)$ in equation 5.7 is brought to the right, $E[U'(\pi)\cdot Ep]$ is deducted:

$$EU'(\pi)\,(p - Ep) = E\{U'(\pi)\,[c'(q)] - Ep\}. \quad (5.9)$$

From equation 5.10 follows condition 5.11:

$$\pi - E\pi = (p - Ep)q, \quad (5.10)$$

$$\pi \gtreqless E\pi \text{ if } p \gtreqless Ep. \quad (5.11)$$

From the assumption of risk aversion the following equation (5.12) results (the opposite is true under $U''(\pi) > 0$):

$$U'(\pi) \gtreqless U'(E\pi) \text{ if } p \lesseqgtr Ep. \quad (5.12)$$

From this follows the weak inequality (5.13) and for the expected values follows the strong inequality (5.14):

$$U'(\pi)\,(p - Ep) \leq U'(E\pi)\,(p - Ep), \quad (5.13)$$

$$E[U'(\pi)\,(p - Ep)] < U'(E\pi)\,\underbrace{E(-Ep)}_{0}. \quad (5.14)$$

46 Theoretical part

The right side of equation 5.14 is zero, the left side of 5.14 is also the left side of equation 5.9; because of the equality in 5.9 this requires that the right side of 5.9 must also be smaller than zero. This happens only if $c'(q) < Ep$.

$$c'(q) < Ep. \quad (5.15)$$

Given rising unit costs (convex costs) the competitive firm under price uncertainty will produce, under risk aversion (risk-loving), less (more) than under certainty. (For non-convex costs the output under certainty is not defined.) This ascertained tendency is recorded in equations 5.16 and 5.17:

$$\hat{q} < q^* \quad \text{if} \quad U''(\pi) < 0, c''(q) > 0, \quad (5.16)$$

$$\hat{q} > q^* \quad \text{if} \quad U''(\pi) > 0, c''(q) > 0. \quad (5.17)$$

The economic interpretation of the differing outcomes, depending on the risk attitude, is the following: once the decision on the output quantity to be produced has been taken, production costs are fixed while profit fluctuates solely because of the differential revenues per unit sold. Through the transition from the known price under certainty to the price range under uncertainty the expected profits remain the same, but their dispersion increases. Risk neutrality means, roughly, indifference *vis-à-vis* greater dispersion, therefore the same quantity can be produced as under certainty. (Profit maximization is effected at the same output as maximization of expected profit.)

Risk aversion attaches co-decisive influence (aversion) to greater variance; maximum utility is attained at lower output. Mathematically, the result derives from the concavity of the objective function.

The result of the shift of optimal output as against certainty (which is shown under strictly convex/concave utility function) must be modified, if there are forward markets. Holthausen (1979) shows that – given the possibility of selling at least part of the output in forward markets at a known price (b) – the output of a firm acting under price uncertainty (even given the firm's risk aversion), will approach output volume under certainty. The output (calculated from $c'(q) = b$) depends solely on future price; if the latter is near the expected value of the current price (Ep), then price uncertainty in conjunction with risk aversion does not influence output.

5.2.4 Competition, Demand Uncertainty, q-mode (= Fix-price Model with Stochastic Rationing)

We have already referred (in section 5.2.1) to the conceptual difficulties of this model, but also to its possible realism. Here we want to present first the case of risk neutrality and then the case of non-linear utility function. In all models we must distinguish between sold quantity (quantity demanded x), and produced quantity q, since – due to price rigidity – output need not necessarily be completely sold. As we are dealing with a one-period model, it is implicitly or explicitly imputed that the 'goods left over' have no value (are not storable), and for the same reason, that no value is ascribed to unsatisfied demand (demand cannot be backlogged).

The profit maximizer's expected profit results from the difference between costs and expected revenue where revenue is the product of price and quantity demanded, or produced (whichever is the smaller, see equation 5.18).

$$E\pi = p \cdot \min[q,x] - c(q) = \int_0^q p \cdot x f(x) dx + \int_q^\infty p \cdot q f(x) dx - c(q). \quad (5.18)$$

By differentiation with respect to output we arrive at the marginal condition (5.19). This latter is subject to the following formally identical interpretations (equations 5.21a–d):

$$\frac{\partial E\pi}{\partial q} = \int_q^\infty p f(x) dx - c'(q) = 0. \quad (5.19)$$

$$\frac{\partial^2 E}{\partial q^2} < 0. \quad (5.20)$$

$$p[1 - F(q)] = c'(q). \quad (5.21a)$$

$$[1 - F(q)] = \frac{c'(q)}{p}. \quad (5.21b)$$

$$F(q) = \frac{p - c'(q)}{p}. \quad (5.21c)$$

$$p = c'(q) + \underbrace{p F(q)}_{\substack{\text{marginal cost} \\ \text{of uncertainty}}}. \quad (5.21d)$$

$$\hat{q} < q^* \quad (\text{if } c''(q) > 0), \quad (5.22)$$

- the expected marginal revenue is equated to marginal cost, expected marginal revenue being defined as marginal revenue (= price) multiplied by the probability that the last produced product can also be sold (5.21a); remember $F(q)$ = distribution function;
- the probability that the last unit will be needed $(1 - F(q))$, should equal the ratio of marginal cost to price (5.21b);
- the probability of overproduction, $F(q)$, should equal the quotient of marginal profit $[p - c'(q)]$ to price (5.21c);
- price is equated with an extended concept of marginal cost in that, beside the marginal cost of production, the probability that q cannot be sold ('marginal cost of uncertainty') is also taken into consideration (5.21d).

48 Theoretical part

The cause for the downward shift of output is that anticipated marginal revenue under uncertainty is not only equated with marginal production costs, but with marginal production costs plus a cost component resulting from the probability of the non-marketability of the production. This model is a special case of the model used in operationalization 3 in chapter 4, where $r'(y) = p$.

Price is exogenous, and to ensure comparability is assumed to be equal in the certainty and in the uncertainty model. For the uncertainty model here under consideration it is the most plausible assumption: it probably gives an adequate representation of entrepreneurial behaviour given uncertainty (the 'prevailing' price is maintained, at least temporarily). But we want to repeat that, generally, the equilibrium price in the uncertainty model need not necessarily equal the equilibrium price in the equilibrium model.

5.2.5 Non-linear Utility Function

For non-linear utility functions, quantity uncertainty and q-mode we follow the presentation of Hymans (1966); again one must distinguish between quantity produced (q) and quantity demanded (x). The objective function (maximization of expected utility) is expressed in equation 5.23; by differentiation with respect to (q) and supplementing both sides by $\int_0^q U'px - c(q)] f(x) dx$, equation 5.25 will result:

$$EU = \int_0^q U[px - c(q)] f(x) dx + \int_q^\infty U[pq - c(q)] f(x) dx. \quad (5.23)$$

$$\frac{\partial EU}{\partial q} = \int_0^q U'[px - c(q)] f(x) dx [-c'(q)] + \int_q^\infty U'[pq - c(q)] f(x) dx [p - c'(q)] = 0. \quad (5.24)$$

By trivial recasting this equation can be made comparable in form to equation 4.3 in the preceding chapter. Now the ratio of marginal profit to price will be equated, not with $F(q)$, but with $L(p,q)$.

$$\frac{[p - c'(q)] \int_0^q U'[px - c(q)] f(x) dx}{p - c'(q)} + \frac{\int_0^q U'[px - c(q)] f(x) dx \cdot c'(q)}{p - c'(q)} = \frac{\int_0^\infty \cdot U'[pq - c(q)] f(x) dx + \int_0^q U'[px - c(q)] f(x) dx}{EU'[pS - c'(q)]}. \quad (5.25)$$

$$\frac{p - c'(q)}{p} = \frac{\int_0^q U'[px - c(q)] fx dx}{EU'[pS - c(q)]} = L(p,q), \quad (5.26)$$

The theory of the firm under uncertainty 49

where S is sales (volume), and $ES = \int_0^q xf(x)dx + q\int_q^\infty f(x)dx$ is expected sales.

The function L (p,q) represents the relation of marginal utility under low demand (cumulated between 0 and q) to expected value of marginal utility from expected revenue (wherefore the denominator is made up of the same term as the numerator plus marginal utility of a produced unit under high demand – cumulated above q to infinity).

For $q = 0$ the function, too, is 0; it approaches 1 when q approaches infinity. It follows that optimal output (if $c'(q)$ does not equal zero) is always finite, and lower than output under certainty (where $p = c'(q)$). This outcome holds true under concave, linear and convex utility function. The following hierarchy exists between output under risk aversion, neutrality, loving and under certainty:

$$\hat{q}_{RA} < \hat{q}_{RN} < \hat{q}_{RL} < q^*; \tag{5.27}$$

where RA, RN, RL represent strict risk aversion, risk neutrality and strict risk loving respectively.

The economic argument for the ranking of the first three choices is this: the risk-averse businessman reduces output in order also to reduce the variance of the eventual outcomes; the risk lover increases output because by so doing his chances will also rise. Reduction in all these three alternatives as against the case of certainty takes place because in the case of uncertainty an additional cost component exists. 'Marginal costs of uncertainty' are positive and proposition 3 determines the outcome.

5.3 MONOPOLY

5.3.1 Conceptual Problems in Monopoly under Uncertainty

The monopolist (and equally the supplier in monopolist competition – cf. Lim 1980, p. 217) faces a negatively sloped demand curve. Uncertainty consists in the demand curve not being known for certain, in other words, that dependence of price on quantity (and vice versa) is only (conditionally) given for every state of nature. The question whether price uncertainty or quantity uncertainty prevails no longer presents itself. However, a new question arises, namely in what manner the relation between quantity and price is overshadowed by uncertainty (the 'type' issue).

Two possibilities present themselves where the second has to be subdivided again):

- uncertainty is additively superimposed over the demand curve $x = f(p) + u$; or
- uncertainty is multiplicatively superimposed over the demand curve type A: $p = g(x) \cdot u$; or type B: $x = f(p) \cdot u$.

50   Theoretical part

Both forms of uncertainty (additive and multiplicative respectively) will in certain circumstances give different outcomes for the behaviour comparison under certainty and uncertainty.[4] This outcome is familiar in the literature (cf. Karlin & Carr 1962, Zabel 1972). The fact, however, that the two different specifications of multiplicative uncertainty will also cause different outcomes has not been pointed out. (On the possibility of different outcomes for types A and B respectively, see sections 5.3.2.3 and 5.3.2.4.)

The second conceptual problem is the question of choice of the action variable (the mode issue).

In monopoly under certainty both a quantity and a price-setting strategy is possible, but both strategies lead to the same decision and the same profit. Under uncertainty this is no longer the case. We therefore distinguish three modes of behaviour:

- the monopolist sets output before demand is known (q *ex ante* mode) and thereafter lets the (actual) demand curve decide the market clearing price;
- the monopolist sets price before demand is known and thereafter lets the (actual) demand curve decide on market-clearing output (p *ex ante* mode);
- the monopolist fixes price and quantity before demand is known (p,q *ex ante* mode), output can be sold or not ($q \geqslant x$), and demand is fully satisfied or not ($q \leqslant x$). Disequilibria may therefore exist.

An additional decision faces the monopolist: whether he shall produce *any* demanded quantity (under p-mode) and /or if he wants to sell any quantity produced (under q-mode). Most studies assume (and so do we) that goods demanded are produced in all cases and that goods already produced are sold in any case.

Production of any demanded quantity under the p-mode offends against profit maximization if the price lies below marginal costs.[5]

The second problem presents hardly any difficulty (as long as price is positive) in one-period models. But in the multi-period model that assumption is very problematical, since storing is a possibly profit-increasing alternative.

The choice of the mode *per se* may either depend on external circumstances (obligation or commitment to supply, price regulation, etc.), or it must, itself, also be subject to microeconomic maximization. Profits and utility may be different under all strategies. Lim stated that the q-mode is definitely preferable to the q-p-mode, but the p-mode not under all circumstances (in view of the danger of high marginal production costs possibly exceeding the yield from greater flexibility, Lim 1980).

The expected profitability of a p- to a q-mode is determined by the cost curve (convex costs will make the q-mode more attractive).

5.3.2 Monopoly, q-mode, Price Taker

In these models the monopolist determines output (q-mode) and (after the veil of uncertainty has lifted) lets demand determine the market-clearing

The theory of the firm under uncertainty 51

price. That decision taken, costs are fixed and revenue alone fluctuates with the state of the market.

Since the letter f stands for the demand function, we shall deviate in this section from the rest of the study and shall use the Greek letter ϱ to express the density function.

5.3.2.1 Leland (1972)

Standard reference for this model is Leland (1972). Leland arrives at his findings with two qualifications of the universality of the problem formulation. The general implicit demand function would be $f(p,q,u)=0$, Leland assumes that the higher values of uncertainty u are connected with higher demand. This implies the following conditions:

$$\text{when } p=p(q,u) \text{ then } \frac{\partial p(q,u)}{\partial u} > 0. \qquad (5.28)$$

$$\text{when } q=q(p,u) \text{ then } \frac{\partial q(p,u)}{\partial u} > 0. \qquad (5.29)$$

Next, Leland introduces the principle of increasing uncertainty (PIU): 'as total revenue increases (for changes in p or q), it seems natural to expect that the "riskiness" or dispersion of total revenue will increase.'

He shows that PIU is tantamount to the condition that for all u the algebraic sign of marginal yield (with respect to u) equals the algebraic sign of expected marginal yield.

Under these conditions Leland comes to the constantly quoted result that – for the quantity-setting monopolist – quantity produced under uncertainty and under certainty are equal.

$$\hat{q} = q^* \text{ given the assumptions: 5.28, 5.29, PIU.} \qquad (5.30)$$

Neither Leland nor his followers in the literature are fully aware of the restrictive character of the *assumptions*, e.g. of the fact that the outcomes are not valid for the multiplicative case of type B. In his footnote 4 (Leland 1972, p. 279), he suggests that the premises (especially 5.28 and 5.29) are fulfilled for all forms of multiplicative demand and that the PIU, 'although not satisfied in all instances, has strong intuitive appeal' (ibid.).

5.3.2.2 Additive Uncertainty

For additive demand Leland's finding may be demonstrated through maximization of expected profit (equations 5.31–5.33) or application of the operationalization 2 (Z_{YXX}, see equations 5.34 and 5.35).

Equation 5.31 defines additive uncertainty, equation 5.32 the expected profit that is to be maximized. Since this corresponds to the profit to be

52 Theoretical part

maximized under certainty, the decision remains unaffected by the given form of uncertainty (cf. equation 5.33, but also application of operationalization 2 in equations 5.34 and 5.35).

$$p = g(q) + u_1 \qquad E(u) = 0. \tag{5.31}$$

$$E\pi = \int_{-\infty}^{\infty} \varrho(u)\{[g(q) + u]q - c(q)\}\,du,$$

$$\int_{-\infty}^{\infty} \varrho(u)u\,du = E(u) = 0,$$

$$\int_{-\infty}^{\infty} \varrho(u)\,du = 1, \varrho(u): \text{density function.} \tag{5.32}$$

$$E\pi = \pi^{\text{cert}} = g(q)\cdot q - c(q). \tag{5.33}$$

$$Z_Y = \pi_q = g(q) + g'(q)\cdot q - c'(q). \tag{5.34}$$

$$Z_{YXX} = \pi_{quu} = 0 \Rightarrow \hat{q} = q^*. \tag{5.35}$$

5.3.2.3 Multiplicative Uncertainty, Type: $p = g(q)\cdot u$

Given multiplicative demand of this type, when price is a function of quantity times an uncertainty term (with an expected value 1, see equation 5.36), uncertainty can change either costs or expected revenue (cf. equation 5.37), and the decision is identical with decision under certainty (equation 5.38). The outcome follows from proposition 2 (see equation 5.39):

$$p = g(q)\cdot u, \qquad E(u) = 1, \; (0 \leqslant u \leqslant 2). \tag{5.36}$$

$$E\pi = \int_0^2 \{\varrho(u)[g(q)\cdot u]q - c(q)\}\,du, \int_0^2 \varrho(u)\cdot u\,du = Eu = 1. \tag{5.37}$$

$$E\pi = \pi^{\text{cert}} = g(q)\cdot q - c(q). \tag{5.38}$$

$$Z_{YXX} = \pi_{quu} = 0. \tag{5.39}$$

5.3.2.4 Multiplicative Uncertainty, Type: $q = f(p)\cdot u$

A minimal change in the specification of uncertainty changes the outcome. If the demand curve under uncertainty is specified in the form of type B, this will result in a different implied price equation than in the preceding subsection (cf. equation 5.31 and 5.36). This formulation formally runs counter to Leland's assumptions (at least for an essential range of demand functions), though to my mind there is no *a priori* plausibility that speaks in favour of one or other type.[6] Nickell (1978), for example, without discussing economic rationality, chooses the type described in this subsection, nor does he emphasize his outcome's difference from that of Leland (1972).

With this type of multiplicative uncertainty expected costs remain unaffected by uncertainty (since they were determined *ex ante* in the

The theory of the firm under uncertainty

decision), but expected revenue is influenced by the form of the demand curve. If marginal revenue is concave in u, expected marginal revenue EMR (q,u) declines. In order to keep it even with marginal costs, output must be reduced to below certainty quantity.

The specific type of uncertainty is described in equation 5.40, the function to be maximized is represented in equation 5.41, the result of the maximization in equation 5.42. We assume f(.) to be invertible. For the shorter derivation of the result from the certainty model according to proposition 2 (operationalization 2) see equations 5.43 and 5.44.

$$q = f(p) \cdot u \Rightarrow p = f^{-1}\left(\frac{q}{u}\right), E(u) = 1. \tag{5.40}$$

$$E\pi = \int \varrho(u) \left[f^{-1}\left(\frac{q}{u}\right) q - c(q) \right] du. \tag{5.41}$$

$$\frac{\delta E\pi}{\delta q} = \int \varrho(u) \underbrace{\left[f^{-1}\left(\frac{q}{u}\right) + \frac{\partial f^{-1}\left(\frac{q}{u}\right)}{\partial q} q \right] du}_{\text{EMR } (q,u)} - c'(q). \tag{5.42}$$

$$Z_Y = Z_q = \text{MR}(q,u) - c'(q). \tag{5.43}$$

$$Z_{YXX} = Z_{quu} < 0, \quad \text{if MR } (q,u) \text{ concave in } u. \tag{5.44}$$

For instance, MR (q,u) is then concave, when the demand function is linear (cf. equation 5.45a–c) or when it is quadratic, or when demand elasticity is constant and smaller than -1 (these are sufficient conditions; for necessary and sufficient conditions see Nickell 1978, p. 91).

Sufficient conditions for MR (q,u) concave in u:

$$f(p) \text{ linear, or} \tag{5.45a}$$

$$f(p) \text{ quadratic, or} \tag{5.45b}$$

$$\epsilon < -1. \tag{5.45c}$$

The statistical background of the outcome consists in the uncertainty term entering into the argument of the implicit demand function (as a quotient) instead of standing 'outside' the demand function. Consequently, the demand function's features become significant and create technological concavity. The economic significance of the specification of uncertainty in this form is that, for a given u, price variation increases with increasing quantity produced, the concavity of marginal revenues resulting in the advantages of higher prices being more than compensated for by the disadvantages of lower prices.

5.3.3 Monopoly, *p*-mode, Quantity Taker

In this model the monopolist sets the price in the course of maximizing expected profit and lets the demand curve decide on the quantity to be produced.

5.3.3.1 Leland (1972)

Again Leland is the standard reference, and he shows that

> ... the introduction of uncertainty does not affect the price decision of the price-setting, risk-neutral firm with constant marginal cost. (Leland 1972, p. 285)

> ... when marginal costs are not constant ... Jensen's inequality may be used to show that if marginal cost is rising at a non-decreasing rate, the optimal price set by risk-neutral firms will be higher under uncertainty than under certainty; the opposite holds if marginal cost is decreasing at a non-increasing rate ($c''<0; c''' \leq 0$). (ibid).

We shall demonstrate that Leland's statements, though much quoted (see Hey 1979, p. 136ff) are, again, valid only under additive and under specific types of multiplicative uncertainty, and, second, that the equals sign for c''' in the final quote is misleading in the additive case.

5.3.3.2 Additive Uncertainty

Under additive uncertainty optimal price depends on the cost function. If $c'[q(p,u)]$ is concave (linear, convex) in u, then optimal price is lower, equal, higher than under certainty.

$$q = f(p) + u. \qquad (5.46)$$

$$E\pi = \int \varrho(u)[p \cdot (f(p) + u) - c(f(p) + u)] \ (du = p \cdot f(p) - \int c[f(p) + u] \varrho(u) du. \qquad (5.47)$$

In view of the symmetry of $\varrho(u)$, the difference between profit maximization and maximization of expected profit can be presented in the form of equation 5.48. The third derivative of the cost curve decides on the chosen price under uncertainty as relative to optimal price under certainty (5.49). This may also be shown through equations 5.50–5.52.

$$\frac{\partial \pi^{\text{cert}}(p)}{\partial p} - \frac{\partial E\pi(p)}{\partial p} = \int \varrho(u)\{\tfrac{1}{2}c'[f(p) + u] + \tfrac{1}{2}c'[f(p) - u] - c'[f(p)]\}f'(p)du. \qquad (5.48)$$

$f'(p)<0$, assumption of negatively sloped demand curve under uncertainty.

$$c''' \gtreqless 0 \Rightarrow \hat{p} \gtreqless p^*. \tag{5.49}$$

$$Z = p[f(p)+u] - c[f(p)+u]. \tag{5.50}$$

$$Z_p = f(p) + u + pf'(p) - c'[f(p)+u] \cdot f'(p). \tag{5.51}$$

$$Z_{pu} = 1 - f'(p) \cdot c''[f(p)+u]. \tag{5.52}$$

$$Z_{puu} = \underbrace{-f'(p)c'''}_{+} [f(p)+u]. \tag{5.53}$$

$$Z_{puu} \gtreqless 0 \text{ if } c' \left\{ \begin{array}{c} \text{convex} \\ \text{linear} \\ \text{concave} \end{array} \right\} \text{ in } u. \tag{5.54}$$

To determine the outcome in equation 5.48 the difference is used between curves Z_p and EZ_p respectively: when c' is convex in u, then the term in the curled bracket is positive, and since $f'(p)$ is negative, curve EZ_p must always lie higher than curve Z_p. It will therefore intersect the x axis later, and hence the price under uncertainty is higher than under certainty.

Equations 5.50–5.54 demonstrate the outcome by calculating Z_{YXX}. The third derivative must be strictly bigger or smaller than zero to guarantee a distortion ($c''' \leq 0$ does not suffice, as claimed by Leland 1972, p. 285, for the more general case).

The economic background to the shift between price under certainty and uncertainty lies in that marginal revenue (which is equal to marginal revenue under certainty) is to be equated to expected marginal costs. When a hypothetical quantity q is replaced by a batch of equally probable higher and lower outputs, expected marginal costs are equal to MC under certainty as long as the marginal cost curve is linear (be the total cost curve convex or concave). Not before the marginal-cost curve becomes convex do anticipated marginal costs rise on replacement of q_0 by $(q_0 + \epsilon)$ and $(q_0 - \epsilon)$. The higher price chosen is insurance to reduce the danger of having to produce in the range of high marginal costs if demand should turn out to be brisk.

5.3.3.3 Multiplicative Uncertainty, Type: $q = f(p) \cdot u$

Given multiplicative uncertainty of the type in equation 5.55, identically with additive uncertainty the cost function determines the outcome. The optimality condition – as in Leland – incorporates a second and third derivative (5.60b and 5.60c). Expected profits under uncertainty equal profits under certainty (equation 5.56), and do not influence the comparison of certainty and uncertainty (equation 5.57).

Theoretical part

$$q = f(p) \cdot u, \quad E(u) = 1. \tag{5.55}$$

$$Z = p \cdot f(p) \cdot u - c[f(p) \cdot u]. \tag{5.56}$$

$$Z_p = u \cdot f(p) + u \cdot p \cdot f'(p) - c'[f(p) \cdot u] f'(p) u. \tag{5.57}$$

$$Z_{pu} = f(p) + p \cdot f'(p) - c'[f(p) \cdot u] f'(p) - f'(p) \cdot u \cdot c''[f(p) \cdot u] f(p). \tag{5.58}$$

$$Z_{puu} = \underbrace{2f'(p)f(p)c''[f(p) \cdot u]}_{+} \underbrace{- f'(p) \cdot f^2(p) \cdot u \cdot c'''[f(p) \cdot u]}_{+} \tag{5.59}$$

$$c'' < 0 \text{ and } c''' \leqslant 0 \Rightarrow \hat{p} < p^*. \tag{5.60a}$$

$$c'' = 0 \qquad\qquad \Rightarrow \hat{p} = p^*. \tag{5.60b}$$

$$c'' > 0 \text{ and } c''' \geqslant 0 \Rightarrow \hat{p} > p^*. \tag{5.60c}$$

5.3.3.4 Multiplicative Uncertainty, Type: $p = g(q) \cdot u$

The multiplicative uncertainty of the stipulated type implies a demand function in the form $q = g^{-1}(p/u)$ assuming that the inverse of $g(\cdot)$ exists. Both marginal revenues and marginal costs will now change under uncertainty. If marginal revenue is concave in u and marginal costs convex in u, both defined as derivatives with respect to p, optimal price will be reduced; in the opposite case it will increase. If both are concave or both convex, then the result remains indefinite. Conditions for concavity or convexity, respectively, remain the same as in the above-named cases.

$$p = g(q) \cdot u \Rightarrow q = g^{-1}\left(\frac{p}{u}\right). \tag{5.61}$$

$$E\pi = \int \varrho(u) \left\{ \left[p \cdot g^{-1}\left(\frac{p}{u}\right) \right] - c \left[g^{-1}\left(\frac{p}{u}\right) \right] \right\} du. \tag{5.62}$$

$$Z_{YXX} = \pi_{puu} = MR_{uu} - MC_{uu}. \tag{5.63a}$$

$Z_{YXX} < 0$ if MR concave in u and MC convex in u. (5.63b)

$Z_{YXX} > 0$ if MR convex in u and MC concave in u. (5.63c)

5.3.4 Evaluation of the Outcomes of the Equilibrium Monopoly Models

All presented models have in common that an *ex post* variable brings about a market equilibrium: all produced goods are sold and all demanded goods are supplied, there remain no involuntary stocks and no demand unsatisfied. Yet the results are manifold, less ambiguous than might be expected from the literature, and dominated by Leland's exposition. The importance of the 'type of uncertainty' for the outcome necessitates a discussion on what is implied by the various assumptions and whether there are indications for a greater plausibility of certain assumptions.

An additive uncertainty means (in each of the two identical forms $p = f(q) + u$ and $q = g(p) + u$) an equal absolute amount of uncertainty under choice of high or low values of the action variables. The quantity-setting monopolist is unable to change absolute dispersion of the prices he has eventually to face, but relative dispersion may be reduced by selecting a smaller quantity hence equal absolute dispersion a higher expected price. Nor can the price-setting monopolist change the dispersion of quantities he may have to produce.

In multiplicative uncertainty there is a type of uncertainty for which the relative dispersion of the *ex post* control is independent of the choice of the action variable, and a type of uncertainty where relative dispersion declines with each smaller value of the action variable. The type of uncertainty that has this effect differs according to mode. For the quantity-setting monopolist the function $p = g(q) \cdot u$ results in a relative degree of uncertainty that cannot be influenced by the action: the relative scatter of contingent prices cannot be reduced even by a 'low' action. For the price-setting monopolist, the function $q = f(p) \cdot u$ will result in a relatively smaller dispersion of quantities to be produced, irrespective of chosen price. These two combinations of one type of uncertainty and one mode of behaviour were considered 'natural' by Leland and the authors who followed in his footsteps.

Conversely, there are two combinations of type of uncertainty and mode of behaviour which – for extensive ranges of demand functions (e.g. the linear and the quadratic – necessitate the choice of a low value of action variables, since this can reduce (absolute and relative) uncertainty. Given uncertainty in the form $q = f(p) \cdot u$, then the quantity-setting monopolist, by means of lower output, will reduce the dispersion of eventual prices. The price-fixing monopolist reduces the dispersion of outputs he will eventually have to produce by choosing a lower price. Due to technological fact (demand curve and cost curves, respectively), decisions will now be different from what they would be under certainty.

One cannot say in advance which type of uncertainty will be a more realistic description of real-world behaviour (there is no 'strong intuitive appeal' for either, therefore also not for the PIU). But at any rate the type of uncertainty (e.g. whether $p = g(q) \cdot u$ or $q = f(p) \cdot u$) does *not* depend on whether the monopolist is a price-setter or a quantity-setter (conversely, a dependence may exist where all modes are technically possible and are used according to profit maximization).

Thus, for example, given a price ceiling (be it fixed by regulation, approved by management/labour agreement or simply dictated by public opinion), we may expect the model $q = f(p) \cdot u$ to be realistic, and also that higher prices will show less dispersion.

58 Theoretical part

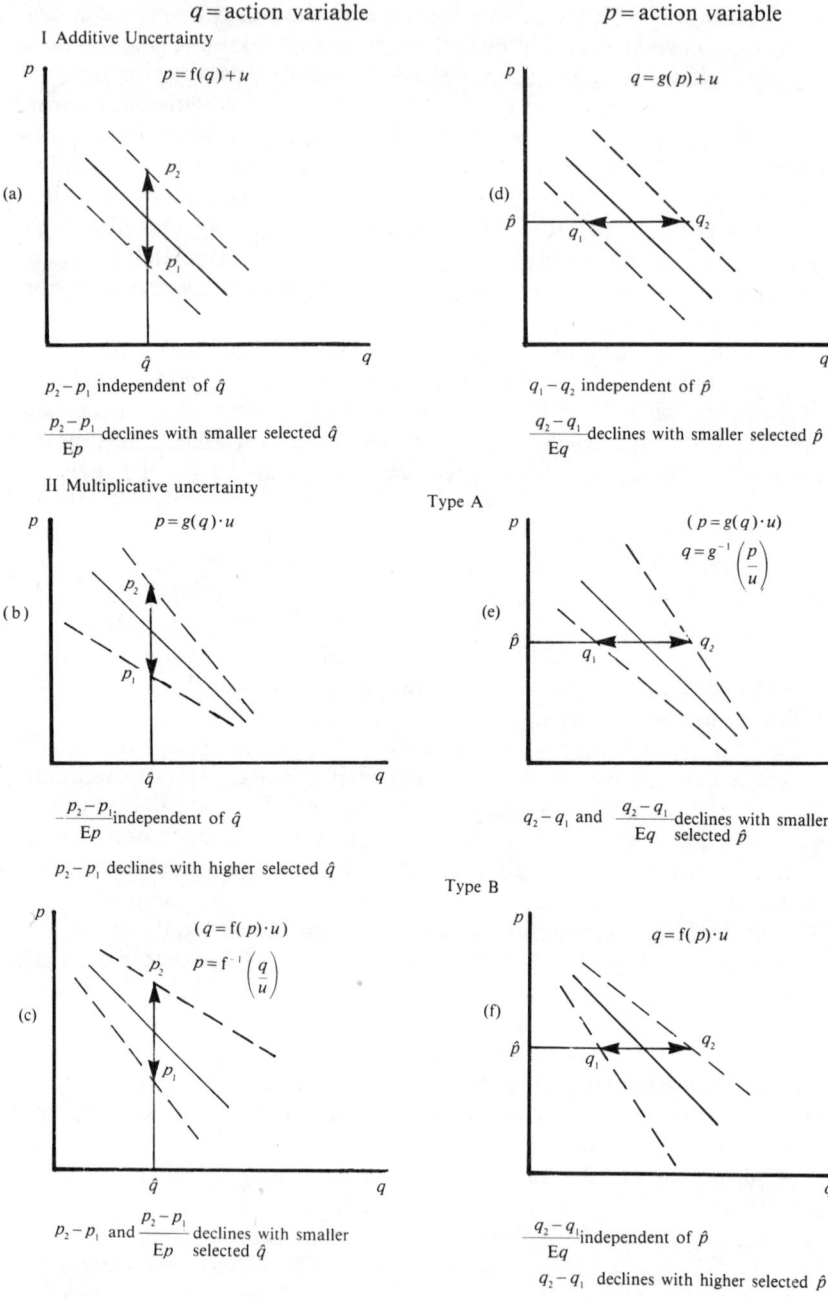

Figure 5.1 The six equilibrium models (two modes, and 3 types of uncertainty) of monopoly under uncertainty

The theory of the firm under uncertainty 59

Of the six models, the price-fixing monopolist will in principle be more susceptible to behave differently under uncertainty as compared to certainty (in all cases cost uncertainty is relevant, because of the unknown quantity to be produced), but there is little hope that universally valid empirical information can be gathered concerning the third derivative of the cost curve. The influence of the demand side is likely to be the more easily assessed (although it makes its appearance in only one model each under price and quantity uncertainty), since the condition of linear quadratic or constantly elastic demand functions appear relatively general. At least it may be assumed that the relevant subjective demand curve should hardly be more complex than linear or quadratic.

5.3.5 Monopoly, *p-q*-mode – Disequilibrium Model

A third 'behaviour' (mode) open to the monopolist consists in setting both price and quantity before the location of the actual demand curve becomes known. Mills (1962) has described this behaviour at an early stage, therefore it is also known as the Mills strategy. It is the behaviour providing least flexibility, since it is not possible – once actual demand becomes known – to react, either by price or by production adjustment; consequently market clearance cannot take place (unsold production or unsatisfied demand will result). This strategy is adopted when other strategies are not possible, but under certain circumstances (see Lim 1980) it may constitute a behaviour that may, at least as against the *p*-strategy, lead even to a higher profit than expected. The outcomes (we follow Karlin & Carr 1962) depend, at least in part, on the type uncertainty; equation 5.64 demonstrates a multiplicative form of uncertainty,[7] equation 5.69 shows an additive form. The second component relevant is a factor comparable to the marginal costs of uncertainty as revealed in proposition 3.

$$x = g(p) \cdot u$$
$$E(u) = 1$$
$$\phi(x) = F\left(\frac{x}{g(p)}\right) x \geq 0$$
$$f(x) = \frac{1}{g(p)} \cdot f\left(\frac{x}{g(p)}\right). \tag{5.64}$$

where ϕ and F are distribution functions.

$$x = g(p) + u, \quad E(u) = 0, \quad x \geq 0. \tag{5.65}$$

Borrowing from Karlin and Carr's derivation (with modification and adopting the present study's notation) the optimal price ($\hat{p}$) for the

60 Theoretical part

multiplicative case will result from the solution of equation 5.66; optimal quantity is arrived at by solution of equation 5.67 (cf. Karlin & Carr 1962, p. 165).

$$(p-c)\cdot g'(p)+g(p) = -\frac{c\cdot g'(p)\cdot N(p)}{D(p)} \quad (5.66)$$

where $(p-c)g'(p)+g(p)=0$ is that equation from which price p^* under certainty will result.

$$D(p) = \int_0^{F^{-1}(v)} [1-F(\xi)]\,d\xi, \xi = \frac{x}{g(p)}$$

$$N(p) = D(p) - F^{-1}(v)$$

$$v = \frac{p-c}{p}.$$

$$\hat{q} = g(\hat{p})F^{-1}\left(\frac{\hat{p}-c}{\hat{p}}\right). \quad (5.67)$$

The value p that satisfies equation 5.66 is always higher than the value under certainty (that value that results if the left side of the equation is zero), since the term on the right side is smaller than zero. Proof thereof (cf. Karlin & Carr): the denominator is positive, c is positive, $g'(p)$ – due to the negative slope of the demand curve – is negative, $N(p)$ is negative for all $p>c$.

$$g(\hat{p})F^{-1}\left(\frac{\hat{p}-c}{\hat{p}}\right) - g(p^*) \lesseqgtr 0 \Rightarrow \hat{q} \lesseqgtr q^*. \quad (5.68)$$

Optimal output q may be bigger or smaller than chosen output under certainty. Under very plausible assumptions, however, it is less than under certainty.

The reduction of optimal quantity results from two factors. Firstly, a lower optimal quantity follows from the higher price p (according to the negative slope of the demand curve under certainty), even if $F^{-1}(\cdot)$ equals 1. Second, the value of $F^{-1}(\cdot)$ is smaller than 1 if p is less than twice c. This latter is the slightly modified condition for the ratio of profit to costs, which was discussed in the competition model under demand uncertainty, and will be discussed in the newsboy model (cf. section 6.2). The modification adopted lies in that the higher optimal price $\hat{p}$ – established by optimization (and not the fixed price) – is put in relation to costs.

For additive uncertainty, optimal price and optimal quantity are derived from equations 5.69 and 5.70, respectively.[8]

The theory of the firm under uncertainty 61

$$\hat{p} \text{ satisfies } (p-c)g'(p) + g(p) = \int_{F^{-1}(v)}^{\infty} [1 - F(u)] \, du. \quad (5.69)$$

$$\hat{q} \text{ satisfies } \hat{q} = F^{-1}\left(\frac{\hat{p}-c}{\hat{p}}\right) + g(\hat{p}). \quad (5.70)$$

The left side in 5.69 would have to equal zero under certainty, the right side is positive, therefore optimal price ($\hat{p}$) in the additive model must be lower than under certainty. Optimal quantity $\hat{q}$ is undetermined. Two forces act in opposition to each other. Under very plausible assumptions the first term in 5.70 is negative, (since we maintain that profit, $p - c$, lies below c^9); on the other hand, price elasticity of demand will now militate in favour of higher output since price $\hat{p}$ is now lower than under certainty (p^*). The condition for the increase – or reduction – of output under uncertainty is given in equation 5.71:

$$g(\hat{p}) - g(p^*) + F^{-1}\left(\frac{\hat{p}-c}{p}\right) \gtreqless 0 \Rightarrow q \gtreqless q^*. \quad (5.71)$$

The present model imputes constant unit costs.

Nevin (1966) shows by numeric simulations that with rising unit costs the price may, also in the multiplicative model, lie below that under certainty.

The general tendency of multiplicative uncertainty rather leading to a price in uncertainty that lies above the price under certainty (thus strengthening a downward bias of output), and conversely, of additive uncertainty tending to lower the price (and therewith to a stricter condition for downwards distortion of output) may be explained (see Zabel 1972) by the fact that, given multiplicative uncertainty, a higher price will also reduce uncertainty (assume, for example, an excessively high price; then demand – and with it also uncertainty about demand – will, in the multiplicative case, drop towards zero).[10]

5.4 UNCERTAINTY ABOUT PRODUCTIVITY (PRODUCTION UNCERTAINTY)

Uncertainty may exist not only about prices or demand but also about the productivity of factor inputs. Breakdown of machinery may reduce productivity of capital, absenteeism or strikes may reduce productivity of labour. We have to distinguish in this chapter between labour, capital and capacity installed (for which we will use the letters L, K, and C) and labour, capital and capacity rendered (L_1, K_1 and q); we will use the term capacity for the maximum production feasible with the factors chosen if we do not relate output to the individual factors but to the combined inputs.

It is no surprise that the same forces which lead to divergent results for price and demand uncertainty are working also in a world of production

62 Theoretical part

uncertainty. Market structure, availability of an *ex post* control and the chosen type of uncertainty decides about the result.

Taking a model with given prices and given demand ($\bar{x}$) which may be interpreted as a model with production on order), expected profits depend on the smaller of order and capacity rendered (equation 5.72). Capacity rendered (q) depends on capacity installed and a random variable u for the uncertainty about the productivity of the combined factor. Optimal capacity installed is smaller than under uncertainty (equation 5.73), due to the extra cost, for example of potential breakdowns of machinery.

This result survives in an economically more important model where demand is the second random variable, whose density function f(x) is known (equation 5.74). The lower capacity planned in this case ($\hat{C} < C^*$) is due to the combined effect of potentially unsold production (in case of low demand) and the irregularities in the productivity (equation 5.74). The characteristic features of the model are the fix-price assumption and that inputs can be described by 'capacity'. There is no *ex post* control which closes disequilibria after the actual values of the random variables become known.

Production uncertainty model with given demand $\bar{x}$:

$$E\pi = \int_{-\infty}^{\bar{x}-g(q,C)} p \cdot q(u,C) f(u)du - \int_{\bar{x}-g(q,C)}^{\infty} p \cdot \bar{x} f(u)du - c(C)$$

$$q = q(u,C) \Rightarrow u = g(q,C) \quad E[q(u,C)] = q(C). \quad (5.72)$$

$$p \cdot q'(u,C) \cdot \underbrace{F(\bar{x}-g(q,C))}_{<1} = c'C)$$

$$c'(\hat{C}) < p \cdot q'(u,C) \Rightarrow \hat{C} < q^*, \quad (5.73)$$

e.g. if q is linear: $c'(\hat{C}) < p$.

Production uncertainty with unknown demand (f(x)):

$$E\pi = \int_{0}^{x-g(q,c)} \int_{-\infty}^{\infty} p \cdot q(u,C) f(u)f(x)dudx - \int_{x-g(q,c)-\infty}^{\infty} \int_{-\infty}^{\infty} pxf(u)f(x)dudx - c(C). \quad (5.74)$$

$$\underbrace{\int F(x-g(q,C))f(x)dx}_{A<1} \cdot q'(u,C) = c'(C) \Rightarrow \hat{C} < q^*,$$

e.g. if q is linear $\Rightarrow p = c'(\hat{C})$. (5.75)

Assuming the more standard competitive assumption that all production can be sold (though we first hold to the assumption of price stickiness), the impact of production uncertainty hinges on the type of uncertainty. For multiplicative of the type $q(C \cdot u)$ and additive uncertainty there is no impact; for a more general form $q(C,u)$ it depends on the concavity, linearity or convexity of the marginal revenue.

$$E\pi = p \cdot E[q(C,u)] - c(C) \tag{5.76}$$

if $q(C,u) = q(C+u)$ or $q(C,u) = q(C \cdot u) \Rightarrow \hat{C} = q^* = C^*$ (since $Z_{Cuu} = 0$)

if $MR_{uu} \lessgtr 0 \; q^* \lessgtr C^*$.

Other models relax the assumption that production uncertainty effects both inputs in the same way (as we did up to now modelling 'capacity'), now the substitutability of the production function becomes relevant. Ratti & Ullah (1976) and Roodman (1972) construct models where strong qualitative results can be derived; the assumptions necessary to do this have been criticized as too narrow by Pope & Just (1978).[11] Turnovsky (1973) and Feldstein (1976) have presented more general models, but were not able to derive strong qualitative results.

Roodman (1972) assumes a fixed coefficient production function. One of the two factors employed is reliable, so that service chosen is identical with service rendered; the second is unreliable in the sense that $F_1 = u \cdot F$, i.e. a service chosen is multiplied with a random variable with unit mean. It can be shown that expected output will be smaller than under uncertainty though the quantity of the unreliable factor chosen will be larger. The rationale for decreasing output under uncertainty is the extra costs of the reserve capacity. Roodman's model fits into our disequilibrium models, since there is no *ex post* control which can be adjusted after the veil of uncertainty has lifted, the extra cost of uncertainty guarantees an unambiguous result.

Ratti & Ullah (1976) investigates uncertainty about the productivity of labour and capital in a competitive model. The firm can choose the inputs of capital and labour (K, L), the actual services rendered by the inputs however, are uncertain ($K_1 = u \cdot K$, $L_1 = v \cdot L$) and therefore the output is also a random variable. u and v are assumed to have a unit mean, and no relation between them is defined. Ratti and Ullah show that, under the condition (i), that the elasticities of the marginal product curves[2] are as defined in equation 5.77a non-increasing functions of factor services (see equation 5.77b), and second condition (ii), that the factors complement one another less and less as more of each factor is employed (see equation 5.77c), the input demands of firms operating in an uncertain environment are less than under certainty and so is output:

$$\eta = \frac{K_1 f K_1}{f K_1}, \qquad \epsilon = \frac{L_1 f_{LL}}{f L_1}. \tag{5.77a}$$

$$\frac{\delta \eta}{\delta K_1} \leq 0, \qquad \frac{\delta \epsilon}{\delta L_1} \leq 0. \tag{5.77b}$$

$$\frac{\delta K_1 L_1}{\delta K_1} < 0, \qquad \frac{\delta f K_1 L_1}{\delta L_1} < 0. \tag{5.77c}$$

64 Theoretical part

This rather strong result is derived from the fact that formally the uncertainty variables are placed 'inside' the production function, therefore the functional form (concavity) of the production function helps to produce results diverging from the certainty case even in cases of risk neutrality. Higher and lower actual services from the chosen input factors are distortions from the optimal input combinations under certainty and these extra costs are 'severe' in the sense that there is no variable which can adjust after the factor service rendered is known.

5.5 CONCLUSIONS

The models presented in this chapter have put the current paradigm of uncertainty theory that 'risk aversion neutrality loving decreases leaves constant increases' optimal decision into perspective. Risk proneness decides about the result if profits are linear (as shown in proposition 1) and this is the case in the competition model with price uncertainty, or in the monopoly equilibrium model with price-taking behaviour and a special type of uncertainty (additive or multiplicative type A).

The results of the model in general however are much richer, since all kinds of technological concavity (convexity) tend to divert optimal results under uncertainty away from the certainty results. For example, in the case of other monopoly models, elements of the cost function or the demand function decide on the outcome. These effects could be exaggerated or mitigated by non-linear utility functions, but the models following proposition 2 show an economic importance of uncertainty independent of the risk attitude.

In models in which prices do not adjust rapidly enough to clear the market, the possibility of shortages and overcapacity becomes the important feature. Risk aversion is not necessary at all to bias optimal output downwards under competition with demand uncertainty, under monopoly with disequilibrium or in models with uncertainty about the productivity. Models in line with proposition 3 therefore show the most clear and unambiguous impact of uncertainty (without any reference to risk aversion). Critics of this type of model will maintain that price stickiness may be suboptimal, one of the principal questions for empirical research is therefore whether these models represent real-world behaviour and why a certain degree of price stickiness may have very economic reasons.

The models presented up to now concentrated on the one-period optimization, on one-decision variable only and on the strict divide between one variable which had to be decided upon *ex ante* without any feasibility to change the decision. The following chapters will deal with these shortcomings one by one.

NOTES

1. More accurately: uncertainty about output price.
2. Hey (1979) rejects quantity fixing under demand uncertainty for competition since profit would be higher in this case if the firms were to be set the price.
3. The term 'linear technology' is used according to the definition presented in section 4 ($Z_{YXX}=0$), not in the narrow sense of a linear cost and production function.
4. In one of the first articles of firm's behaviour under uncertainty, Leland (1972) characterized its form thus: that uncertainty ought to increase with rising expected sales (principle of increasing uncertainty – PIU).
5. Cf. Leland (1972); though he points out that the outcomes should tendentially remain intact if this is taken into consideration. This study, in conformity with the prevailing literature, assumes that demand will be satisfied, given available output.
6. The potential violation of PIU shall be demonstrated for the quantity-setter and for the alternative functions $p(q,u) = (q) \cdot u$ and $p(q,u) = h\left(\dfrac{q}{u}\right)$. As shown by Leland, PIU is equivalent to stating that (following the terminology of this study) R_{qu} has the same algebraic sign as $E(R_q)$. In the first case, R_{qu} and ER_q are identical and therefore also have the same algebraic sign.
   In the second case $R_{qu} = h'\left(\dfrac{q}{u}\right)\dfrac{-q^2}{u^2} + q \cdot \dfrac{1}{u} \cdot h''\left(\dfrac{q}{u}\right)\dfrac{-q}{u^2} + q \cdot h'\left(\dfrac{q}{u}\right)\dfrac{-1}{u^2}$,
   where the first and third terms are positive, and also the second under concavity of the demand function (therefore the whole term also under linear demand function).
   $ER_q = E\left[h\left(\dfrac{q}{u}\right) + q\dfrac{1}{u}h'\left(\dfrac{q}{u}\right)\right]$, the first term being positive and the second negative. Under linear demand curve of the type $p(q \cdot u) = \dfrac{q - a \cdot u}{bu}$, $b < 0$ R_{qu} is in any case positive $\left(R_{qu} = \dfrac{2a}{b} \cdot \dfrac{-1}{u^2}\right)$, $ER_q \dfrac{2q}{b} E \dfrac{1}{u} \dfrac{q}{b}$ only if $|2\dfrac{q}{b}\left(\dfrac{1}{u}\right)| < |\dfrac{-a}{b}|$, which is not generally the case.
7. The type of multiplicative uncertainty is not of the same importance in the p-q-mode as in equilibrium models, because one differentiates simultaneously with respect to p and q.
8. It is always assumed that price is 'sufficiently' high in the sense of $p > c$, and $\hat{p} > c$ respectively.
9. In this case the lower price (lower as compared with certainty), enters into the calculation.
10. Zabel shows also that – qualitatively – the statements and effects of uncertainty remain similar in the one-period model and the dynamic model, but that stricter conditions are needed in the multiplicative case, in order to guarantee that the solution be unambiguous. In another article (Zabel 1970, p. 215), Zabel deals with the difference between constant and rising marginal costs. In optimization conditions for the dynamic case Karlin & Carr exclude the feasibility of backlogging and obtain a value as in equation (6.27) in section 6.7. In our opinion, use of the right side of (6.14) would be more realistic.

66 Theoretical part

11 Pope and Just criticize the assumption that capital rendered is a multiplicative function of capital installed. This implies that the variance of capital rendered increases also with higher capacity installed, which contradicts some notion of greater flexibility. I do not find this criticism very convincing, since flexibility does not refer to the one input alone but to the substitutability of two inputs, and this effect is fairly dealt with in the model.

6 Inventory Models under Uncertainty

6.1 THE RELATION BETWEEN INVENTORY THEORY AND THE THEORY OF THE FIRM

Most models relating to firms' behaviour under uncertainty are limited to one-period optimization (static models), yet they are applied to a variety of market structures, modes, cost curves, etc. When facing more sophisticated versions, we cannot really bypass problems resulting from dynamic effects and have to enter the world of stock models. To avert complexity other simplifying assumptions are made, for example in most cases fixed prices.[1] This follows the specialization between a dynamic inventory theory (assuming fixed prices) and a static theory of the firm under uncertainty (allowing for different market structures and modes) which is also reflected in the choice of publication media: inventory theory is mostly published in operations research journals (*Management Science, Operations Research Procedure, Naval Research Institute*) and utilizes the technique of dynamic programming, and further on that of lattice programming.[2] The theory of firms under uncertainty is published in the journals of mainstream economics and is admitted to the more sophisticated textbooks of microeconomics[3] (where inventory theory has not 'arrived'). Of this division in the field there are exceptions – the studies, in the 1960s, of Arrow & Mills (who both were set on combining economics and operations research), and the work of Zabel (1970, 1972) in the 1970s.

Our main emphasis in the present study is on looking for the answer inventory theory has to offer to the question whether more or less is produced under uncertainty than under certainty. Inventory theory does not answer this question directly but rather aims at ascertaining the optimal 'goods in stock plus production but before demand' (stocks on hand); from this magnitude it is possible to infer the volume of output.

A critical survey of the literature related to output under certainty and uncertainty reveals that this problem does not excite the main interest of this special branch of our science.[4] This may be due to most authors having a definite preconceived opinion in this matter (e.g. that stocks should be higher under uncertainty, as shown in section 6.7); or it may be that the problem whether more complicated dynamic systems have

68 Theoretical part

unique solutions has more appeal from the theoretical point of view than does the question whether empirical parameters lie within certain boundaries. The scanty interest evinced for this problem has, we feel, led to totally unrealistic assumptions (e.g. to the unquestioned assumption that orders cannot be backlogged: the no-backlog = lost-sales case), and in some otherwise seminal articles even to some startling errors (see appendix 4).

Most results of the inventory models relevant to this question do not depend on the form of the cost curve. Therefore a linear cost-curve behaviour pattern is adopted for most of the models. Constant unit price is also assumed as a rule, and inventory models are usually notated as cost-minimizing models. To show that modelling inventories are only the dynamic extension of the firm's model, we mould them into profit-maximization models, whenever possible. The standard of comparison for the uncertainty model is accordingly not the certainty optimum (since as for linear models under competition, there is no unique optimal value under certainty), but the expected value of demand. In section 6.6 we discuss the extension to non-linear models and are able to compare the optimal decision under certainty and uncertainty.

6.2 THE NEWSBOY MODEL

The starting point, as a rule, for inventory models (see for example Johnson & Montgomery 1974, p. 45ff, or Hillier & Lieberman 1980, p. 514ff) is still the newsboy model (which of course is a static model). The newsboy faces uncertain demand, he must ask a fixed unit price p and must commit himself to purchasing a definite quantity at a fixed unit cost c.[5]

The newsboy model is virtually identical with the competition model under uncertainty (section 5.2.4.), except for constant unit costs being assumed. In inventory literature, discussion is absent on what market form this model is supposed to represent (and whether quantity-setting is a rational strategy).

Optimal production (order) is determined by the ratio of cost share to profit share. Costs under insufficient output are the foregone profits $(p-c)$; under overproduction (or too large orders), actual costs of production or ordering costs (c) must be taken into account. By definition at this stage the value of stocks is not assessed. If unit costs and unit profits are equal ($p = 2c$), then optimal production is equal to the expected value of demand,[6] if unit costs are bigger (smaller) than unit profit, then less (more) than expected demand will be produced.

$$E\pi = \min\ [p \cdot x, p \cdot q] - c \cdot q. \qquad (6.1)$$

Inventory models under uncertainty   69

$$F(q) = \frac{p-c}{p} \Rightarrow \hat{q} \lesseqgtr Ex \text{ if } p \lesseqgtr 2c. \qquad (6.2)$$

Formally this model is a subcase (for linear costs) to the competition model with demand uncertainty (section 5.2.4). For linear costs the comparison with the certainty model is inapplicable (since the latter offers no unique optimum), and we need a new reference point. The qualifications for lower output as against expected value of demand are more rigid than those in section 5.2.4, where optimal output is compared with certainty output. Here the advantages and disadvantages of low output (i.e. costs against forgone profits) are set off, whereas the invariable positive marginal costs of uncertainty must definitely result in a lower value of output as against certainty in the competition model with demand uncertainty.

6.3 APPROXIMATION OF THE DYNAMIC EFFECTS RESULTING FROM GOODWILL COSTS AND HOLDING COSTS (MILLS 1962)

The first step to incorporate dynamic effects may be seen in allowing for the cost of storing unsold goods; alternatively in eventual reduction of future demand due to current inability of supply (goodwill cost). The former will be a function of the difference between produced and demanded quantity if the difference is positive, the latter if the difference is negative. The inventory carrying costs will certainly include holding costs in the narrower sense (storage space, obsolescence, finance, etc.); these may possibly be balanced against discounted expected sales revenue. The goodwill cost can be interpreted as loss of customers, due to doubts about the firm's future supplying capability, or efficiency. The goodwill cost may also be assessed as a surcharge on production costs, generated by the commodity being obtained by emergency procurement. It would be unusual to allow a discount against goodwill cost for expected revenues from demand postponed to the next period (parallel to that due to expected revenues from today's unsold stocks).

Optimal output is the outcome of maximization of expected profits (equation 6.3). Equation 6.4 demonstrates condition for optimal output, which is rearranged in equation 6.5. The optimal stock on hand will be the greater, the higher the price (p) and goodwill costs (g), and the smaller, the higher production costs (c) and holding costs (h).

When goodwill costs and inventory costs are equal ($g = h$), then they cannot change optimal output in relation to expected demand. If optimal output was bigger (smaller, equal) in the newsboy model, then so it will be now. If costs were considerably higher in the newsboy model than profit (e.g. $p - c = 0,1$), then even high goodwill costs in relation to holding costs (e.g. $g = 0,4$, $h = 0,2$) cannot lead to optimal stocks (output) above the expected value of demand.

$$E\pi = \int_0^q pxf(x)dx + \int_q^\infty p \cdot qf(x)dx - c \cdot q - \int_0^q h(q-x)f(x)dx \int_q^\infty g(x-q)f(x)dx. \quad (6.3)$$

$$(c+h)F(q) - (p+g-c)[1-F(q)] = 0. \quad (6.4)$$

$$F(q) = \frac{p+g-c}{p+g+h} \text{ e.g.} : p=1, \ c=0,9, \ g=0,4, \ h=0,2 \ F(q)=0,31 \Rightarrow \hat{q} < E(x). \quad (6.5)$$

6.4 DYNAMIC MODELS USING THE DYNAMIC PROGRAMMING METHOD

More sophisticated dynamic models do not attempt to estimate future revenue and costs resulting from the production decision by evaluation of holding cost and goodwill loss: they set out on long-term optimization using the technique of dynamic programming.

A dynamic model cannot assume a zero starting stock, I, at the beginning of each period, since the existence of stocks after demand is the essence of the model. The starting stock shall be designated I. The decision variable is again the optimal 'stock on hand', which is designated by $\hat{y}$. Now optimal production will implicitly result from the difference $\hat{q} = \hat{y} - I$.

Out of the many inventory models those shall be dealt with where demand distribution[7] is identical from period to period and is not altered by past realizations (i.i.d. assumption). The decision is to be made for an infinite planning horizon, inventory costs shall depend on the level of the inventory at the end of the period (after demand has been disclosed and output been delivered). Fix costs in one order (start of production) and delivery lags are neglected.

The technique employed for solving this problem is that of a recursive equation and the technique to solve it is supplied by dynamic programming. It can be shown that the optimal quantity $\hat{y}$ is equal in each period and can be determined as the joint minimum of costs of the next period and of all future periods ('principle of optimality', see Howard 1966). Among the pioneers of the application of this method we may name Bellmann et al. (1956), Arrow et al. (1951), Dvoretzky et al. (1953), Wagner (1962), Iglehart & Karlin (1962).

The presentation follows that of Veinott (1966), one of the most frequently quoted survey studies, which on the one hand conveys a precise exposition of the method and the literature, but which also contains an error in the treatment of backlogged orders that is also found in a large number of other studies. For a more recent exposition see Hey (1981, pp. 133ff.); however, we have incorporated the possibility of an order backlog in the flow-maintenance equation, take cognizance of revenues from backlogged demand and of goodwill and inventory costs.

Inventory models under uncertainty 71

We use x again for (uncertain) demand, y denotes inventory level after production (q), I denotes inventory level before production. V(I) is maximum expected profit due to an inventory I. Initial stock before production is determined by the flow-maintenance equation (6.6).

$$I_{t+1} = \begin{cases} a(-x_t + q_t + I_t) & \text{if } x_t \leq q_t + I_t. \\ b(-x_t + q_t + I_t) & \text{if } x_t \geq q_t + I_t. \end{cases} \quad (6.6)$$

The recursion formula spells out (q = y − I)

$$V(I) = \max_{q \geq 0} \int_0^{q+I} \{[px - h(y-x)] + \alpha V[a(-x+y)]\} f(x) dx + \int_y^{\infty} \{py + bp(x-y) - g(x-y) + \alpha V[b(-x+y)]\} f(x) dx - cq. \quad (6.7)$$

Differention with respect to q yields

$$0 = \int_0^{\hat{q}+I} \{-h + \alpha a V'[a(-x+\hat{q}+I)]\} f(x) dx + \int_{\hat{q}+I}^{\infty} \{p - \alpha bp + g + \alpha b V'[b(-x+q+I)]\} f(x) dx - c. \quad (6.8)$$

The q in equation 6.8 always appearing in the form of $\hat{q} + I$, there will be a post-order stock $\hat{y}$. If I is smaller than this value, then production will be carried on until this value is reached. For $I \leq \hat{y}$ we can write equation 6.7 as equation 6.9:

$$V(I) = \int_0^{\hat{y}} \{[px + h(\hat{y}-x)] + \alpha V[a(\hat{y}-x)]\} f(x) dx + \int_y^{\infty} \{p\hat{y} + \alpha bp(x-\hat{y}) + g(x-y) + \alpha V[b(-x+\hat{y})]\} f(x) dx - c(\hat{y}-I). \quad (6.9)$$

From this follows:

$$V'(I) = c \text{ for } I < \hat{y}. \quad (6.10)$$

The case $\hat{y} < I$ need not concern us since, given optimal behaviour starting out from zero inventory, it never arises.

If we insert equation 6.10 in equation 6.8, this will give us:

$$(-h + \alpha ac)F(\hat{y}) + [p - \alpha bp + g + \alpha bc][1 - F(\hat{y})] = c. \quad (6.11)$$

$$F(\hat{y}) = \frac{p - \alpha bp + g + \alpha bc - c}{p - \alpha bp + h + g + \alpha bc - \alpha ac} = \frac{(p-c)(1-\alpha b) + g}{p + g + h - \alpha b(p-c) - \alpha ac} \quad (6.12)$$

Let us first interpret the functional equation 6.7 and then the result (equation 6.12). The first term in each curled bracket represents the sales revenue as in the one-period model. The $h\,(\cdot)$ and $g\,(\cdot)$ terms represent holding and goodwill costs, the argument in both cases is the difference between the post-order stock ($y = I + q$) and the demand. The $V\,(\cdot)$ terms calculate the properly discounted future expected consequences from an item stocked or a demand backlogged. In the first case the consequence is positive since an item stocked decreases future production costs (depending on the discount parameter, α, and the durability parameter, a.) In the second case it is a cost since backlogged demand has to be produced in the next period (depending on the degree of backlogging b). The second term in the second line is the term often forgotten in the literature; it represents the expected revenue of backlogged demand (see section 6.5).

The result (equation 6.12), which firms have to follow according to their optimal strategy, defines an optimal post-production (order) stock y. Some of the implications of the formula are:

- if $\alpha = 0$ (infinitely high time discount), or if a and b equal zero (perishable commodity and loss of all unfilled demand) then the formula is identical with that of the static case. This is an eminently logical outcome;
- if $b = 1$ (total backlogging), then foregone profit (the opportunity cost of lower output) is greatly reduced. The quantity that should optimally be produced, decreases. The outcome is in contradiction to Veinott, who takes only the cost of additional production into account;
- if $b = 0$ (no backlogging), but at the same time stocks are not completely perishable (a is larger than zero), then optimal production will – also under $g = h$ – be larger than in the static case, since stocks save subsequent costs (whereas an unfilled order brings no revenue); and
- optimal output (stocks on hand) declines with rising b (contrary to Veinott, see chapter 6.5.

Generally, the forces that applied in the static case remain the basis of the decision. If the profit share was relatively low, rather less than expected demand will be produced (under symmetrical behaviour of goodwill cost and inventory cost, or of b and a respectively). This will be seen, for example, if it is assumed that $g = h = 0$ and $a = b = 1$. In this case the formula collapses to the newsboy result:

$$F(y) = \frac{(p-c)(1-\alpha)}{p(1-\alpha)} = \frac{p-c}{p} \quad \ldots \text{equation 6.2} \quad (6.13)$$

It can further be shown that in general the consequences both of high and low output are of less significance in the dynamic case, since foregone profit opportunities may be caught up later (under discount), and remaining stock can (under discount) be profitably utilized.

6.5 THE CRUCIAL ROLE OF BACKLOGGING

Inventory literature learned a long time ago to distinguish between the case where excess demand can be postponed into the next period (backlog case, BL) and the alternative case where demand which is not provided for by stocks on hand is lost (lost-sales case, LS). But the importance of the feasibility of backlogs as to the production (order) volume and especially on its relation to expected demand, has not been stressed adequately. Secondly, we will show that most models intending to deal with the backlogging case, do not do it adequately, forgetting the revenues from backlogged demand.

The formulas for the backlogging case and the lost-sales case implied by equation 6.12 from the last section are presented in equations 6.14 and 6.15, the partial derivative of equations 6.14 with respect to b shows that the optimal inventory decreases with the feasibility of backlogging. This is a logical result, since the feasibility of backlogging reduces the cost of an eventually too-small inventory (demand is now lost only to a certain extent). To demonstrate how important the influence

$$BL: F(y) = \frac{(p-c)(1-\alpha b)+g}{p+g+h-\alpha b(p-c)-\alpha ac}, \quad (6.14)$$

$$LS: F(y) = \frac{p-c+g}{p+g+h-\alpha ac}, \quad (6.15)$$

$$\frac{\partial \hat{y}}{\partial b} < 0, \quad (6.16)$$

of backlogging can be, we further simplify our model to assume that $g = h = 0$, $a = 1$ and b is 0 respectively 1 in the two cases to be distinguished. For the lost-sales case we arrive at formula 6.18, which tells us for large α (a small time discount) that nearly all demand that can be imagined should be provided for, and optimal stocks are far higher than expected demand. On the other hand, if we take $b = 1$, we arrive at the newsboy formula 6.17, implying that we should produce less than expected demand as long as profits $(p-c)$ are smaller than unit costs, which as we have argued is quite likely. The outcome of the models in respect of optimal inventory is different depending on the assumption about backlogging. This is not surprising from the economic point of view since backlogging softens the problem of shortages quite a lot. If this cushion against uncertainty is feasible to the same extent as the other one (inventories allow overproduction to be transferred into the next period), then we have a symmetric influence of the dynamic forces and are back to the forces governing the

74 Theoretical part

static case. If dynamics work asymmetrically in one direction (too-large inventories can be carried over, too-small production is demand lost) then the result will be biased in one direction.

$$\text{BL case for } g=h=0,\; b=1:\; F(y) = \frac{p-c}{p} \quad . \tag{6.17}$$

$$\text{LS case for } g=h=0,\; b=0:\; F(y) = \frac{p-c}{p-\alpha c} \tag{6.18}$$

i.e. for
$\alpha \to 1 \Rightarrow y \Rightarrow \infty$.

In the light of this crucial role of backlogs, we have to raise the question, why such important studies (like Hillier & Lieberman 1980, p. 529f, Johnson & Montgomery 1974, p. 52ff, Hey 1981) refer implicitly to the lost-sales case without making this crucial assumption explicit. One of the answers is that many models referring to the BL case do not accomplish this task in a correct way. They model the costs of backlogging (the production costs for that part of excess demand, which can be carried over into the next period) but they forget the revenues of backlogs. An especially clear example of this error is the otherwise excellent paper of Veinott (1963), in which he omits the revenues of expected sales from backlogged demand and arrives at the formulas 6.19 and 6.20, which imply that the feasibility of backlogging increases optimal inventory (6.21):

$$F(y) = \frac{p + \alpha cb - c}{p + h + \alpha(cb - ca)} \text{with backlog } (b>0). \tag{6.19}$$

$$F(y) = \frac{p - c}{p + h - \alpha ca} \text{without backlog } (b=0). \tag{6.20}$$

$$\frac{\partial \hat{y}}{\partial b} > 0. \tag{6.21}$$

We have classified in appendix 4 the articles concerning inventory strategies in Management Science Literature according to (a) their explicit reference to the LS case, (b) their implicit reference without mentioning it, (c) their explicit and correct treatment of backlogs, and (d) their explicit and wrong treatment of backlogs. We found only four papers and textbooks out of twenty-seven sources scrutinized in which backlogs were treated correctly, and none of them was concerned with the comparison of optimal stocks with expected demand.

The only case in which no error would be made by Veinott would be if his p is interpreted to incorporate an element of expected sales out of backlogs $p = (1 - \alpha)P$, where capital P may serve for a moment as the 'product price proper'. In that case $\dfrac{\partial \hat{y}}{\partial b}$ would become negative. However, p was introduced in the LS case by Veinott and not changed after backlogs were incorporated. The presentation of a formula in which b is partly made explicit and partly hidden in another variable (introduced as a constant) is at least very unusual and misleading. Above all, textbooks and papers following Veinott did not reveal the hidden component of p.

6.6 AN EXTENSION TO NON-LINEAR MODELS

We have demonstrated the influence of (increasing) uncertainty on optimal inventory with the help of linear models. Non-linearity of production costs does not change the results qualitatively, but it can solve one of the main disadvantages of linear models, namely that they do not allow comparison with optimal decisions under certainty (since there is no single optimal point under certainty).

The comparison can be made if we assume non-linear production costs. This will be shown first for non-linear production costs in a model approximating the long-run effects of uncertainty with goodwill and holding costs only (see section 6.3). The comparison may be of limited value since there is no very compelling interpretation for goodwill and holding costs under certainty, they are assumed to be zero in the certainty model. Optimal decision under uncertainty can be written in a form allowing to interpret the components of 'marginal cost of uncertainty' (operationalization 3).

$$E\pi = p \int_0^q x f(x)dx - h \int_\infty^q (y-x)f(x)dx + p \int_q^\infty q f(x)dx$$

$$- g \int_q^\infty (x-q)f(x)dx - c(q). \qquad (6.22)$$

$$p - pF(q) = c'[q] \underbrace{- g[1 - F(q)] + hF(q)}_{B}. \qquad (6.23)$$
$\underbrace{}_{A}$

If $g = h \Rightarrow B = 2gF(q) - g;$ and if $F(q) \approx \tfrac{1}{2} \Rightarrow B \approx 0.$ (6.24)

Component A represents the usual extra cost of uncertainty as seen in the competition model with demand uncertainty; B is an extra component increasing the marginal cost if inventory costs are high and decreasing if goodwill costs are high. In general, B will be less important than A from the empirical point of view. In the case where g and h are approximately the same and production lies somewhere near expected demand, B becomes zero.

76 Theoretical part

This simple non-linear model demonstrates that the forces working are the same whether we compare optimal inventory with expected demand in a linear model or with the outcome under certainty in a non-linear model. The results from the non-linear, one-period model with demand uncertainty, where uncertainty had unambiguously decreased production, can be generalized to the result that this is very likely in this case since goodwill and holding costs will not be high enough in relation to the price to change the result.

Finally, in a non-linear model of the type of equation 6.22, but with non-linear cost, we get the solution of equation 6.25:

$$p - \underbrace{pF(q)}_{A} + \underbrace{\alpha a c'(\cdot)}_{C} + \underbrace{\alpha b c'(\cdot) - \alpha b p}_{D_1}$$

$$\underbrace{-\alpha b c'(\cdot) F(q) + \alpha b p F(q)}_{D_2} = c'(q) + B. \qquad (6.25)$$

where $|A| > |C|$ since $p > c'(\cdot)$; $D_1 < 0$, $D_2 > 0$, $|D_1| > |D_2|$ since $F(q) < 1$.

A very interesting interpretation of this equation is feasible. On the left side we get A, which are the extra costs of uncertainty in a non-linear, one-period model. These extra costs are reduced by the components C and D, but cannot be equated. C is positive (reducing the unfavourable effect of uncertainty) and can be interpreted as the opportunity of using products left from the last period to meet today's demand. D is negative, it consists of the negative part D_1 and the positive D_2, but in absolute terms D_1 is larger than D_2. The economic interpretation of D is the mirror image of C namely the opportunity to use backlogged demand from yesterday for profit-making today. The total influence of D and C is the reduction of the static 'marginal costs of uncertainty'. A part of the negative influence of uncertainty is recovered under dynamic conditions, since cost and profits are not sunk or lost for ever in a dynamic process. But uncertainty is still unarbitrarily reducing production in a dynamic model as compared to certainty since the C and D components cannot match the A component.[8]

A generalized version of operationalization 3 for the dynamic case:

p	−	A	+	[C	+	D]	=	c'(q)	+	B
MR certainty		marginal costs of uncertainty recovered in a static model		marginal costs of uncertainty recovered in a dynamic system				MC under certainty		goodwill/ holding costs asymmetry

(6.26)

We want to sum up these results in equation 6.26. Under the restrictive conditions we used to develop operationalization 3, but now incorporating

Inventory models under uncertainty 77

some dynamic effect of the inventory models (storing products and backlogging demand) we can arrive at a dynamic analogue. It tells us (a) that uncertainty will add costs to those costs given under certainty but that (b) in a dynamic model under plausible empirical conditions a part of those costs can be recovered.

6.7 TRADITIONAL PREJUDICES OF MAINSTREAM LITERATURE ON THE INFLUENCE OF UNCERTAINTY ON THE OPTIMAL INVENTORY LEVEL

The results of the preceding sections have shown that the inventory level (starting stock plus production) depends on the level of several parameters. An *a priori* evaluation of the parameters (for additional empirical indications see chapter 11) led to the conjecture that optimal stock on hand is below the level of expected demand and should thus be lowered by increasing uncertainty. This conjecture rests on the surmised asymmetry of profit $(p-c)$ and cost (c), as well as – in the absence of other information – on a supposed similarity of holding costs and goodwill costs $(h \approx g)$, and/or of consumer loyalty and product durability $(a \approx b)$.

Contrary to this conjecture, the mainstream literature almost universally maintains that the level of stock on hand increases under uncertainty, and that more than expected demand is produced. This becomes apparent from interpretative remarks, from the choice of the optimization approach (where the backlogging possibility is left out, or at any rate the revenue therefrom), and from numerical assumptions of parameters in the chosen examples.

The opinion, that non-satisfiable demand is 'very expensive' moves Arrow *et al.* (1951, p. 257) to write: 'The penalty for depleted stocks may be very high: "A horse, a horse, my kingdom for a horse" cried defeated Richard III.' The prejudice is apparent in the approach of many authors who do not consider the possibility of an order backlog at all. Some emphasize that they make the assumption (e.g. Zabel 1972, p. 526), sometimes models that exclude order backlogs are presented simply as the outcomes in mainstream literature (e.g. De Groot 1970, p. 405ff and Hey 1981, p. 133ff). In both cases the authors arrive at a result in the form of equation 6.27. The equation implies that – given a low discount rate (a factor close to one, which will be likely for monthly planning – even the most unlikely demand must be met. This event, unlikely in view of supply bottlenecks and production on order, results from the assumption that goods are infinitely durable but that orders cannot be backlogged even to the slightest extent. The formula results as a special case from the above (in equation (6.12)) for $b=0$, $a=1$, $h=g=0$.

78 *Theoretical part*

$$F(y) = \frac{p-c}{p-\alpha c} \text{ for } \alpha \Rightarrow 1,\ y \Rightarrow \infty. \qquad (6.27)$$

Consideration of the effect of inventories as a buffer between output and demand with simultaneous neglect of order backlogs has persisted in disequilibrium literature. Thus Benassy (1982, p. 47) writes that rationing is rarer and stock is higher in an economy with stockholding than in an economy without.[9]

Beside the deliberate assumption of the impossibility of order backlogging, forgetting the revenue of backlogged revenue (with simultaneous consideration of the cost for the production for backlogs), e.g. in Veinott (1966), points in the direction of these prejudices. Arrow *et al.* (1951) place the costs of non-delivery in two examples as 100 and ten times that of the marginal costs of higher production and show that this is equivalent – assuming normal distribution – to a 'service level' of 95% and 99.7%. All the examples in the books of Arrow *et al.* (1958 and 1962) follow this trend. Maron (1961) tests probabilities of demand fulfilment of 67%, 83%, 94% and 98%. It is particularly surprising that a conclusion of tendentially low demand has not been drawn from the newsboy model. Lange (1971) explicitly assumes values of more than half of price for the profit rate ($p-c$). Petersen & Silver (1979) quote samples above and below that value. Johnson & Montgomery (1974) relate examples where prices (the bottleneck costs) are double (p. 53) and five times (p. 51) the price of production (procurement) costs. In Hillier & Lieberman (1980) they are also double, and Bell (1977) also claims as a matter of course that production surpasses the expected value of demand.

As a rationale for the opinion that uncertainty must in any case increase optimal stockholding, let us formulate the following hypotheses:

- historically, the level of inventory was initially a measure of personal wealth rather than an activity, the costs of which ought to be minimized (Tichy, 1976, p. 8; ibid. also references);
- subsequently it was the task of inventory literature to explain stockholding as an efficient economic activity (precautionary and transaction motive);
- the assumption of inventory theory that production planning under certainty must fully satisfy demand (and that therefore given seasonal demand peaks and strictly convex production costs, inventories are needed), was initially modified to the extent only that an *ad hoc* determined 'service level' (assumed at over 90%) would be required;
- the (further) development of inventory theory was largely conducted under the aspect of military demand (cf. the frequency of relevant articles appearing in the *Journal for Naval Research*, etc., or the above

quote from Arrow *et al.*). A high cost is here ascribed to the 'non-satisfaction of demand';
- implicitly and explicitly inventory theory is frequently concerned with input inventories.[10] Indeed, the cost of one critical input might be smaller than forgone profits due to bottlenecks (a tendency, that is unlikely for production costs as a whole); and
- a firm's balance sheets and national accounting systems record, by definition, positive inventory levels. A negative stock (after demand = initial stock in next period) is only conceivable if one considers backlogged orders as a negative inventory.

As a matter of fact, it is precisely those authors who interpret orders, at least in principle, as negative inventories who tend to consider the effect of uncertainty on stockholding to be neutral. Simon (1951) mentions that positive or negative inventories are feasible, depending on the type of good.[11] Zarnowitz (1973, p. 11) expressly cites stable or sporadic demand as reasons for production on order (negative inventory).

In contradiction to the above prejudices we hold that the dynamic models demonstrate that due to the difference between profits (main costs of low production decision) and production costs (the main costs resulting from a decision for a large stock on hand) an optimal volume for stock on hand below expected demand cannot be excluded. The critical parameters (relative level of profit to production costs, of inventory cost to goodwill cost, and of durability to backlogging opportunity) will be examined in chapter 11). If stocks on hand are below expected demand, then initial inventories eventually resulting will on average be negative.

6.8 LIMITATIONS OF THE MODELS PRESENTED SO FAR – REFERENCES TO FURTHER LITERATURE

The models presented in the preceding sections display characteristics in several respects:

- linear costs were assumed in most models;
- constant product prices were assumed;
- costs are stable across the total forecast horizon;
- probability distribution of demand is identical and independent (i.i.d.) for each period;
- risk neutrality was assumed; and
- delivery lags were excluded.

80 Theoretical part

These restrictions were justified by our intention to establish in the first place how far the static results under uncertainty are changed by stockholding. The influence of stockholding possibilities depends both on the model used for optimization (with or without backlogging opportunity) and also on the empirical range of the parameters (goodwill v. inventory carrying cost, ratio of profit and costs, discount rate).

If the linearity of the cost pattern is abandoned, then this will primarily raise the question whether there is still a unique optimal inventory value (see the studies in Arrow *et al.* 1958, 1962, Scarf *et al.* 1963, Veinott 1966, Zabel 1970); nothing will change in respect of the tendential influencing factors. A convex cost pattern facilitates comparison with the solution under certainty, whereas assumed linearity only allows comparison of the starting stock (and thereby implicitly of production) with the expected demand. Cost increasing over time (expected cost increase) favours stockholding (Veinott 1966, p. 754f). The assumption of variable prices involves the dependence of the solution on demand elasticity (as in the static p-q-mode, literature to be found in Karlin & Carr 1962, Zabel 1970, 1972).

The most important outcome of this chapter for the optimal production decision is that the results of the static theory of firm may be carried over to the dynamic case not under all logical circumstances, but if some empirical characteristics are given. A fixed price and the possibility of disequilibria is one condition (which proved also important in the static case for unambiguous results). We modelled inventory behaviour as a part of optimal production, whereas it could be regarded as a speculative occupation in view of rising costs (and/or prices). The third condition is that goodwill costs are not much larger than inventory holding costs and the fourth that backlogging is feasible to a similar extent as the durability of goods. These are empirical issues which will be tested in chapters 11 and 12.

NOTES

1 See Arran & Moses (1982) for a critique of the fix-price assumption of inventory models.
2 See Veinott (1975).
3 See Henderson & Quandt (1973) and Koutsoyiannis (1979).
4 The same is true for the question whether stocks on hand (stocks after ordering or after production but before demand) are lower or higher than expected demand.
5 The newsboy model (with total costs if the goods cannot be sold) is considered to be a plausible model for goods becoming obsolete quickly, or goods with a future quite uncertain beyond a single period (Hillier & Liberman 1980, p. 515).
6 This holds for symmetric density functions. In the case of asymmetric densities p larger (equal, smaller) 0.5 yields production smaller (equal to, larger) than the median of the demand distribution.

7 More exactly 'new demand', to distinguish it from backlogged demand or from the sum of these two components.
8 Assuming additionally that B will be small.
9 Benassy (1982, p. 46) reports a result similar to that presented in equation 6.27; production costs are represented by a combination of a wage and a productivity parameter.
10 Cf. Lange (1971): 'But since the use of raw material is a random variable, common sense tells us that an additional stock should be held to meet any unexpectedly large demand for the raw material.'
11 Simon (1951, p. 250): 'Depending on the commodity produced, the optimal inventory may also be positive or negative . . . the former ships from stock, the latter on orders.'

7 The Impact of Uncertainty on the Optimal Choice of Inputs

7.1 INTRODUCTION

The impact of uncertainty on the input of the production factors is a wide field of research, and its findings are indirectly dependent on the output and price decision – as described in chapter 5 – with new aspects added. It demands attention in the present context in that the downward distortion of empirically surveyed investment plans is very well documented, and more pronounced than that of the output decision.

The number of feasible models is larger than of those for the output or price decisions. What is added are the possibilities that the input of either one or both (all) production factor(s) must be determined before the veil of uncertainty is lifted, that this choice can be binding for output or not (fix or variable factor output relation), the production factors may be substitutable *ex ante* only, or *ex ante* and *ex post* (putty–clay assumption, putty–putty assumption), to which is added the impact of further attributes of the production functions (e.g. returns to scale). There may also be uncertainty – besides that on price and demand – in respect of the production factors' pay (wages) or their performance (and efficiency). Long-term considerations are important especially concerning the choice of the production factor capital, which means that one-period models would appear to be insufficient. Thus, in view of the large variety, the choice of models to be presented must be arbitrary to a certain degree. Our selection is intended to demonstrate that partly similar, partly additional factors, all out of the group of 'technological causes' can lead to different decisions, compared with the certainty model.

The first subsection among the static models (7.2.1) shows the dependence of the input decision on the output decision made under uncertainty in that case where the employment of both production factors must be decided *ex ante*. The following subsections assume that one factor must be determined *ex ante*, the other *ex post*. Opportunity of *ex post* control over one factor is first described for a competition model with demand uncertainty (under fix price and limitational production function) (7.2.2), then for price

Optimal choice of inputs under uncertainty 83

uncertainty (and two distinct assumptions concerning substitutability) (7.2.3). Next we discuss wage uncertainty under a given demand curve in a monopoly model (7.2.4).

Out of the equally numerous choice of dynamic models (7.3) we report on two of Nickell's (1978) models, where the effects of uncertainty on the course of investment are deduced, first with disregard to any irreversibilities, then under consideration of the fact that capital stock can often be reduced only to the extent of the depreciation. The determinants of a downward distortion of the course of investment are the same in principle as in static models, just as Hartman's (1972, 1973) models show that the opposite outcome is equally (depending on the same parameters as in the static case) possible.

7.2 STATIC MODELS

7.2.1 Both Inputs as *ex ante* Control

If the use of both production factors must be decided on before the realization of the random variables is known and when the price of the production factors is known for certain, then the input decision is arrived at by the same laws as under certainty – though in respect of an output chosen under uncertainty. If the output determined under uncertainty equals output under certainty (Batra & Ullah 1974, Hartman 1975, Hey 1979, p. 151ff), then the input of the production factors is the same (e.g. in the competition model under price uncertainty).

$$\text{If } q^* = \hat{q} \Rightarrow L^* = \hat{L}, \; K^* = \hat{K}. \tag{7.1}$$

If the output chosen under uncertainty is lower than under certainty (be it because of risk aversion in the competition model under price uncertainty, be it under the impact of maybe unsold output in the competition model under demand uncertainty, or due to technological concavity in the monopoly model), then the consequence will not necessarily be a reduction of both inputs. But this possibility is not necessarily due to the specific effect of uncertainty; rather, it follows for every input decision in relation to a lower output, even if this decrease should happen under certainty. A lower output leads to a reduction of both inputs, if the production factors are complimentary ($f_{KL} > 0$). The latter condition is sufficient and is often used to characterize a production function as 'well behaved' (cf., for example, Lippman & McCall 1981, p. 255). For the necessary condition (cf., for example, Hartman, 1975, p. 1290) for the factor labour see equation 7.2, for factor capital see equation 7.3.

$$\hat{q} < q^* \Rightarrow \hat{L} < L^* \quad \text{if } F_L(K,L)F_{KK}(K,L) - F_K(K,L)F_{KL}(K,L) < 0. \tag{7.2}$$

84   Theoretical part

$$\hat{q} < q^* \Rightarrow \hat{K} < K^* \quad \text{if } F_K(K,L)F_{LL}(K,L) - F_L(K,L)F_{KL}(K,L) < 0.$$
(7.3)

Ratti & Ullah (1976) show that a firm facing perfect competition will use less of both inputs if the performance of both factors are tainted with uncertainty; Turnovsky (1971) shows that a firm faced with uncertainties in her supply of raw materials will plan a higher quantity of inputs. Both models demonstrate particular cases where under certain assumptions specific impacts of uncertainty on the choice of the production factors will be effective, when both (or several) are considered *ex ante* controls. In general (i.e. assuming a 'well-behaved' production function, certainty concerning the factor productivity and availability of inputs), a result concerning the optimal output decision determines also the input of production factors (that are to be determined *ex ante*).

7.2.2 Optimal Capacity with Labour as an *ex post* Control – The Case of Limitational Production Functions

This model (Nickell 1978, p. 72ff) assumes that the production factor capital must be determined before demand is disclosed, and that this constitutes an upper limit for output too (limitational production function). The only advantage of the flexibility of labour input rests on the fact that in the case of overproduction only capital cost is lost and not total production costs. Labour is put in only to the extent that it is needed. Linear costs, constant unit price and competition are assumed in this one-period model.

$$E\pi = \int_q^\infty (p-w)q \cdot f(x)dx + \int_0^q (p-w)xf(x)dx - iq,$$
(7.4)

where i = unit cost capital and $p > w + i$.

$$F(q) = \frac{p-w-i}{p-w} \Rightarrow \hat{q} = K \gtreqless E(x) \text{ if } i \lesseqgtr \tfrac{1}{2}(p-w).$$
(7.5)

The result, as must be expected of a competition model with fix price and demand uncertainty, resembles the newsboy model. This model, however, tends to a higher production plan (capacity), since capital cost only is lost in case of overproduction. Here q must be understood as *ex ante* fixed production capacity K.

7.2.3 Optimal Capacity with Labour as an *ex-post* Control – The Case of Substitutability between Labour and Capital (Competition Under Price Uncertainty)

Price uncertainty in a competitive market is the feature in these models (Hartman 1976, Nickell 1978, model 5, Kon 1983). The decision on capital to

Optimal choice of inputs under uncertainty 85

be invested is taken *ex ante*, labour input can be decided on after the price has been ascertained. In the Hartman–Nickell model there are no limits to adjustment (except those devolving from profit maximization), in Kon's model the capital/labour ratio must be fixed simultaneously with the capacity decision (putty–clay assumption). To obtain optimal results both models initially assume general concave production functions (decreasing returns to scale) and eventually CES functions. The input of labour is decided by maximization of short-term profits (π_{sr}), in the Hartman–Nickell model the optimal labour input L is determined by equations 7.6 and 7.7, therefrom follows, equation 7.8, the short-term profit function g, after choice of optimal labour input L.

$$\pi_{sr} = pF(K,L) - wL; \quad F_K, F_L > 0, F \text{ is concave.} \tag{7.6}$$

$$\frac{\partial \pi_{sr}}{\partial L} pF_L(K,L) - w \Rightarrow \tilde{L} = \tilde{L}(K,p,w). \tag{7.7}$$

$$g(K,p,w) = pF[K, \tilde{L}(K,p,w)] - w \cdot \tilde{L}(K,p,w). \tag{7.8}$$

The long-term profit (after choice of optimal labour input in the short-term profit function) is given in equation 7.9. Equation 7.10 shows the maximization condition of the first order (Z_Y in the terminology of chapter 4), equations 7.11 and 7.12 determine whether these solutions are concave or convex in respect of the price (Z_{YXX}). Since the first term in equation 7.12 is negative in any case, the third positive in any case, it is the second term that determines the algebraic sign of Z_{YXX} (see equation 7.13).

$$\pi_{lr} = p \cdot F(K, \tilde{L}) - w\tilde{L} - iK = g(K,p,w) - iK. \tag{7.9}$$

$$Z_Y = \pi_K = \frac{\partial q}{\partial K} I = p \cdot F_K[K, \tilde{L}(K,p,w)] - i. \tag{7.10}$$

$$Z_{YX} = \pi_{Kp} = F_K + pF_{KL} \frac{\partial \tilde{L}}{\partial p} = F_K - F_L \frac{F_{KL}}{F_{LL}}. \tag{7.11}$$

$$Z_{YXX} = \pi_{Kpp} = -F_L \underbrace{\frac{\partial (F_{KL}/F_{LL})}{\partial L}}_{-} \cdot \underbrace{\frac{\partial \tilde{L}}{\partial p}}_{+}. \tag{7.12}$$

$$Z_{YXX} \gtreqless 0 \text{ if } \frac{\partial (F_{KL}/F_{LL})}{\partial L} \gtreqless 0. \tag{7.13}$$

Hartman (1976, p. 678f) shows that on the assumption of a CES production function this magnitude depends on the relation between substitution elasticity σ and the degree of the diseconomies of scale (the scale parameter μ is smaller than one), to wit, in the shape of equation 7.14. If the substitution elasticity is relatively large and there are great diseconomies of scale, then the capital input will be rather smaller than under certainty. If substitutability is relatively low and/or if the production function approaches the linear homogeneous production function, capital input will be higher than under certainty:

$$\frac{\partial(F_{KL}/F_{LL})}{\partial L} \gtreqless 0 \quad \text{if} \sigma \gtreqless (1-\mu)^{-1}. \tag{7.14}$$

The economic interpretation of this outcome will be found in the fact that, when the factors can easily be substituted, a low capital input can be cheaply compensated for by means of *ex post* variable labour input; alternatively, given large diseconomies of scale, a contingently high price will lead to only a moderate increase of optimally profitable output. Generally it can be assumed according to the present model that capital input may be rather higher than under certainty. For example, given a substitution elasticity of 2, μ would have to be smaller than half in order to lead to a lower capital input. Not below a substitution elasticity of 4 might μ approach 0.75. For such seemingly realistic values of the scale parameter as 0.8 or 0.9, unrealistic substitution elasticities would have to be attained. If on the other hand the production function approaches linear homogeneous, then the possibility of reducing the capital input evaporates completely in this model of price uncertainty.[1]

Kon's (1983) model permits free choice of the input ratio between capital and labour only before the price becomes known (putty–clay model). Capacity utilization may be selected as an *ex post* control, whereby other than full utilization ($\theta < 1$) permits savings of labour costs. The short-term profit function (see equation 7.15) serves to determine optimal capacity, where $L_0(=\beta K_0)$ denotes the maximum labour employment constraint.[2] For the long-term profit function see equation 7.16.

$$\pi_{sr} = p \cdot F(\theta K, \theta L_0) - w\theta L \Rightarrow \tilde{\theta}. \tag{7.15}$$

$$\pi_{lr} = p \cdot F[\tilde{\theta}(p,K,L)K, \tilde{\theta}(p,K,L)] - w\tilde{\theta}(p,K,L)L - iK. \tag{7.16}$$

The effect of price uncertainty on optimal capital input is the outcome of combining the utilization risk effect and the flexibility effect (equations 7.17 and 7.18).

Utilization risk effect (Kon 1983):

$$h' + zh'' \gtreqless 0 \text{ tend to lead to } \hat{K} \lesseqgtr K^*, \tag{7.17}$$

where $F(K,L) = h[f(K,L)] = h(z)$, $f \ldots$ is a linear homogeneous production function, and $h(z)$ has characteristics $h'(z) > 0$, $h''(z) < 0$.

'Flexibility effect' (Kon 1983):

$$F_{KL} \gtreqless 0 \text{ tends to lead to } \hat{K} \gtreqless K^*. \tag{7.18}$$

Proposition 2 (Kon 1933, p. 188):

$$\hat{K} \geqslant K^* \quad \text{if} \quad h' + zh'' \leqslant 0 \text{ and } F_{KL} \geqslant 0.$$
$$\hat{K} \leqslant K^* \quad \text{if} \quad h' + zh'' \geqslant 0 \text{ and } F_{KL} \leqslant 0. \tag{7.19}$$

The 'utilization risk effect' shows the impact of changes of utilization on the marginal productivity of capital. For general production functions it could increase or lower the optimal capital stock $\hat{K}$ (the latter, if there are severely negative returns of scale and little increase of marginal capital productivity through enhanced utilization). For CES production functions the left side of equation 7.17 will always be positive and the optimal capital stock under uncertainty, under this impact, will never be larger than under certainty. This partial effect is in the nature of marginal costs of uncertainty after operationalization 3.

The flexibility effect corresponds to that effect which, in the Hartman-Nickell model, is *solely* decisive for the impact of uncertainty, namely the degree of substitutability of the production factors. Equation 7.14 did this for CES functions.

Kon's model permits an unambiguous statement of the impact of uncertainty on capital input only if both effects go in the same direction (proposition 2, according to Kon 1983, p. 188, see equation 7.19). This puts the Hartman-Nickell outcome decisively in perspective, since there is now a greater likelihood for CES functions that capital input is lower under price uncertainty.[3]

What is the economic background of this change of outcome? An increased capital stock does not only provide the opportunity, after the price has been disclosed (by increasing the labour input), for offering a large output volume at relatively low price, but a larger capacity might conceivably be left unused (because such labour input might turn out to be uneconomical at a low realized output price, thus also creating idle capital). That risk is evaluated in the utilization risk effect – and tendentially leads to a lower capital input under uncertainty.

The question, which is the more realistic the Hartman-Nickell model or the Kon model is an empirical one. According to the Hartman-Nickell model any installed capacity would in any case be utilized, in which case substantial fluctuations in labour input would cushion the effects of price fluctuations. In the Kon model there would be fluctuations in capacity utilization and relatively moderate changes in labour input (compared with the Hartman-Nickell model).

7.2.4 Optimal Capacity under Wage Uncertainty (Monopoly Model)

In this model it is assumed by Nickell that the demand curve is known but that the capacity decision must be taken under uncertainty concerning the wage level w. After disclosure of the actual wage level, the input of labour is decided on, and hence the output decision too. Constant returns to scale are assumed.

The optimal choice of capital stock ($y = K$) is determined by setting the expected marginal product (value) of the capital equal to capital costs (equation 7.20).

$$\mathop{E}_{w} [\text{MR}\{p(K,w)\} F_K[K,L(K,w)]] = i. \tag{7.20}$$

Nickell (1978, p. 80f) shows that optimal capacity under uncertainty is bigger or smaller than under certainty, depending on whether substitution elasticity is greater or smaller than the absolute extent of demand elasticity (for derivation of $Z_{YXX} = Z_{Kww}$ see proposition 5, Nickell 1978, p. 88).

$$\hat{K} \lesseqgtr K^* \text{ when } \sigma \gtreqless |\epsilon|. \tag{7.21}$$

The fact that optimal capital input declines with high substitutability goes parallel with the situation under price uncertainty in the competition model (cf. section 7.2.3). But the causation (and the gauge whereby the 'height' of the elasticity of substitution is measured) is distinct.

The economic reason why capital stock should possibly be higher under uncertainty is that – given lower substitution opportunity and high price elasticity of demand – profit chances offered by contingently low wages cannot be utilized. This tendency may be described – for example, in case of low elasticity of substitution – by the development of the marginal product of capital: 'When the wage falls the output effect dominates the substitution effect, and, if capital were a variable factor, its use would rise. Since it is fixed its marginal product rises and, what is more, rises at an ever-increasing rate.' (Nickell 1978, p. 81).

7.3 DYNAMIC INVESTMENT MODELS UNDER UNCERTAINTY

In this section we describe the choice of an optimal investment strategy under uncertainty. The restriction of the planning horizon by the one-period model is especially problematical for that production factor whose most important impact derives from its characteristic as a stock variable that is variable only step by step. This is why most dynamic models concentrate on determining an optimal investment strategy, which is then

Optimal choice of inputs under uncertainty

assumed – we simplify – as solely decisive for the firm's capacity development. Among the multitude of possible models of investment decisions, we present two models of Nickell which show the connection between the outcomes of dynamic and static models. First, a model without irreversibility is described, thereafter a model where the likelihood of overcapacity arises because the selected capital stock can only be reduced to the extent of the write-offs. In both cases there exists a certain period of uncertainty concerning the increase of demand. It is important to emphasize with Nickell that uncertainty alone does not cause a change in the capacity path; it only occurs if there are either adjustment costs (of actual to desired capacity), or if there is a lag in deliveries during the installation of new capacities.

7.3.1 Demand Uncertainty without Irreversibility

The firm maximizes its expected discounted net earnings. The planning horizon consists of three periods: to begin with, the first 'equilibrium period' when demand rises with a known trend ($\beta°$). This is followed by a non-recurring change in the growth path about which only a probability distribution is known (β_1 – the rate of demand increase prevailing from t on – is the random variable). The effect of this change lasts until the date $t+m$ (m being the delivery lag), thereafter the actual capital stock will have adjusted to the rate of growth, known since the advent of the change. From this date on, a new 'equilibrium period' prevails.

The condition for maximization of expected earnings is the outcome of equation 7.22. On the left side we find the (expected) marginal net earnings before the change in the trend of demand (N_Y^0), during the delivery period (EN_Y^1), as well as thereafter ($E\pi_Y$).[4] On the right side we find an 'extended' capital cost term (see Nickell 1978, p. 98f.), with the 'customary' capital costs (with the elements interest rates, depreciation and inflation) assumed to be constant (c). The equalization of expected revenue and capital costs may be reformulated in equation 7.23.

General condition:

$$g(t)N_Y^0 + [1-g(t)]EN_Y^1(\beta_1) + \theta(t-m)E\pi_Y = \theta(t+m)q + c. \quad (7.22)$$

$$g(t)N_Y^0 + [1-g(t)]EN_Y^1(\beta_1) = c + \theta(t-m)(q - E\pi_Y), \quad 7.23$$

where m is the time lag between order and productive implementation; $g(t)$ and $\theta(\cdot)$ are defined in note 4.

Without irreversibilities the second part of the right side of equation 7.23 is dropped, since the free variability of capital stock makes it possible to equate the value of an additional unit after completion of the uncertainty period with its costs ($\pi_Y = q$).

90 Theoretical part

Without irreversibility, with uncertainty: $q = \mathrm{E}\pi_Y$:

$$g(t)N_Y^0 + [1 - g(t)] \mathrm{E}N_Y^1(\beta_1) = c. \qquad (7.24)$$

Without irreversibility, without uncertainty:

$$g(t)N_Y^0 + [1 - g(t)] N_Y^1(\mathrm{E}\beta_1) = c. \qquad (7.25)$$

The only difference between certainty and uncertainty is that between the expected marginal revenue and the certain marginal revenue during the delivery lag.

The effect of uncertainty in this model is thus dependent on the same set of circumstances as in the one-period model: if the marginal revenue is concave (linear, convex) with respect to the growth path β_1, then the optimal growth path in uncertainty will decline (remain even, be higher). Nickell assumes a situation that corresponds to the model in section 5.3.2.4 (multiplicative uncertainty, type B) and comes to the conclusion that the growth path will most probably lie lower than under certainty. This is due to the choice of a specific monopoly model, as we know from the discussion of the static models. What is more generally applicable in this result is that the effect of uncertainty depends, also in the dynamic model, on the concavity (linearity, convexity) of the marginal revenue with respect to the random variable.

$$N_Y^1(\beta_1) \begin{Bmatrix} \text{concave} \\ \text{linear} \\ \text{convex} \end{Bmatrix} \text{ in } \beta_1 \Rightarrow \hat{y} \lessgtr y^*. \qquad (7.26)$$

7.3.2 The Case of Downward Irreversibility

The model assumed that a possibly too-high capacity can be reduced by the sale of investment goods in the secondary market. That, however, is possible only for a small part of investment goods.[5]

The absence of a second-hand market for investment goods (downwards irreversibility of the investment decision) has its impact on maximization insofar as the expected discounted yield of the last unit of an investment programme ($\mathrm{E}\pi_Y$) is now smaller than its cost (c) and the second part of the right side in equation 7.27 becomes positive. The optimal investment path is then always lower under irreversibility than under full reversibility, whenever there is even the smallest likelihood that a capacity unit may not be used. The effect of irreversibility can become (given concavity in the model with reversibility) as an additional factor for a lowering of the investment path under security, or counteract its increase in the case of convexity of the marginal revenue in respect of β_1.

Optimal choice of inputs under uncertainty 91

With irreversibility and uncertainty:

$$g(t)N_Y^0 + (1-g(t))EN_Y^1(\beta_1) = c + \underbrace{\theta(t-m)(q-E\pi_Y)}_{>0}. \quad (7.27)$$

$$\hat{y}_{\text{IRREV.}} < \hat{y}_{\text{REV.}} \quad (7.28)$$

where IRREV. and REV. respectively signify impossibility and possibility of negative gross investments.

The question of the irreversibility of investments is extensively dealt with in the literature, where widely different model specifications and methods of solution were chosen. As a rule, irreversibility distorts investment decisions downwards, (cf. Arrow & Fischer 1974, Henry 1974, and especially Bernanke 1983). Bernanke formulates the 'bad-news principle', namely that of all possible future realizations only the most unfavourable ones influence today's investment decision (Bernanke 1983, p. 91).

Because of this characteristic of the optimization process, any increase of uncertainty reduces the investment level, even if the mean revenue of all projects should rise (since new information may shift the hierarchy profit rates of the projects).

7.3.3 Summing Up the Results for Investment Models

Nickell's models show that a downward change of the investment decision through uncertainty is also possible from the point of view of a dynamic model. But this outcome – just as with parallel outcomes in the static model – is only one of many theoretically possible results, and other specifications of the uncertainty would have led to other results. We may mention the studies of Hartman (1972 and 1973) on price and wage uncertainty as examples of the increase of investment due to uncertainty in a dynamic model (where, again parallel to the static model, the result depends partly on the algebraic sign of F_{KL}). The crucial statement of all the named studies without irreversibilities is that the outcomes of the static models are tendentially preserved if a dynamic strategy is chosen.[6] The effect of the irreversibility of the investment decision (downwards) introduces an additional asymmetry, unknown in the static model. A similar effect would come about if one assumed that investments are more easily increased than reduced (asymmetrical adjustment costs).

NOTES

1 For exactly linear homogeneous production functions the model does not give any determinate demand functions for the production factors.

92 Theoretical part

2 Capacity utilization and labour input (on the auxiliary condition that the selected capital/labour ratio must not be changed) are *ex post* controls, where price, as usual under competition, must be accepted (and) capacity is optimized in the second plan.
3 More accurately: only in this case is an unambiguous result available. If the two effects go in different directions, then assessing the tendency becomes 'extremely complicated' and is no longer pursued (Kon 1983).
4 The earnings are multiplied with (conditional) probabilities which result from Nickell also defining the date of trend reversal as a random variable:

$$g(t) = G(t)/G(t-m); G(t) = \int_t^b f(t) \mathrm{d}t \ f(t)$$
$$\theta(t) = f(t)/G(t)$$

f(t) density function of the date of trend reversal; f(t) = 0 if $t \leqslant a$ or $t \geqslant b$.
5 Nickell mentions buildings and vehicles as goods with functioning secondary markets (1978, p. 48). As proof of the reality of irreversibilities he quotes statistical data showing that in capital assets gross purchases of £7077 million (1970–3) are counterposed by a mere £286 in asset disposals, whereas – in a more 'perfect' secondary market (real estate, buildings, vehicles) – purchases of £1113 are counterposed by £683 in disposal revenue obtained by industry (UK Census of Production).
6 Another model combines the problem of optimal investment strategy with that of adjustment costs: Pindyck (1982) assumes that future demand is increasingly uncertain and shows that the third derivation of the adjustment cost function is decisive for the level of capital stock. Abel (1983), however, shows that Pindyck's analysis refers to the 'target' rate of investment, which in general is not optimal.

8 *Ex post* Flexibility of Production Decisions

The models presented in chapter 7 could be ranged by their 'degree of flexibility'. Models with *ex post* substitution among production factors or an *ex post* output determination are more 'flexible' than those where technique and output are fixed *ex ante*. In this chapter we shall deal briefly with the case wherein the decision variable can be partly revised *ex post* (readjusted).

Were one unreservedly to accept the basic concept that 'expected' production (such as is reported in surveys) constitutes a final production plan under uncertainty, then production plans and actual production would always coincide and there could be neither random nor systematic errors in the production expectations (as long as production is an *ex ante* control). To explain the differences between planned and actual output, which come to light largely on the level of the individual firm and to a smaller extent in the aggregate, one must stipulate an *ex post* flexibility of production decisions in the shape of a readjustment of the *ex ante* control variable.

If there is *ex post* flexibility then it must optimally enter already into the planning of the 'preliminary' figure. There is a particular need for *ex post* flexibility in those models in which there is no *ex post* control variable, these being the disequilibrium models. In models with *ex post* control there is, as a rule, no unfilled demand or unsold output. This means that profit opportunities from additional flexibility are usually smaller.

By means of a fix-price model with fixed unit costs under demand uncertainty, we demonstrate how a production decision operates that makes allowance for later revision.

Let us assume three cost categories: (constant) unit costs in normal production (in the first plan) are termed c; c_1 are the costs of production cutback,[1] c_2 are additional costs of additional production (emergency production: thus costs of an additionally produced good are $c+c_2$). We further assume parameters a and b which state the technical possibilities (between 0 and 1) of lowering or increasing preliminary output.

Maximization of expected profit will give us a first production plan q_1 according to equation 8.2.

Theoretical part

$$E\pi = p \int_{q_1}^{q} xf(x)dx + p \int_{q_1}^{\infty} q_1 f(x)dx - cq_1 +$$
$$(c-c_1) \cdot \int_{0}^{q_1} a(q_1-x)f(x)dx + (p-c-c_2) \int_{q}^{\infty} b(x-q_1)f(x)dx, \quad (8.1)$$

where $0 \leq a \leq 1$, $0 \leq b \leq 1$, $0 \leq c_1 \leq c$ is cost of production cutback, and $0 \leq c_2 \leq p-c$ (additional costs of increase).

$$F(q_1) = \frac{p-c-p\ b+c\ b+c_2\ b}{p-c\ a+c_1\ a-p\ b+c\ b+c_2\ b}, \quad (8.2)$$

special case: $b=a=1$	special case: $b=a=0$
$F(q_1) = \dfrac{c_2}{c_1+c_2}$	$F(q_1) = \dfrac{p-c}{p}$

special case: $c_2=0$, $b=a=1$	special case: $a=0$, $b=1$
$F(q_1) = 0$	$F(q_1) = \dfrac{c_2}{c+c_2}$

This equation has the following properties:

- given the technical possibility of completely revising the first decision – both up or down ($b=a=1$) – then the relative level of additional costs decides whether more or less than the expected value of demand is to be produced. If the additional costs of emergency production are lower than those of lowering (production) ($c_2 < c_1$), less than the expected value will be produced (if c_2 approaches zero, then nothing will initially be produced). The actual production (q_2) after revision will here always correspond to actual demand, x, therefore, on average. If q_1 lies below $E(x)$ but q_2 on average at $E(x)$, then an upward revision will, on average, be made;
- if no *ex post* revision is possible ($a=b=0$), then the formula reduces to the newsboy result (this is merely the consistency check);
- if emergency production is technically possible ($b=1$) and feasible without additional costs, then nothing is produced under the first plan and actual demand awaited;
- if increase of output is technically substantially easier than lowering, then less will be produced, even given equal costs for adding and cutting production; in the extreme case ($a=0$, $b=0$) an output below expected

Ex post flexibility of production decisions 95

value will be planned as long as the additional costs of increase are below normal costs (i.e. as long as additional production is less than double the cost of normal production).

It is hard to find indications concerning the actual possibilities and costs of changes in production plans. As a rule, the increase of labour input causes higher costs (in the form of overtime premiums, hiring or training costs), a lowering is often impossible at short notice in view of labour protection legislation (especially in Europe, where short-notice layoffs are not tolerated). Where the production factor capital is concerned, increase is also expensive (a smaller choice of tenders and technical opportunities, higher delivery and/or installation costs), while a lowering (apart from and beyond the depreciation) is often quite out of the question at short notice. Thus emergency production[2] is more expensive than normal production. A reduction, however, is often impossible (produced output cannot be undone).

Allowing non-linear costs does not change the story. Let us assume the non-linear cost of producing in the first plan, $c(q_1)$, and non-linear profits due to a later downward revision, $c_3[a(q_1)]$, respectively, due to emergency production $c_4[b(x-q_1)]$. Maximizing equation 8.3, we get equation 8.4, which is in the tradition of operationalization 3. A goes to zero, if $a = B$, $F(q)$ is near 0.5, and c_4 and c_3 are symmetric (and evaluated at similar points). Since most probably $F(q_1)$ will tend to be smaller than 0.5, A may well be negative in the majority of the cases, adding an extra cost (lowering the optimal first plans). Asymmetries in a and b resp. in c_4 and c_3 may add to or reduce these extra costs, starting to work from a reference point where optimal first plans are well below optimal production under certainty:

$$E\pi = p\int_0^{q_1} xf(x)dx + p\int_{q_1}^{\infty} q_1 f(x)dx - c(q_1) + \int_0^{q_1} c_3[a(q_1-x)]f(x)dx +$$
$$\int_{q_1}^{\infty} c_4[b(x-q_1)]f(x)dx. \quad (8.3)$$

$$\frac{\delta E\pi}{\delta q_1} = p - pF(q_1) - c'(q_1)$$
$$+ \underbrace{a\int_0^{q_1} c_3'[a(q_1-x)]f(x)dx - b\int_{q_1}^{\infty} \cdot c'_4[b(x-q_1)]f(x)dx}_{A} = 0. \quad (8.4)$$

where c_3 is contribution to profit due to emergency reduction of a first plan, and c_4 is contribution to profit due to emergency production.

The signifance of flexibility is known in literature. Stigler (1939) and Hart (1942, 1950) emphasized the advantages of plant with a flat average cost curve in the minimum, Marshak & Nelson (1962) have worked this idea into a sequential decision model. In the context of the production decision under uncertainty Turnovsky (1973) constructed a decision model with *ex post* variation of production decision depending on actual price. Turnovsky initially picks out the symmetrical case where plans can be varied equally up or down, then he mentions the case where already planned output cannot be reduced (there being only upward flexibility), or else the probability that higher flexibility of plans may be given in an upwards (increasing) direction.

Then Turnovsky analyses the symmetrical case in more detail: the firm decides, under price uncertainty, on a first plan, and thereafter is in a position to vary the price up or down after the veil of uncertainty has lifted. In Turnovsky's model, the costs of correction are higher than the original production, but they are symmetrical. Comparison with certainty shows that, in principle, all three possibilities are given (higher, lower or equal output), both for the first production plan and also for the sum of the first production plan plus expected revision. The outcome depends on a third derivation, *viz.* on c_{221}, a variation of marginal emergency production costs dependent on the first plan. Turnovsky holds it to be plausible that this term is positive and that the output level is thus lower than under certainty. The second problem (production plus expected revision) depends on the conjunction of two third derivations. Turnovsky's complex conditions – compared with those of equation 8.2 – are not surprising, since we are dealing here with an equilibrium model and the probability of unsold output alone does not suffice to distort the plan. A possibility to overcome the discrepancy between optimal production planning and demand, that lies on average above (or below) the former, may be found in a two-sector model. The one sector of the economy – say, large enterprises – must determine its optimal production before the uncertainty becomes known (the *ex ante* control is enforced by high fixed costs, price regulation, by the 'social partner's' joint commission, dismissals protection law); the second sector – the small firms – is fully flexible in that sense: that these firms can determine their production plans after the uncertainty has been disclosed. When optimal production plans decline in the large-enterprise sector – as seems likely under plausible conditions – then the market shares and profits of the smaller firms will rise under uncertainty. In actual fact empirical studies show, especially in recent times, rising shares of smaller- and medium-size enterprises and a decline of 'optimal' enterprise size (cf. Aiginger & Tichy 1984). This may well be due, beside technical, organizational and sectoral causes, to increasing uncertainty.

NOTES

1 Here exactly c_1 is the cost of lowering output *ex post*.
2 Here exactly c_2 is the extra cost of producing the output *ex post*, the total cost of emergency production is $c_2 + c$.

9 Summing Up the Results of the Theoretical Models

9.1 EVALUATION OF THE OVERALL RESULTS

In chapters 5 - 8 we have described several models on optimal decisions of a profit-maximizing firm (mostly under risk neutrality). The majority of the models are well known in the literature, though there they are scattered in numerous articles and specialized fields of economics (theory of the firm, inventory theory). In these articles, Leland's conclusions on monopoly decisions in the theory of the firm and the opposite conclusions, developed by Nickell (1978), in the context of investment theory, can coexist without being ever confronted. The same is true for the logical reservations against the competition model under demand uncertainty in the theory of the firm on the one hand, and on the other hand the dominance of the same model (of fixed prices and uncertain demand) in inventory theory.

Greater attention than in the literature was paid in this study to the problem of *ex post* flexibility of the production decision. Whereas a strict distinction is made as a rule in the literature between *ex ante* and *ex post* control, it may be considered closer to reality to speak of a preliminary first decision on an *ex ante* control, which may thereafter, in the light of new information concerning the random variable, be corrected in part. That aspect is of particular importance for the second aim of this study: the attempt to interpret reported production and investment plans as optimal plans. If the variable elicited in surveys was indeed subject to *ex ante* control, then there could be no deviations from the realizations. Tied up with the assumption of a certain degree of *ex post* flexibility we encounter the theoretically unattractive question whether that flexibility be symmetrical or asymmetrical. If an asymmetry exists, in the sense that increases were easier than reduction, this would bias down the first plan trivially. Instead of enumerating the individual models, we summarize them in Table 9.1.

We describe action and random variables, the model's first presentation in literature, the main result and its restricted range of validity. We note whether the outcome follows from the technological concavity (linearity, convexity) or from the marginal costs of uncertainty. The comparison of the outcomes under uncertainty concentrates primarily on the production

Table 9.1 Summary of the theoretical models

Mode	Literature	Main result	Condition for main result	Economic rational	Empirical implication (EI) Caveats (C) Critical parameters (CP)
Competition – price uncertainty $Y:q$ $X:p$	Sandmo (1971)	– q *ex ante* mode $\hat{q} = q^*$		$\left.\begin{array}{c} E(p) = c'(q) \\ p^* \end{array}\right\}$	EI: no involuntary inventories, no fluctuations of involuntary inventories, no (involuntary) fluctuation of capacity utilization, expected production = actual production, actual price differs randomly from expected one, many competitors
Competition – demand uncertainty – q *ex ante* mode $Y:q$ $X:x$	Hymans (1966)	(1) $\hat{q} < q^*$	$c^*(q) > 0$	expected unsold quantity can be reduced; opportunity cost of unsatisfied demand smaller than sunk cost	C: is this a competitive model?
	'Newsboy model'	(2) $\hat{q} < \text{Ex}$	$p - c < c$ $(= p < 2c)$		CI: disequilibria inventories, forecast errors even in competitive markets, fixed prices CP: profit share v. costs

(continued)

Table 9.1 *(continued)*

Mode	Literature	Main result	Condition for main result	Economic rational	Empirical implication (EI) Caveats (C) Critical parameters (CP)
Monopoly Y:q X:$p=f(q,u)$	– demand uncertainty – q *ex ante* mode				
	Leland (1972)	$\hat{q}=q^*$	additive uncertainty, multiplicative uncertainty + PIU	additive uncertainty, production can do nothing to reduce price uncertainty	EI: no disequilibria, expected production = actual production, actual price differs from expected one randomly
	Nickell (1978)	$\hat{q}<q^*$	multiplicative uncertainty of type: $q=f(p) \cdot u \Rightarrow$ $p=f^{-1}(q/u)$ and one of these conditions: $\epsilon<-1$, q_p *linear or quadratic*	indirect influence via demand curve	C: depends on specific type of multiplicative uncertainty: is uncertainty additive or multiplicative (if the latter: is $p=g(q) \cdot u$ or $p=f^{-1}(q/u)$?)
Monopoly Y:p X:$q=f(p,u)$	– demand uncertainty – p *ex ante* mode				
	Leland (1972)	$\hat{p} \geqq p^*$	if $c''' \geqq 0$ and $c''>0$ PIU or additive demand	high price insures against eventually expensive production	EI: no disequilibria, expected price = actual price, actual production differs from expected one randomly

(continued)

Table 9.1 Summary of the theoretical models *(continued)*

Mode	Literature	Main result	Condition for main result	Economic rational	Empirical implication (EI) Caveats (C) Critical parameters (CP)
Monopoly $Y:p,q$	– demand uncertainty – p and q *ex ante* mode additive uncertainty Karlin & Carr (1962)	$\hat{p} < p^*$ $\hat{q} \gtreqless q^*$	$c'(q) = c$	smaller price to reduce additive uncertainty, quantity smaller if $p - c$ very small but larger according to demand elasticity	EI: disequilibria inventories and backlogs, expected variables = realizations
	multiplicative uncertainty	$\hat{p} < p^*$; q likely to be smaller than q^*	$c'(q) = c$	higher price (chosen to reduce multiplicative uncertainty) and small profits reinforce each other to lower production	EI: disequilibria inventories and backlogs, expected variables = realizations C: assumption of constant costs
Inventory models – demand uncertainty – fixed prices following the line of Veinott (1966) $Y: q + I$ $X: x$		$\hat{q} + I$ likely to be smaller than $E(x)$	$c'(q) = c$ p fixed	small $p - c$ and symmetric holding and goodwill costs as well as symmetric backlogging and durability parameters	EI: disequilibria inventories and backlogs, net inventories negative, procyclical movement of planned net inventories, decreasing net inventories with increasing uncertainty CP: $p - c$:c:g:h:a:b

(continued)

Table 9.1 *(continued)*

Mode	Literature	Main result	Condition for main result	Economic rational	Empirical implication (EI) Caveats (C) Critical parameters (CP)
Factor demand models					
$Y:K,L$	see, e.g. Hey (1979)	$\hat{K}=K^*$	$\hat{q}=q^*$	implication of the result for output	C: both factors under *ex ante* control, equilibrium model
$X:P$	Hartman (1975)	$L=L^*$	'well-behaved' production function		
$Y:K,L$		$\hat{K}<K^*$	$\hat{q}<q^*$	implication of the result for output	C: the same as for the competitive model under demand uncertainty
$X:x$		$L>L^*$	$c''(q)>0$		
$Y:K,q^{\max}$ $X:x$	Nickell (1978, p. 72f.)	$\hat{K}\lessgtr K^*$	$i \gtreqless \frac{1}{2}(p-w)$	i fixes upper limit of production, forgone profits have to be balanced only against i, since wages can be saved if demand is low	C: constant prices, constant unit wage, investment cost EI: strong fluctuations of wages (and unemployment) disequilibria inventories

(continued)

Table 9.1 Summary of the theoretical models *(continued)*

Mode	Literature	Main result	Condition for main result	Economic rational	Empirical implication (EI) Caveats (C) Critical parameters (CP)
Y:K X:p	Hartman (1976)	$\hat{K}$ likely to be larger than K^*	$\sigma < \dfrac{1}{1-q}$ competition; *ex post* control	marginal product of labour rises with increasing rate	EI: uncertainty increase capital stock, fluctuations of wages (employment), investment anticipation = actual investment C: equilibrium model
Y:K X:p	Kon (1983)	$\hat{K}$ likely to be smaller than K^*	large utilization effect	possibility of unused capacity outweighs advantages of large programmes	C: disequilibrium in the sense of unused capacity
Y:K	Nickell (1978, p. 80f.)	$\hat{K}$ likely to be larger than K^*	$\sigma<|\epsilon|$ monopoly, L *ex post* control	low substitutability favours 'reserve capacities'	EI: as in last case above
Asymmetric *ex post* flexibilities Y:l° or q° X:x	e.g. Nickell (1978, p. 105ff.)	$\hat{K}<K^*$ $\hat{q}<q^*$	upward revisions easier than downward revision	irreversibility of investment or production, cost differences in emergency reactions ($c_2>c_1$)	C: easy results often dependent on constant price and cost assumptions EI: investment anticipation and production plans biased downward

plan, on optimal starting stock (after production) and optimal capital invested. The reference standard used is the value of the action variables under certainty or – where there is none (because of the linearity of costs in the competition model) – expected demand.

The overview of the models shows, in the first place, a multitude of possibilities as to why uncertainty decision should diverge, for technological reasons (in the wider sense as defined in chapter 4), from the decision under certainty, and why the enterprises' optimal plans should diverge from the expected value of the random variable. On balance – and this may be the author's subjective impression – the findings appear to favour a production decision below that in the certainty model; in the inventory models (there, especially, contrary to traditional prejudice), the empirical parameters suggest a decreasing starting stock under uncertainty; however in the decision on an input that must be fixed *ex ante*, in favour of a 'larger' capital stock (as long as disequilibria are closed by an *ex post* control).

Generally, equilibrium models (where a flexible *ex post* control guarantees complete selling of the output, or complete satisfaction of demand, respectively) lead to more ambivalent outcomes of the models (they depend on the third cross derivative of a function, and therefore the direction of the distortion is often not known). Conversely, disequilibrium models (where no *ex post* control bridges the difference between planning and realization) lead to greater (usually downward) distortions. It is therefore a central objective of the following chapters to determine whether the empirical indicators rather favour an equilibrium model, firms in the real industrial world having to face persistent disequilibrium[1] devoid of a quick *ex post* control. Short-term price flexibility would point to the equilibrium case, price rigidity and involuntary variations in the finished goods' inventories and capacity utilization would militate against the case.

The forecast of ample capital endowment is also partly dependent on the problem of full resource utilization (cf. the different results of Hartman and Kon). A robust forecast of low capacities follows only when there are asymmetries: either if one assumes that the investment decision is reversible upwards but not downwards, or if one assumes asymmetries in the *ex post* flexibility costs. It will therefore be the task of the empirical part to look for indications of such asymmetries, especially in the light of the tendency of investment plans – hardly disputed in the literature under review – on average to underestimate the actual capital inputs.

9.2 'PETTY' v. 'SEVERE UNCERTAINTY': ELEMENTS OF AN ALTERNATIVE DICHOTOMIZATION

We want to use this structure of the model results to propose a new tentative dichotomization for situations (types) of uncertainty. On the one

104 Theoretical part

hand there is a type of uncertainty where uncertainty is some sort of an 'intermediate' problem. That means a decision about one part of the variables has to be made before the veil of uncertainty is lifted, some other variable(s) adjusting thereafter. This type includes models:

- where there is an *ex post* control, which adjusts automatically (market price, output given by the demand curve);
- where there is an optimization process feasible for some variable after the realization of the random variable is known (short-run profit maximization for the variable factor).

Related economic consequences (to that of *ex post* control) are given if a decision does not have a one-shot character but is of a repeated nature, especially if the realization of the random variable is not correlated over time[2] or if there exist insurances and/or future markets[3] and there are no irreversibilities.[4] If some or all of these *ex post* strategies are feasible there will be no disequilibria between supply and demand, at least not for some longer period. Since this type of uncertainty is relatively easy to cope with we will label it 'petty uncertainty'. The optimal decision parameters are different nevertheless from those under certainty, however probably not 'too far'. For example, for models following the type of operationalization 2, the third cross-derivative of the objective function determines. We can conjecture that for firms with approximately linear costs the effect of uncertainty in such models will be a minor one.

On the other hand, there is a type of uncertainty where there is a lack of *ex post* adjustments in some very broad sense. This lack of *ex post* adjustment starts either with a lack of a formal *ex post* control in the model or with price stickiness, thereby generating disequilibria. The possibility of a final negative event like bankruptcy or dismissal is another one. Irreversibility of investment or the immutability of a production technology chosen are further constraints. One single decision is crucially important so that later decisions in the next periods cannot change the outcome; sometimes even the risk cannot be insured. If some or all of these characteristics hold the economy will experience a lot of disequilibria between supply and demand and between factors employed and factors warranted. Firms will regard this type of uncertainty as especially unfavourable, since they do not have many opportunities to react to the realization of the random variable. We will therefore label it as 'severe' uncertainty. The optimal decision will differ from certainty much more than for petty uncertainty, since a cost component is added in the uncertainty model (cost of uncertainty, for example probability of excess demand or supply, information costs, bankruptcy feasibility) which does not even exist under certainty. Under 'severe uncertainty' it seems very probable that optimal production is less than under certainty, according to the arguments following propositions 3 (marginal costs of uncertainty) and 4 (less downward than upward flexibility). In general, severe uncertainty generates a pressure to change the model to a larger extent than just to substitute a known value by a probability function. We would like to add information costs, goodwill and holding costs, the probability of bankruptcy, the cost of changing the technology, etc.

Some examples where uncertainty is mitigated by some *ex post* control or by rapid price changes and where it has its full impact are the following:

- in the competitive model with price uncertainty (where *ex post* prices clear the market), decisions under uncertainty and certainty are identical (for risk-neutral firms). In the competitive model under demand uncertainty (with disequilibria) firms produce less under uncertainty;
- in the monopoly model with market-clearing there is little room for different behaviour under certainty and uncertainty. The outcome depends on the 'technological concavity', where the third cross-derivative of revenue and cost functions (about which we do not know much empirically) decides. In the monopoly disequilibrium model under nearly all circumstances the decisions will be different between certainty and uncertainty (due to a component labelled marginal costs of uncertainty, which represents the expected cost of unsold production or unsatisfied demand);
- in models in which disequilibria (stocks or backlogged demand) can be transferred into the next period, decisions are more similar to certainty than in those where they are 'lost'. This stems from the fact that part of the 'marginal costs of uncertainty' can be recovered in the dynamic context (goods can be sold, demand satisfied);
- in models where one factor is to be chosen *ex ante*, the other *ex post*, uncertainty tends to lower capital input (Nickell 1978); in models where the *ex post* adjustment is limited (Kon 1983) a tendency to provide less capital is seen;
- if a preliminary production decision can be partly revised in the light of new information, if investment goods can be sold in a second-hand market, the outcomes are more similar than with inflexibility and irreversibility of investment decisions.

Our distinction between 'petty' and 'severe uncertainty' resembles that between risk and uncertainty or between expected utility maximization and Keynesian uncertainty. However, we think it is necessary and feasible to use the formal structure of Neumann–Morgenstern to derive results for situations like Keynesian uncertainty at least as a first approximation. If we have derived a preliminary qualitative result by this procedure we can still argue that the situation may be 'worse' than modelled insofar as people do not know the probability distribution exactly or at least not with great confidence (Falkinger 1986), that there are extra costs of uncertainty not yet considered, or that even the type of model

Table 9.2 Petty v. severe uncertainty

	Petty uncertainty	Severe uncertainty
Definitions	Uncertainty is an intermediate problem, some variables have to be decided before realization of x is known, some thereafter in a short-run optimization or they adjust automatically	Lack of *ex post* adjustments – no *ex post* control – price stickiness
Characteristics	Repeated (or small) decisions, lack of serial correlation for realizations of x, insurances, future markets	One-shot (large) decisions, x serially correlated Lethal events (bankruptcy, dismissal) Irreversibilities of investment and technologies
Consequences	Minor differences to certainty depending on facts difficult to evaluation (Z_{Yxx})	Important consequences (usually biasing down the optimal value of the decision variable), pressure to change the model to include new cost components and strategies
Empirically testable conclusions for relevance of the model	Equilibria, flexible prices and quantities, uncertainty does not depress economic activity	Disequilibria, price stickiness, uncertainty depresses economic activity, pressure to change 'the rules'

used should be changed. All these factors, already stressed by Keynesians, will gain more acceptance if we have proved that under 'severe uncertainty' behaviour really changes even within the Procrustean bed of models inherited from the world of certainty and treated by expected utility maximization.

9.3 INVENTORY MODELS

Inventory holding is an important link between the one-period models and dynamic models. From out of the enormous multiplicity of inventory models represented in the literature we selected some which neglect speculative stockholding (cost and price expectations are not taken into account), we concentrate on 'Keynesian causes' (cf. the classification by Walrasian and Keynesian inventory-holding models, Winckler 1977): we compare costs of unintentionally low inventories (goodwill costs, unsatisfied demand) with those of too-high inventories (production and inventory carrying costs). The question, whether – assuming constant unit cost and price – more or less is produced than the expected demand depends mainly on the ratio of profit (opportunity costs of low production in the one-period model) to production costs (opportunity costs of high production in the one-period model), and on the technical possibilities for backlogging of unsatisfied orders compared to the storability of the products. If backlogging of orders is not possible then a dynamic approach will increase the optimal inventory level in the one-period model and, as a rule, also above expected demand. If complete-order backlog is possible, then the newsboy model with its tendency to low stocks (and production) retains its validity.

This interpretation, which deviates from the literature, leads among other things to the testable implication of negative, and under uncertainty, declining net inventories. It will therefore be the main task of Part III to find clues for backlogging possibilities of orders and – in case they are substantial – to check implications arising therefrom for the net inventories.

NOTES

1 Disequilibria in the sense of unutilized capacities or in the sense of order backlog which are not due to optimizing behaviour.
2 i.i.d. assumption.
3 See Holthausen (1979).
4 See Nickell (1978).

10 Decision Theory and Empirical Evidence

Studies on decision theory usually do not confront models with empirical data. Optimal decisions are considered primarily a matter of logic; therefore results carefully derived from explicitly documented axioms should be obeyed by rational agents. Empirical evidence contradicting the results can indicate that agents do not behave rationally but it cannot defy the normative value of the theoretical models.

Within the minority of studies which do not neglect empirical tests, the evidence is predominantly gathered by experiments like questionnaires to be answered by students in the course of a seminar. Experiments are used to investigate the relevance of the axioms (for example, transitivity, continuity, substitutability) or to test whether individuals follow some implications of the theory developed (for example by comparing the consistency of choices in two sets of alternatives as in the famous Allais paradox). In respect of the current paradigm of decision theory, namely the expected utility theory, empirical evidence is currently growing fast. For decades the so-called Allais – or the St Petersburg – paradox has been tested. Since the emergence of prospect theory and regret theory some more decisions inconsistent with expected utility theory have been revealed. Conflicts between evidence gathered by experiments and the theory are solved by proposals to modify or generalize the theory. The role of empirical evidence in this book is somewhat different. We by and large accept that people (should) behave in a way indicated by expected utility theory. We interpret the evidence supplied by the experiments as being that in fairly sophisticated situations (where the alternatives are either not very different or where the outcomes are of a qualitatively different nature – like small income changes v. death) there could be some deviations from the normative theory (as demonstrated in the experiments), but over time and across individuals for real-world situations expected utility maximization should not be a bad guide. This may be a daring presumption but we used it in part II and maintain it in part III (though we do not want to denigrate the importance of all those experiments undertaken to find alternatives to expected utility theory). Having made this assumption, we use empirical data to reduce the ambiguity of the theoretical results. We have posed two questions, namely whether rationally formed expectations

Decision theory and empirical evidence

could on average be lower than outcomes, and whether production will be lower under uncertainty than under certainty. The answers to these questions cannot always be the same logically and therefore the models offered a wide range of possible answers, depending on the assumptions as well as on empirical values for some parameters. We can show that the answer will tend to be yes for a broad range of models in which prices are relatively constant and where disequilibria persist at least for some period. In these models according to our proposition 3, marginal costs of uncertainty – a cost component not existing under certainty – lowers optimal production. We can furthermore show that uncertainty will lower optimal stocks on hand (production plus stocks) if backlogging of unsatisfied demand is possible or if profits are small in relation to costs. On the other hand, the effect of uncertainty is less clear if market prices adjust quickly and no disequilibria are to be anticipated. We have seen that with two production factors, one of which has to be decided *ex ante* and one *ex post*, there are good arguments to provide more of the fixed one; but on the other hand if the preliminary decision can be adjusted to some extent after the veils of uncertainty are lifted ('*ex post* flexibility'), and if the upward adjustment is cheaper than the downward adjustment (asymmetry), then the opposite is true.

The role of empirical evidence in this book therefore lies in selecting the relevant models and in narrowing the range of the results with the help of information about the parameters involved. Empirical data are used to determine the importance of models by checking their assumptions and their implications. Chapter 11 focuses primarily on inventory-related problems. What is the rationale for inventories? How large are inventories for finished goods in relation to sales? Do they fluctuate cyclically (thereby indicating that inventories are a disequilibrium phenomenon), or are these fluctuations assessed by entrepreneurs as voluntary? Are price and cost changes the important determinants of inventory variations (indicating that the speculative element dominates)? Is backlogging an important factor in the industrial world? Do empirical variations of inventories follow the implications of the dynamic inventory models (have we chosen the right models?)? Do inventories empirically increase or decrease with increasing uncertainty?

In chapter 12 we focus on the question whether prices are fixed exogenously, and whether they are a decision parameter or a market-clearing device. We try to discover whether the competitive model with price uncertainty is empirically valid or whether the competitive model with demand uncertainty may be a good description of real-world behaviour, and whether monopoly or competition dominates. Since the results of the theoretical model were different depending on the market structure, the empirical importance of fixed *v*. flexible prices determines the real-world impact of uncertainty. Chapter 13 addresses the question of flexibility: firstly, whether investment plans are flexible, and then whether

110 Theoretical part

the upward and downward flexibility is different. We collect further information as to the question which parameter is usually set *ex ante* and which *ex post*. Finally we try to sum up which features (fitting to which models) seem to be stylized facts of modern industrial production in developed countries.

The methods used in part III could best be labelled as method mix. We use econometric techniques to estimate aggregate inventory functions, which will tell us to what extent inventories are a disequilibrium phenomenon and to what extent they are part of optimal price speculation. We use econometrics to assess price formation behaviour. We use simple statistical measures to assess the importance of backlogs in relation to finished goods' inventories. We use surveys among entrepreneurs concerning their production and price expectations and their assessment of the inventories as voluntary or not. We use reported expectations to get information about the flexibility and asymmetry of the investment decision. We use a questionnaire to ask firms to describe their particular decision situation under uncertainty, their modes, which variables they consider as uncertain, and how they choose between projects with different risks.

A large part of the evidence refers to aggregates and could be twisted by aggregation biases. The aggregates even sometimes sum up over quantities or prices without discriminating between price-setters and price-takers, between monopolists and competitive firms. In some cases we can disaggregate the material into smaller and more homogeneous groups to demonstrate that this aggregation bias will probably not be too large. The questionnaire on firms' strategy under uncertainty (see appendix 5) is the method nearest to that of experiments usually applied for testing the axioms of decision theory.

Against a (large) subset of the evidence we can argue that it refers to market outcomes but not to *ex ante* decisions in a carefully set up decision framework. Evidence derived from market outcomes has advantages and disadvantages in comparison to experiments. An advantage always stressed in the rational expectations' literature is that market outcomes tell us what people really have done, and not only what people intended to do or what they told an interviewer after a lot of rationalizing – see Lahiri (1976) and McCallum (1976) for statements along these lines. Questionnaires and experiments have other advantages: they can specify more carefully the choices and the environment, but usually there are no direct economic consequences (gains and losses) following from the answers (see appendix 2 for a discussion of the advantages and disadvantages of questionnaires). In the rational expectations' literature a consensus seems to emerge that both sources of evidence should be utilized (see Maddock & Carter 1984). Actual inflation gives us some clue as to the implied 'price expectations' but only after we accept some other hypothesis like 'inflation is the sum of a constant real rate and inflationary expectation'. Inferring expectations from actual inflation has the advantage that data are used from markets

Decision theory and empirical evidence 111

in which people actually acted with consequences for their wealth, but it has the disadvantage that we have to assume a theory of how expectations can be derived from the actual date.

Direct measurements of price expectations in surveys or experiments do not need the presumption of a theory, but the results may not be reliable and the questionnaire may not be taken seriously enough. In some experiments (e.g. Hey 1986) the experimenters pay a small fee to the participants depending on the results of the strategies used.

Using a method mix hopefully increases the validity of the evidence. One obstacle however cannot be overcome. Stylized facts can at best tell us about the empirical behaviour in the real world. They cannot answer normative questions. We can investigate whether markets *are* cleared or not, and whether backlogs *do* exist or not, but not whether they *should* be cleared or disequilibria *should* exist.

Part III

Empirical Information on the Relevance of the Models and on the Range of Critical Parameters

11 Empirical Evidence on the Function of Inventories (and Order Backlogs) under Uncertainty

11.1 THE EVIDENCE REQUIRED

The theoretical models of the microeconomic production decision of the firm under uncertainty have assigned different functions to inventory-holding. The one-period models abstract by definition from consideration of inventories and order backlogs, but implicitly they leave the question wide open as to whether all the results might not come out differently if inventory aspects were introduced. Even the one-period models, however, have diverse implications for the start of the (disregarded) second period. In the competition model with price uncertainty supply and demand were adjusted by means of price, in the competition model under demand uncertainty the entrepreneur was left with unsold goods, or demand could not be fully met. Similarly, disequilibria were disregarded in the monopolist's p-mode and q-mode, and in complete *ex post* flexibility, whereas they were the essence in the p-q *ex ante* mode (and increase with decreasing *ex post* flexibility, cf. chapter 8).

The first question to be answered by the empirical data is whether actual inventories are a disequilibrium phenomenon in the sense that they increase if demand proves weaker than anticipated and decrease if demand proves stronger. Alternative rationales for inventories would be that they are either technically fixed – for example in relation to sales – or that all inventory fluctuations follow from intentional optimizing behaviour – for example firms increase their stock if they expect rising prices and vice versa. Winckler (1977) has denoted the position that inventories are a disequilibrium phenomenon as 'Keynesian', while inventories resulting from intentional and carefully planned optimization are 'Walrasian'. The dominant empirical motive for inventories is important for the selection of the relevant models from amongst the theoretically feasible ones. If inventories (of finished goods) represent disequilibria, then a competitive model with demand uncertainty or a monopoly model with p-q mode will be the better representation of real-world behaviour. If, alternatively,

116 Empirical information

inventories are always at that level planned by firms, and prices always clear the market, then the competitive model with price uncertainty will be the relevant one and monopoly models should incorporate an *ex post* control. In the latter case, we would have made a bad choice in dealing with inventory models in which prices were assumed to be exogenous.

In section 11.2 we discuss the rationales for inventories in the theoretical literature, in section 11.3 we report which econometric tests of the determinants of inventories are proposed, and present new econometric evidence on the determinants of inventory investment in the Austrian manufacturing industry.

In section 11.4 we use business surveys from several European countries to see whether firms usually regard their inventory as satisfactory or whether they assess them – varying over time – as either too large or too small. The second important information which empirical data could supply is in assessing the range for some crucial parameters in the inventory model used in part II. We have seen that stocks in hand (inventory after production or ordering) will be relatively low in relation to expected demand, if the profits are relatively small, holding costs are high, and if backlogging was feasible. In section 11.5 we therefore try to evaluate the empirical range of profits and holding costs, and the importance of backlogging.

The optimal inventory policy following the theoretical model has several implications as to the net stock position (once the empirical range of the parameters is known). These implications are developed in section 11.6 and tested in section 11.8 after a small digression on orders as negative inventories (11.7). If reality confirms the implication of the theoretical model it is more likely that we have chosen the right model for deriving our conclusions as to the influence of uncertainty on optimal production and inventory.

Though it is trivial that the decision on the level of stocks on hand and the decision on *ex post* inventories are closely related, we want to stress that theoretical literature usually refers to the optimal stocks on hand (before sales), while empirical literature deals with stocks after sales are deducted (which again are identical with the inventory stock at the beginning of the next period – called 'initial inventory' in theoretical models).

In section 11.9 we sum up what empirical data suggest as to which models seem more realistic and in which range the parameters necessary to determine the optimal stocks on hand will probably lie.

11.2 WHY DO FIRMS CARRY INVENTORIES?

11.2.1 Overview on Inventories

The reasons for inventory-holding may be grouped by different (and partly overlapping) criteria. The following are some of the possible approaches to classification:

Inventories under uncertainty 117

- by transaction motive, speculative motive, precautionary motive. This classification emphasizes the similarity between the motives for holding money and holding stocks – for examples for applying that classification to motives for stockholding see, for example, Arrow *et al.* (1958) and Rowley & Trivedi (1975);
- by causes for inventory holding under certainty, uncertainty;
- causes of inventory-holding in the Walrasian and Keynesian models. Winckler (1977) emphasizes, as a significant difference between them, that inventories in the Walrasian models have the function of increasing profit, whereas in the Keynesian models they are consequences of planning errors;
- a classification related to the last item is that of motives of 'desired', 'planned' and '*ex post*' inventories, where desired stocks are defined as a longer-term target level, to be approached step by step through planned inventories; unexpected events (demand surprises) cause the *ex post* inventories (actual stock) to deviate from the planned level. This last classification is dominant in macroeconomic thought (econometric functions, analysis of business cycles).

In keeping with the aims of our study we shall follow the classification by inventories under certainty and uncertainty.

11.2.2 Inventory Theories under Certainty

The transaction motive is considered an argument for inventory-holding under certainty. It explains inventories as the outcome of insufficient synchronization between the purchase and sale of goods (or between output and delivery) and between income and consumption (in its use as an explanation of money-holding). Both in monetary theory and in inventory theory it is the basis for assuming a fixed (mostly linear, often even proportional) relation between inventories and revenue. Arrow *et al.* (1958) point out that, given certainty about future demand, the transaction motive does not strictly necessitate inventory-holding since, for example, money can be continuously borrowed or lent and thus no net money-holding is necessary. Such a need arises only the moment transaction costs for this operation arise. One is inclined to concede the necessity of 'technical' inventories in the case of intermediate inventories, and paralleling these (see, for example, Rowley & Trivedi 1975, p. 45) the need of 'stock (needed for) sample and display purposes'.

Transaction-conditioned inventories of raw materials or of final goods originate from concave cost components. Under this category we may classify all motivations of inventories by 'fixed' ordering costs, such as are encountered, for example, in the famous 'square-root formula' at the beginnings of inventory theory. In this formula, inventories are determined by the trade-off between ordering costs and unit inventory-holding costs,

118   Empirical information

where constant costs for each order independent of the quantity ordered are assumed. Concave ordering costs would also justify a positive inventory, but not constant unit costs.

A second set of motivations declare inventories as buffers (for production) against fluctuations in demand, which latter may, in principle, be predictable with certainty (seasonal fluctuations), or uncertain. Within the present subsection (inventories under certainty) the predictable seasonal or cyclical sales' fluctuations are dealt with. The motivation for inventory-holding rests now on a convex production cost component (rising unit costs). Given proportional unit costs, it would be possible to produce in time for demand, however much this demand may fluctuate.

A third related motive may arise from the costs of changing the volume of production, when it may be cheaper, even with a linear cost curve, to offset part of the demand fluctuations by means of inventory fluctuations (production smoothing). Mathematically, the cost function will in this case be a function of two variables – production costs and the cost of changing production volume.

To justify inventories both by concave and convex costs appears contradictory at first sight. This result becomes reasonable when we remember that, given concave costs, production ought to be as compact as possible, whereas convex costs will cause a minimum of costs with the most evenly spaced output. Thus the argument for convex costs needs demand fluctuations if it is to serve as a motive for stockholding, and the argument for concave costs requires smoothness of sales.

The speculative motive explains stockholding as due to the expectation of cost increase. Under certainty, stockholding is rational (Arrow *et al.* 1958, p 9) when the expected price rise is higher than the interest rate. Martirena-Mantel (1971) presents a further argument for inventory-holding under certainty: she sees in it an alternative to investment in capacity expansion. Investments in capital stock are irreversible (gross investments do not decline below zero); inventory investments save capacity adjustment to each fluctuation in demand. This argument is a special case of costs connected with the change of one variable (usually of production or prices), the costs of change in this case deriving from the irreversibility of the investments.

11.2.3 Inventory Theories under Uncertainty

The speculative motive has already been cited as a stockholding motive under certainty; a price rise cannot, as a rule, be assumed with certainty.

But the traditional inventory motive under uncertainty is the precautionary motive. Arrow *et al.* make the limiting proviso that the precautionary motive alone does not motivate stockholding if the desired good (money), when needed, can be obtained instantly and without extra cost. That is a logically unimpeachable statement, but today it is a generally accepted characteristic of uncertainty that at least a partial decision must be taken before the veil of uncertainty is lifted (part of the variable(s) is/are under *ex ante* control and can be revised, at best, at additional cost).

The precautionary motive was originally developed for money-holding, Arrow mentions Edgeworth (1978) who cites risk as a reason for caution in the banks' money stockholding. It leads to the distinction between *ex ante* planned inventories and actual inventory-holdings after the impact of demand. Second, the precautionary motive suggests that inventories must on average be positive. Third, it leads implicitly to the assumption that the inventory level should rise with the degree of uncertainty. These two latter consequences are understandable in the context of the dominant discussion of the motive relating to money and its application to safe banking, but as applied to goods' inventories (where order backlogs can be interpreted as negative inventories) its suggestions are not as valid.

The further development of the precautionary motive led to the construction of formulae about optimal inventory levels as shown, for example, in section 6.4. Some of the formulae make allowance also for expected price increases (cf. Veinott 1966), thus linking the speculative motive with that of caution.

11.3 MACROECONOMIC INVENTORY FUNCTIONS

11.3.1 The Accelerator – Buffer-Stock Model

The most popular macroeconomic explanation of changes in inventory-holding is the combination of an accelerator model with an 'unplanned' inventory movement resulting from sales surprises.

The accelerator motive in its simplest form assumes a linear relation between desired inventory level and sales,[1] it can be interpreted in the sense of the transaction motive[2] in justifying inventory-holding under certainty. Also, when applied to inventory formation the acceleration concept is criticized for lack of microeconomic foundation of a rigid relation between inventory level and sales; at an early stage Modigliani (1957) provided reasons for accepting it as rational, similarly (cf. Nickell for investment functions) convex adjustment costs (Nickell 1978, pp. 25 – 49) may be mentioned as rationalizing the behaviour that a part (δ) of the gap between desired and actual capital stock should always be closed. The only partial closing may thus be seen either as a consequence of optimal 'inventory smoothing' or as mere inertia (Feldstein & Auerbach 1976, Rowley & Trivedi 1975).

The buffer element assumes that a part (λ) of the sales surprise is compensated by countervailing inventory variations, another part ($1 - \lambda$) by output (*ex post* flexibility during the planning period).

Both elements of this explanation of inventories necessitate an estimation of expected sales. Here there remains a further spectrum of possible

120 Empirical information

assumptions: static and extrapolating expectation forming, weighted rule-of-thumb formulae or actually surveyed sales anticipations (Lovell 1967, Feldstein & Auerbach 1976) were carried out. Depending on the accuracy of the specification, different estimation equations may easily result, whereof equations 11.1 and 11.2 for inventory level (LB), or inventory investments (LI) respectively, are typical.

$$LB_t = \underbrace{\delta(LB_t^* - LB_{t-1})}_{a + bS_t^e} + LB_{t-1} + \lambda(S_t^e - S_t), \qquad (11.1)$$

$$LI_t = \delta a + \delta bS_t - (\delta b + \lambda)(S_t - S_t^e) - \delta LB_{t-1}, \qquad (11.2)$$

where δ and λ represent adjustment parameter, S_t and S_t^e represent actual expected revenue, and LB and LI represent inventory level and inventory investments, respectively.

Besides accelerator- and buffer-stock elements, price indicators are often incorporated into macroeconomic inventory equations (cf. Tichy 1976a, p. 92), though the theoretical foundation of an equation incorporating accelerator and price elements may be criticized (Winckler 1977, p. 92). We want to include prices to test the importance of the speculative element and we want to include profits as well as interest rates because our inventory model demonstrates that these elements influence the optimal desired inventory. See table 11.1 for the construction of the correct equation, and for the econometric results in the Austrian manufacturing industry. The overall results show that approximately 40% of the variations of investment in the finished goods' inventory can be explained by the equations. The surprise term has the correct sign in most equations, but its coefficients were not too high and not always significant. This may be either due to the unsuccessful approximation of the true surprise by the difference between the trend value and actual change or to the fact that in the real world a substantial part of the surprise can be absorbed by last-minute changes in production volume (*ex post* flexibility). A strong determinant of inventory investment is the last period's inventory stock, its coefficient suggests that three-quarters of the gap between desired and actual stock can be closed within a period.

Price change, simultaneous or delayed, is of no significance, therefore speculative inventory movements cannot be proved. Conversely, both the cash-flow trend and the preceding period's cash-flow share and its trend deviation make a significant contribution (t-values 2.79 and 2.00 respectively); bringing them into the stock-adjustment function also increases the significance of the variable that should signal unplanned stock movement. The prime rate, too, contributes significantly and shows the expected sign.

Inventories under uncertainty   121

Table 11.1 Stock-adjustment models with alternative assumptions about desired stocks

---

I   Models

Assumptions about inventory stock: A1, B1, C1

(A) Simple stock-adjustment model
(A1) $LB^*_t = a + bS^e_t$

(A2) $LI_t = \delta(a + bS^e_t - LB_{t-1}) + \lambda(S^e_t - S_t) = \delta a + (\delta b + \lambda)(S^e_t - S_t) + \delta bS_t - \delta LB_{t-1}$

(B) 'Microeconomic augmented' stock-adjustment model
(B1) $LB^*_t = a + bS^e_t + \mu_1 CF^e_t + \mu_2 PRIME_t$

(B2) $LI_t = a + (b + \mu_1)(S^e_t - S_t) + bS_t + \mu_1 CF^e_t + \mu_1 PRIME_t - LB_{t-1}$

(C) Stock-adjustment model with speculation
(C1) $LB^*_t = abS^e_t + \mu_3 PREIS, R_t$

(C2) $LI_t = a + (b +)(S^e_t) + bS + \mu_3 PREIS.R_t - \delta LB_{t-1}$

II   Regression estimates for Austrian manufacturing (1955–81)

(A2) $LI = 1.372 + 0.04\ (S^T_t - S_t)\ + 0.05\ S_t - 0.77 LB_{t-1}$
       $\quad (1.07)(1.72) \quad\quad\quad (3.65)(-3.52)$
       $\quad\quad\quad\quad\quad\quad\quad\quad R^2 = 0.34,\ S_e = 2.083$

(B2.1) $LI = -398 + 0.07\ (S^T_t - S_t)\ + 0.05\ S_t + 0.37 CF_{t-1} - 0.37 LB_{t-1}$
       $\quad\quad (0.31)(2.83) \quad\quad\quad (3.87)\quad (2.79)\quad\quad (-2.79)$
       $\quad\quad\quad\quad\quad\quad\quad\quad R^2 = 0.50,\ S_e = 1.822$

(B2.2) $LI = -4.947 + 0.06\ (S^T_t - S_t)\ + 0.05\ S_t + 221 CF - Q_{t-1} - 0.82 LB_{t-1}$
       $\quad\quad (1.47)(2.41) \quad\quad\quad (4.23)\quad (2.00)\quad\quad (-3.97)$
       $\quad\quad\quad\quad\quad\quad\quad\quad R^2 = 0.43,\ S_e = 1.954$

(B2.3) $LI = 4.053 - 0.06\ (S^T_t - S_t)\ + 0.06\ S_t - 387\ PRIME_{t-1} - 0.90 LB_{t-1}$
       $\quad\quad (2.50)(-2.51) \quad\quad\quad (4.43)\ (-2.38)\quad\quad (-3.97)$
       $\quad\quad\quad\quad\quad\quad\quad\quad R^2 = 0.46,\ S_e = 1.892$

(C2.1) $LI = 1.684 + 0.05\ (S^T_t - S_t)\ + 0.04\ S_t + 256\ PREIS, R_t - 0.70 LB_{t-1}$
       $\quad\quad (1.35)(1.82) \quad\quad\quad (2.96)\ (1.57)\quad\quad (-3.22)$
       $\quad\quad\quad\quad\quad\quad\quad\quad R^2 = 0.39,\ S_e = 2.017$

(C2.2) $LI = 1.608 + 0.06\ (S^T_t - S_t)\ + 0.06\ S_t + 272\ PREIS, R_{t-1} - 0.89 LB_{t-1}$
       $\quad\quad (1.32)\ (2.12) \quad\quad\quad (4.12)\ (1.83)\quad\quad (-4.08)$
       $\quad\quad\quad\quad\quad\quad\quad\quad R^2 = 0.41,\ S_e = 1.981$

S^e resp. CF^e, expected sales resp. cash flow.
CF-Q, ratio of cash flow to value added.
LB, LB^*, actual, desired inventories of finished goods.
LI, inventory investment.
$PREIS$, $PRIME$, manufacturing prices, prime rate.
R after a variable: relative difference.
Assumption: $CF^e = CF_{t-1}$ resp. $CF^e = CF - Q_{t-1}$.
S_e standard errors of regression (t-values in brackets).

Table 11.2 Inventory assessment and capacity utilization in peaks (P) and troughs (T) in EEC countries

	Capacity utilization				Assessment of finished-good inventories[1]			
	1972/73(P)	1974/75(T)	1979/80(P)	1982/83(T)	1972/73(P)	1974/75(P)	1979/80(P)	1982/83(T)
Belgium	85.4	70.4	79.1	74.4	−14	+37	+2	+18
Germany	88.1	74.8	86.0	75.3	−7	+43	−2	+31
France	87.8	76.6	85.3	81.1	−14	+50	+3	+42
Italy	78.8	68.0	77.3	69.1	−24	+53	−8	+32
Netherlands	86.0	76.0	83.0	75.8	−3	+57	+3	+39
United Kingdom	90.6	75.5	87.6	79.0	—	—	−1	+42

Source: Business test of European Economic Community, Europäische Wirtschaft, Beiheft B/5/1986.
[1] Balances of firms reporting them as too low/too high.

Inventories under uncertainty 123

The main conclusions from the estimations for Austrian fixed-stock inventory (and the literature about econometric function in other countries) is first that prices are not too important in the explanation of inventories, and secondly that inventories do contain disequilibria elements (a smaller one due to recent surprises and a larger one due to the impossibility of adjusting inventories quickly to the desired stock). Profits and interest rates contribute significantly to the inventory fluctuations as predicted by the inventory models.

11.4 SURVEY INFORMATION ON THE ROLE OF INVENTORIES

In several European countries firms are asked in surveys (called 'business tests') whether they consider their inventories as satisfactory, as too large or as too small. If inventories are a disequilibrium phenomenon we would expect firms to make frequent use of the 'too large' and the 'too small' category and these assessments should fluctuate over time. Where inventories are carefully planned and these plans can be carried out, the answers should be concentrated in the category 'satisfactory'.

Let us first look at the German data which have the advantage that the survey asks separate questions for raw-material inventories and finished-good inventories. Table 11.5 shows that while raw-material inventories are always approximately as high as intended, for finished-good inventories the proportion of firms reporting imbalances is comparatively large. In February 1983, 78 per cent assessed their raw-material stock as normal, but only 45 per cent did the same for their finished goods. We checked that this difference prevails for other periods.

As far as the cyclical variation of the assessments are concerned table 11.2 tells us for six EEC countries the maximum and the minimum of the inventory valuations. At the peak of a business cycle the majority of the firms assessed their finished-good inventories as too low, see for example the survey result in Belgium, where for 1972/73 a negative balance of −14 was reported (that means that the proportion of firms assessing their inventories as too small was fourteen percentage points larger than the proportion which reported them as too high), the same balance turned to +37 in the next trough (1974/75). A similar switch in opinion can be seen in other cycles and for other countries. If firms could manage to be in approximately that inventory position which they wanted according to their *ex ante* optimization, then the balances should be small and invariant over time (as they are roughly for raw-material inventories).

11.5 EMPIRICAL INFORMATION ON PROFITS *v.* COSTS AND GOODWILL *v.* INVENTORY-HOLDING COSTS

Whether, in the linear inventory model stocks will be finally higher or lower than expected demand, depends on the empirical values for some

124 Empirical information

parameters. We examine information on the relation between profits and costs and on goodwill and inventory-holding costs in this section.

The relation between price, p, and unit cost, c – or what is its complement – between unit profit and revenue per unit can be approximated by several measures. As a first measure we want to use the relationship of cash flow to sales, which is often reported in business reports. This relationship varies over time and over countries and branches but on average between 5 and 10 per cent of sales are reported as cash flow (for Austria the ratio lies between 5 and 6 per cent).

This would imply profits to be by far the smaller part in relation to costs.

Table 11.3 The ratio of cash flow to value added in six countries as a percentage

	1976	1977	1978	1979	1980	1976–80
USA	15.2	15.6	15.2	15.0	14.4	15.1
Germany	17.3	15.0	15.4	16.0	14.4	15.6
Japan	14.3	14.5	15.5	17.9	—	14.7[1]
France	13.6	12.6	13.8	14.7	—	12.7[1]
Norway	12.7	11.8	10.9	17.1	—	12.5[1]
Austria	25.0	18.9	19.1	21.8	20.2	20.6

Source: *Financial Statistics*, Part 3/1981, and Hahn (1987).
[1] 1976/79.

This estimate may be considered as a lower limit, in that whereas the model requires all costs (including taxes) connected with production to be subject to *ex ante* control – a good deal of flexibility obtains for some cost components. An obvious candidate for exclusion from cost which has not to be fixed *ex ante* may be purchases of primary products. This could lead us to compare cash flow not to sales, but to value added; data on this ratio are available for six countries for 1976–80 (table 11.3). Cash flow as a percentage of value added lies between 12.5 per cent in France and 20.6 per cent in Austria. It is 15 per cent in the USA and Japan. In all countries it remains well below 50 per cent. Additionally, we have also to remember that cash flow is a wide concept for profits, including depreciations and provisions (for pensions, dismissals, etc.), which could be considered as cost components and not as profit components.

Very scant and diverse information is available as to the relationship between inventory-holding costs and goodwill costs (the relationship of h to g).

Holt et al. (1960) conducted a field enquiry among firms on the relative costs of order backlogging and stockholding, and have also computed hypothetical values by model simulations for these cost categories. Order backlogging is more expensive according to firms' replies whereas a model simulation showed higher inventory costs (cf. Holt *et al.* 1960, p. 24).

Inventories under uncertainty 125

Tichy (1976a, p. 38) assumes that the relative costs of the inability to deliver show cyclical variation: in boom times they are supposed to be lower than during recession, because the loss of customers is improbable during a general shortage.

In an empirical survey of the extent of costs of shortages, Walter & Grabner (1975) come to the conclusion that a unique once-only non-delivery results approximately in the loss of one-quarter of revenue. Silver (1981, p. 631) reports that firms undertake 'all that's possible' to avoid non-delivery (speed-up of production, additional purchase from competitors, substitution by qualitatively higher-valued articles): in this case the loss of goodwill is converted to an excess cost for the 'emergency measure'.

Based on very specific assumptions' Reisman *et al.* (1972) establish stockholding costs – depending on the scope of the term – of between 9 and 28 per cent, and goodwill costs of less than 5 per cent of the price.

In an enterprise survey on possible reactions (to demand surprise) within the planning period, 60 per cent cited stock cuts (under positive shock), but only 36 per cent mentioned inventory build-up (under negative shock) as a primary reaction (see also section 12.4.2). Such asymmetry would point to dearer inventory costs compared to goodwill costs.[3]

Estimates of the relative significance of inventory costs as against goodwill costs thus vary greatly. Generally, both components, and especially possible differences between them, are likely to be slight relative to the asymmetry of profits and production costs[4] respectively.

11.6 TESTABLE IMPLICATIONS OF THE INVENTORY MODEL

When summing up the findings of section 11.5, in that

- profits and costs are asymmetric, setting up a tendency for the right side of the formula to be well below one half;
- inventory costs and goodwill costs are low with slight indications of asymmetry; and
- order backlogging is possible in large areas of industry, and at least equally as feasible as building up stock (see table 11.4);

then it may be concluded that most probably the right side in equation 6.12 will show a value of less than one half. This has two implications, amenable to testing:

- net inventories (stocks of finished goods minus deliveries, less order backlog) are negative on average, since stocks on hand (before deliveries)

are lower than expected demand (because $F(q+I)<0.5 \Rightarrow q+I<E(x)$); and
- net inventories must decline with increasing uncertainty (must grow more negative).

The latter characteristic is a consequence of the former (if net inventories were positive then they would rise with increasing uncertainty). A situation is more uncertain than another, if it is characterized by a random variable Y whose symmetrical density function is less concentrated – 'more weight in the tail' (Hey 1981, p. 30) – than that for X. For the distribution functions F and G (of X and Y respectively) the following will hold for all t:

$$\int_{-\infty}^{t} [G(s) - F(s)] \, ds \geq 0. \qquad (11.3)$$

This inequality tells us that X is less uncertain than Y, we further assume that $E(X) = E(Y)$ and that the difference $F - G$ changes its sign once only – 'mean preserving spread', (Lippman & McCall 1981, p. 215). The intersection of the distribution functions is reached at their expected value, for $F(s) < 0.5$; $F(s)$ is lower than $G(s)$, the optimal value s^* is therefore lower, for the distribution characterizing greater uncertainty (G distribution).[5]

As a third implication of inventory formula (6.12) there would follow differential developments of the stock position in individual branches. Branches that usually carry a positive net inventory such as homogeneous goods (non-durables) would have to increase stocks with rising uncertainty, branches with negative net inventory (order backlog, e.g. consumer durables, capital goods) would have to reduce stock (allow it to grow more negative).

All three implications are examined below, with the assumption that recent years may be considered the period of increased uncertainty and that difference between inventories of finished goods and order backlog can be considered as 'net inventory level'. The last assumption is discussed.

11.7 DETERMINANTS OF ORDER BACKLOGS – ARE BACKLOGS NEGATIVE ORDERS?

The question whether uncertainty lowers inventories – as is assumed in general – or increases them, depends as was shown in the last section, on whether the inventories are on average positive or negative. The latter is only possible if orders can be understood as negative inventories (a component that is largely missing in monetary theory).[6]

The interpretation of the order stock as negative inventory has been known for a long time – cf. Simon (1951) on the feasibility of positive or negative inventories. The empirical statement that there are branches that produce to order and others that produce to stock is established in the economic literature at any rate since Abramovitz (1948) and Zarnowitz (1962).

Zarnowitz cites as typical fields of production to order:

- production of non-homogeneous goods with unforeseeable specifications;
- physically or economically non-durable goods; and
- branches with unstable or sporadic demand.

Typical stock goods listed by Zarnowitz are staple commodities, shelf or rack goods, homogeneous goods and products requiring a long production period.

From the point of view of uncertainty, the diversity of who carries the risk impact is conspicuous. In production for stock, the firm must produce before uncertainty has lifted. A q-mode in terms of chapter 5 prevails: given fixed prices, and in competition under demand uncertainty, price and quantity produced are fixed *ex ante*.

In consequence, the risk of demand fluctuations is fully borne by the producer. In production to order, demand uncertainty is eliminated,[7] some elements of cost uncertainty remain but they can be reduced by a sliding price clause.[8]

In times of increasing uncertainty the entrepreneur (given risk aversion or technological concavity) would be likely to favour, as far as possible, production to order. The most recent business literature therefore stresses the importance of 'just-in-time' production.

Some authors raise the question of whether inventories and order backlogs are symmetrical. Belsley (1969) mentions that the determinants of inventory costs are substantially different from that of order backlogs. Reagan *et al.* (1982) determined in a time series analysis that order backlogging and inventory holding in the US do not have equal spectral properties nor do they have good coherence. Amihud & Mendelson (1983) and Blinder (1982) in their theoretical contributions consider inventory and order backlog to be elements of the same optimization process. Despite the tendency present in the theoretical studies to treat positive and negative inventories as symmetrical, to my knowledge there exist no empirical functions with net inventory movement as the variable to be explained.

Some part of every order backlog is not subject to economic optimization but is technologically conditioned (production period). Something similar applies – though not to the same extent – to finished-good inventories. But the borderlines between the 'economic option' and 'technological fact' are fluid since there is choice between different techniques. Unplanned variations of inventories and order backlogs should go in the same direction (in terms of net inventory considerations).

128 Empirical information

Unexpectedly strong demand will bring an unplanned order-backlog increase and cause an unplanned decline of the stock of finished-goods. Whether the reactions turn out strong or moderate depends on the option of alternative reactions (price fluctuations, *ex post* quantity flexibility), or maybe on inventory, order (and output) changes. The net inventory movement is pushed in the same direction by stock reduction and by increase of the order backlog.

The arguments do not permit us to expect full symmetry of inventories and orders since factors exist that go in the same direction and others that go in opposite directions.

11.8 TEST FOR FINISHED-GOOD INVENTORIES IN THE US, GERMANY AND AUSTRIA

In this section we shall test the three implications of the inventory formula concerning level, movement and branch differences under the assumption that the years under consideration (1980 – 2) can be taken to be a period of uncommonly strong demand uncertainty.

The three implications presented in section 11.6 are:

- net inventories will be negative on industrial average;
- net inventories will diminish (will grow more negative) in periods of increasing uncertainty, and
- depending on the net inventory position in the branches, inventory dynamics should go in opposite directions across branches in periods of stronger uncertainty.

Data concerning order backlogs and the level of finished-good inventories are, as a rule, surveyed by different institutions, according to differing methods and even for a varying selection of branches of industry. Statistics in table 11.4 shall serve to exemplify this.

In the US, the average (finished-good) inventory – sales ratio is slightly above 14.2 per cent of annual revenue, the average order backlog near 28.9 per cent the net inventory position is clearly negative (– 14.7 per cent). Since the order data here, too, refer only to a smaller selection of branches, comparing the surveyed order positions and the inventories of all branches enables us to determine a lesser, though still a negative (– 2.1 per cent), net inventory level.

In recent years (average 1980 – 2), the inventory – revenue ratio (14.08) has remained static or declined, depending on whether we compare it with the 1970s (14.09) or with the total period (1954 – 72: 14.22), the order backlog has risen to 31.39 per cent, which is higher than in all comparative periods.[9]

Inventories under uncertainty 129

Conforming to the hypothesis, the net stock position has therefore declined (grown more negative: 1980 – 2: – 17.3, 1954 – 82: – 14.7). In accordance with the third implication, the order backlog of durable goods has risen whereas orders declined and inventories rose for non-durables.

Data on order backlogs in industry are available since the 1960s for the Federal Republic of Germany. Unlike the US the backlogs declined there in recent years. In 1980–2 they amounted to 23.9 per cent of annual output, in the 1970s they were about 25.9 per cent. However, an evaluation of order backlogs in a business survey shows that the decline of order backlogs must not be interpreted as the desired development, since a large majority of business enterprises rate these backlogs as too small (net balance – 40 per cent).[10] The survey even indicates that the desired order backlog may have risen, since an order backlog of equal size in 1972 (23.5 per cent of annual output) had been considered less unsatisfactory (hangover of the 'too little' reports in 1972: 25 per cent).

Data on finished-good inventories are available for the last three years only; they amount to 7.5 per cent of annual output, which means that the net inventory position in the FRG was also distinctly negative (see table 11.5).

Stocks of finished goods in Austria were 7 per cent of output on average, their level had hardly changed in 1980 – 2. But now they are described as distinctly excessive, indicating that – unlike the 1970s – they are likely to contain more involuntary elements. The order backlog for overall industry has risen distinctly (from 33.4 per cent at the beginning of the survey to 39 per cent in the years 1980 – 2); this tendency is primarily due to the machine-building and electrical engineering industries. The net inventory position is distinctly negative, order backlog being five times the volume of finished-good stocks – without machine it is still three-and-a-half times.

The net inventory position declined in conformity with hypothesis (with and without machine-building industry it grew more negative), the backlog increase – conforming to the third implication – was bigger for branches with more emphasis on order production (machinery, electric engineering).[11] Yet the overall rise in satisfied orders over finished-good stocks (diminished net inventories) does not seem to correspond to the 'desired' movement, since orders are presently declared to be too low and finished-good stocks too high.

The results of this section confirm that the net inventory position is manifestly negative confirming the first implication. The actual net inventory position has not risen in recent years but has rather declined, the desired net stock position probably having declined even more than the actual position. This would conform with the second implication if indeed the start of the 1980s was a period of increased uncertainty. The sectoral changes of the net stock position, according to production to order

Table 11.4 Inventories (finished goods) and order backlog in % of annual sales

USA

	(1) Inventory – sales ratio	(2) All	Order-shipment ratio[1] (3) Durables	(4) Non-durables	(5) Net inventories (1) – (2) = (5)
1954–9	14.58	28.29	33.42	8.02	–13.71
1960–9	14.17	27.09	32.40	6.09	–12.86
1970–9	14.09	10.32	36.15	6.52	–16.23
1980–2	14.08	31.39	38.08	5.03	–17.31
Ø 54–82	14.22	28.90	34.49	6.53	–14.68

Source: Economic Report of the President
1. For firms which do have backlogs
Unfilled orders in % of sales (including branches without backlogs): 16.30
Net inventories: 2.08 (14.22 – 16.30)

Germany

	(1) Inventory – sales ratio	(2) Evaluation as too high (+) or too low (–)	(3) Order backlog	(4) Evaluation as too high (+) as too low (–)	(5) Net inventories (3) – (1)
1972	—	+13	23.5	–25	—
1980–2	7.5	+29	23.9	–40	–16.4
1970–9	—	+12	25.9	–24	—

Source: IFO-Munich

Austria

	(1) Inventory – sales ratio Total	(2) Evaluation as too high (+) as too low (–)	(3) Order backlog Total	(4) Order backlog excl. machinery	(5) Evaluation as too high (+) as too low (–)	(6) Net inventories
Ø 73/4	6.8	+ 9.4	33.4	22.9	– 4.2	–15.0
Ø 80/2	7.1	+26.5	39.0	25.8	–25.9	–17.4

1. Excluding machinery and those branches not covered by order statistics

Table 11.5 Volume and 'voluntarity' of raw-material and finished-good inventories in German manufacturing (February 1983)

	Raw materials					Finished goods			
	Volume in weeks	Assessment in %			Volume in weeks	Assessment in %			
		Too large	Normal	Too small		Too large	Normal	Too small	
Basic goods	5.1	8	75	14	4.3	21	50	2	
Investment goods	6.0	10	79	9	4.9	30	42	1	
Consumer goods	4.2	6	84	8	3.6	32	38	2	
Food and beverages	6.3	13	66	3	3.6	20	51	1	
Total manufacturing	5.4	9	78	9	4.3	26	45	2	

	Raw-material inventories	Finished-good inventories
Share of 'normal'	78	45
Share of 'too large' 'plus' 'too small'	18	28
Share of 'usually no inventories'	4	27

Source: IFO-Schnelldienst 10 – 11/1983, p. 4f.

132 *Empirical information*

and to stock, respectively, correspond tendentially to the prediction that the net position should become more negative for branches in which backlogs already dominate stocks.

Tendencies that arise through increase of uncertainty or decline of the (expected) demand trends cannot be separated in the data. However, the results are less contradictory to the hypothesis of this study (declining net position given greater uncertainty) than they are to the hypothesis that high precautionary inventories should be built up in times of uncertainty.

11.9 THE EVIDENCE WE GOT

In summing up the main results of this chapter we want first to stress the limitations. The concepts for inventories used in the theoretical models (stocks on hand, backlogs) are not easily identified in real-world balance sheets. The simplifying assumptions of models (i.i.d. demand, linear costs and revenues) may be unrealistic. Empirical data are subject to a variety of problems whether they are collected by central statistical agencies or by surveys among firms.

If we nevertheless accept that empirical data can help us to choose between different models and determinants of the inventory process, we obtained information that inventories are a disequilibrium phenomenon. Sales surprises contribute to the variation in inventory investment, desired inventories cannot be achieved immediately, firms assess (alternatively and in a degree varying over time) their finished goods' position as too large and too small.

Cash flow is indeed a determinant of the inventories investment, the same seems to be true for the interest rate, but not for price changes.

In the real world, profits seem to be by far the smaller part of sales or of value added, goodwill costs v. holding costs will not be too asymmetric or both will be too small to negate the tendency for smaller inventories (after production) as compared to expected demand. Backlogging seems to be at least as easy as storing finished goods.

Three implications can be derived from the empirical range of these parameters. The first, overwhelmingly confirmed by the data, is that net inventories are negative; the second is that optimal inventories should decrease with increasing uncertainty; the third that in branches where the net position is negative it should decrease (in the sense of becoming more negative) while in others where it had been positive it should increase. Further empirical work is needed to supply more evidence, but at least the implications are not contradicted by facts. The role of prices has been important in this chapter to assess the function of inventories – especially in the conflicting position between Walrasian and Keynesian inventories. It will need more attention when we have to discriminate between fixed-price and flexible-price models and is therefore dealt with in the following chapter.

NOTES

1 Concerning the usually disregarded question of whether value added might be the correct reference figure, see Winckler (1977, p. 94f.).
2 Clark (1917), Metzler (1941).
3 Amihud & Mendelson (1983) developed the testable hypothesis that higher inventory costs (relative to goodwill costs) can be recognized by the fact that the prices are then more flexible downwards than upwards. According to the business survey quoted this can be spotted only in a very restricted sense because price reductions and price increases are both seen to an equal extent as first reactions. Nevertheless, a price increase, even given a large deviation, was reported as rare by 43 per cent of firms, a price reduction by only 32 per cent.
4 Asymmetrical goodwill (with dearer goodwill) is arrived at if inventory costs are reduced by a future scrap value (e.g. Mills (1962) arrives at negative costs for inventory-holding), or if one includes forgone revenue (profits) in the costs of inability to deliver (supply). The former becomes negligible within the planning horizon, the second effect is already discounted in the formula part $(p-c)$ (goodwill costs are only the loss of future demand based on the experience that the firm cannot supply, not forgone present revenue).
5 More accurately: s^* is not higher. The variation of inventory level is here affected by a variation of the distribution function, but under equal parameters on the right hand side of equation 6.12. Uncertainty could, however, also change the parameters, e.g. through variation of the forward discount (α), or through a greater desire for constancy of supply contracts (which could manifest itself in a higher or a lower b), or through a quicker tendency to obsolescence of products (a lower a). Since there are few indications of such variations of parameters, the main effect of increasing uncertainty concerning the variation of the distribution function is assumed.
6 This statement, too, is confined to cash-holding. A current account balance may already be negative.
7 What is eliminated is the chance that variable production costs arise 'unnecessarily'; the fixed costs for installed capacities remain.
8 Remaining uncertainties result from production technology and delivery risk.
9 There is also a longer-term trend in evidence towards rising order backlogs (a structural shift in favour of technical processing goods branches), but the decline in 1980-1 is too strong to be (considered) solely as caused by this shift.
10 Balance of shares of firms naming order backlogs as too big and too small respectively. Negative balance signifies overhang of evaluation as too little.
11 The rank correlations between net stock position level and variation is positive but not significant ($R=0.14$). If the steel industry and the related metal-casting industry are excluded (where the object of avoiding unemployment frustrated the desired strategy of developing a growing order backlog), the rank correlation rises to $R=0.56$, yet remains insignificiant.

12 Empirical Evidence on Whether Prices are an Action Variable, a Random Variable or a Relatively 'Stable' Exogenous Variable

12.1 THE QUESTION TO BE ANSWERED

In the competition model, theory arrives at different answers concerning output volume under uncertainty, compared with certainty, depending on whether price is an *ex post* control or fixed (it will be unchanged or lower, respectively). In the monopoly model, too, different results emerge depending on whether prices and quantities are fixed before the demand curve is determined. The inventory models usually assume constant prices. In this chapter evidence will be gathered on whether prices are in fact an *ex ante* control in industrialized countries, if after demand becomes known they are used to close the gap between supply and demand (*ex post* control) or if in fact they are relatively rigid in the sense that they change slowly and according to generally known laws (e.g. wage dynamics). In the latter case the prices, though not 'absolutely rigid', would in decision-making have to be considered part of the information input (neither as action variable nor as *ex post* control).

In section 12.2 a short overview is given of the controversial issue of how enterprises determine prices and whether supply or demand factors play a more important role in this. Surveys and econometric estimations will round off the findings.

The cost curve typical for industrial production, and pricing too, are subject to sharp controversy in the literature. The competition model under certainty requires convex costs (for achieving well-defined optimal production), which latter under demand uncertainty imply lower optimal production. The cost curve affects optimal pricing in all forms where quantities (in monopoly) are *ex post* controls and will also influence the optimal choice of the action parameter (price or quantity) if the monopolist can make a choice between strategies (Lim 1980). Again a brief survey

The nature of prices 135

of the literature concerning the divergent opinions is supplemented by findings of a field survey of Austrian industry; although we cannot hope thereby to obviate dispute on the cost curve, and even less to obtain hints for the third cross-derivative of the cost curve, which is important under models following operationalization 2 (see section 12.3).

Then we first examine by means of a technique proposed by Hay 1970 whether prices or quantities react more strongly to demand shocks, thereafter scanning the results in a field survey (section 12.4). Relative rigidity of quantities and prices after an unexpected price development is also gone into dependent on the direction of the shock and difference in enterprise size.

In section 12.5 we test the relative price and quantity rigidity by statistical measures and by differences between expected and real prices.

In section 12.6 we search for indicators for the relative closeness of branches of industry to the competition model and examine how flexible are prices in those particular branches where changes in price should, according to the model, close gaps quickly and where unwanted inventories ought not to exist. Signficant price rigidities and unwanted vigorous fluctuations of inventories in markets, which in view of the number of suppliers and of competitive pressures (e.g. through imports) should be 'competitive', would imply that demand uncertainty (model 5.2.4) may well be present in the 'competitive sector' too. Equally, free capacities and their cyclical variations would be contradicting the equilibrium models.

The whole chapter is not written for purists. Evidence stems from different countries, periods and sources. The tentative conclusions drawn by the author out of this foggy evidence are presented in section 12.7.

12.2 PRICING IN THE LIGHT OF SURVEYS AND ECONOMETRICS

The discrepancy between the theoretical pricing model and industrial practice occupies economic literature at any time since Hall and Hitch. These authors established in a survey that most enterprises arrive at their pricing by adding a profit margin to direct unit cost. Forty per cent of enterprises never revise this margin in the light of demand while 60 per cent normally stick to the principle of full costs while assigning demand a certain role if and when they vary the price.[1] Numerous empirical studies (Andrews 1949, Hague 1949, Fog 1960, Fitzpatrick 1964, Skinner 1970, Laden 1972, Alfred 1972) confirm such full-cost pricing in one variant or another.

This method of pricing is in contradiction to the competition model (where the price is exogenously given) and tendentially it also contradicts the monopoly model under certainty since the customary optimization rule (marginal revenue = marginal costs) can be represented as a combination of supply

136 *Empirical information*

and demand factors, whereas the full-cost principle considers supply factors only. However, pricing by the 'full-cost-plus-profit-margin' rule need not offend against the profit maximization of the standard model, if the profit margin chosen is the exact equivalent of the price elasticity of demand (for the exact condition see Hay & Morris 1979, pp. 115 – 21).

For a summary of the discussion in the literature of full-cost pricing see Hay & Morris (1979) or Nowotny *et al.* (1978), for a spirited defence of the marginal principle and, in conjunction with it, a repudiation of the findings of business surveys generally (see Machlup 1966, p. 66ff.).

Surveys on pricing behaviour may give an indirect pointer as to whether the price is an action variable or an exogenous one. Both Lanzillotti (1958) and Shipley (1981) report a certain return on the invested capital (target return) as the most important objective; fair prices, according to Shipley, take second place, prices similar to the competitor's third.

The last-named motive (48 per cent of respondents) points to a rather passive mode of pricing. Achieving a stable sales' volume is cited as the aim of pricing by 25 per cent of respondents. This group may be taken as an indicator of the importance of firms using price as an *ex post* control. Shipley states that only 16.5 per cent of firms consider price stability to be the goal of pricing, whereas Lanzillotti's survey (conducted in times of stable prices) names this aim more frequently.

In an Austrian survey of 200 medium-sized firms (Nowotny *et al.* 1978), 26 per cent of firms were found to calculate price by strict full-cost principle, 49 per cent by flexible full-cost principle. Several forms of passive acceptance of price (market price; price-setting by the principal customer; price regulation) was named by 49 per cent of respondent firms. Contrary to theoretical assumption – *viz.* that polypolists are price-takers whereas monopolists are, at least potentially, price-setters – the share of these 'passive' categories rise from 43 per cent in firms with a small (1 – 10 per cent) market share to 61 per cent in firms with more than 30 per cent market share. Only 16 per cent of those in the latter group cited the rigid full-cost principle.

Questioned on causes for price *changes* (Nowotny *et al.* 1978), a majority of respondents name institutions (58 per cent: 'Joint Commission', a semi-official body of management/labour representatives); 17 per cent: start of new financial year, cost shifts follow (35.5 per cent), then wage contracts (19 per cent); and shifts in competitive situation (18 per cent).

The three supply categories[2] taken together easily outrank the sum of demand categories. Taking into consideration the joint commission's substantial bias in favour of considering cost increases, we see that the relative weight of supply factors grows still further.

The predominance of supply over demand factors in pricing, while not directly precluding the use of prices as an *ex post* control, lowers the plausibility that prices promptly react to demand shocks. Yet another

The nature of prices 137

survey of Austrian industry (conducted by the Austrian Institute of Economic Research – WIFO) gives a further indication on whether prices are in fact actively fixed or passively accepted. Seventy-three per cent of respondent firms reported that their domestic prices are fixed in the market, 84 per cent report the same concerning their export prices. This indicates that Austrian firms are predominantly price-takers; and it brings into perspective the surveys enquiring about active pricing modes.

Price-fixing by a large competitor on the domestic market is considered realistic by 54 per cent of respondent entrepreneurs, for abroad by 68 per cent. Price regulation by the Joint Commission must be added for domestic prices as another passive category (36 per cent).

Whether prices are rather cost-determined or demand-determined may be scanned in three reply categories of the WIFO survey. 'Full cost plus a relative constant profit margin' was affirmed by 54 per cent, 'pricing mainly according to demand' by 44 per cent; the compromise solution 'slight adaptation of profit margin according to changing demand' was affirmed by 57 per cent. These findings weight the influence of demand slightly more than the findings of the surveys reported on above; in export markets even a slight preponderance is ascribed to the influence of demand. Weighting of influence factors by econometric functions is an alternative to surveys.

An approach in that direction can be made by means of econometric equations that attempt to explain the actual price development from determinants attributable either to the supply side (e.g. actual unit costs, 'standard costs' in normal capacity utilization, or divergence of unit costs from trend), or to the demand side (e.g. excess demand, backlog of orders, full capacity load). Such studies are available from Eckstein & Fromm (1968) McFetridge (1973), Ripley & Segal (1973), Lund & Rushdy (1967), McCallum (1979); for a summary of these studies see Hay & Morris (1979, pp. 126 – 35). Generally, these studies give a somewhat equal significance to supply and demand factors, the results often depending on the approach and the exactness in constructing the two components.

For the Austrian case, Guger (1978, in Nowotny *et al.* 1978 equations, cf. p. 299) juxtaposes explanatory variables based on supply factors, demand factors and price leadership. Of the three groups of hypotheses, Guger finds demand proxied by trend deviations in production of least importance: the development is best explained by labour costs and in later years additionally by raw-material costs. Import prices and FRG-producer prices have a significant explanatory influence, which is taken to confirm the price leadership of foreign producers.[3]

Guger's equations relate to a time of comparatively small demand fluctuations, as already noted by Nowotny *et al.* (1978, p. 35) in their summing-up of Guger's findings. A reassessment of the functions up to and including 1982 shows that Guger's findings retain their validity also for the whole period 1948–82 and that labour costs contribute significantly

Table 12.1 Regression estimates for price behaviour in Austrian manufacturing–the importance of costs, demand and international prices

	Constant	Wages	Raw-material prices	Import prices	Foreign prices (West Germany)	Trend deviation of industrial production	R^2	DW
1958–82	0.65 (1.51)	0.29 (4.04)		0.48 (6.69)			0.79	1.65
1958–76	0.66 (1.33)	0.30 (3.57)		0.47 (5.40)			0.78	1.61
1974–82	1.06 (1.33)	0.21 (2.32)		0.51 (5.33)			0.85	1.22
1958–82	1.09 (2.78)	0.42 (6.50)	0.14 (7.27)				0.81	1.00
1958–76	0.74 (2.22)	0.40 (7.68)	0.14 (9.14)				0.90	1.85
1974–82	2.48 (3.13)	0.37 (3.64)	0.11 (4.34)				0.80	0.80
1958–82	1.60 (2.27)	0.43 (3.61)				0.08 (0.99)	0.40	1.21

1958–76	0.95 (1.45)	0.34 (3.06)				0.62	1.18
1974–82	3.98 (2.63)	0.34 (1.71)		0.29 (3.18)		0.33	1.25
1958–82	0.92 (2.50)	0.45 (7.41)	0.16 (8.00)	0.14 (1.01)		0.84	1.42
1958–76)	0.73 (2.00)	0.39 (6.74)	0.13 (6.66)	−0.11 (−2.26)		0.90	1.86
1974–82	1.36 (1.82)	0.42 (5.40)	0.15 (5.85)	0.05 (0.80)		0.90	1.89
1958–82	0.44 (1.25)	0.29 (5.07)	0.04 (1.59)	−0.20 (−2.47)	0.57 (4.26)	0.91	1.94
1958–76	0.71 (2.04)	0.36 (5.02)	0.10 (2.72)		0.22 (1.05)	0.93	2.34
1974–82	−0.37 (−0.41)	0.24 (3.39)	−0.03 (−0.65)		0.92 (3.65)	0.94	2.22

Dependent variable: industrial prices in Austria, relative change.

140 Empirical information

to explaining prices even for the sub-period 1974–82. The deviation from trend of industrial output (used as a demand proxy), on the other hand, shows no influence – except in one specification, where it is negative. The variables covering the price-leader thesis (producer prices in West Germany's industry, and Austrian commodity import prices) contribute – as they do in Guger – to explaining the development of prices in industry for the whole period (1958–82) and also for the years since the energy crisis (1974–82) (cf. table 12.1).

The more pronounced role of price-takers in exports on the part of smaller countries follows the findings of Appelbaum & Kohli (1979), and also of Browne (1983), who did not find US and Canadian but indeed Irish exports to be price-takers.

Contrary to the above-quoted studies, which are largely intended to explain price variations and which do not – at least explicitly – refer to uncertainty, we find other studies that explain price changes simultaneously with decisions on output and inventories under uncertainty.

The studies of Holt *et al.* (1960) and Hay (1970, 1972) are examples of total-cost minimization. Total costs consist of the cost of order (cf. equation 12.2 according to Hay's (1970) model) and stocks (equation 12.4) deviating from desired volumes at any given time, cost of production changes (equation 12.5) and price changes (equation 12.6). Equation 12.7 represents the demand curve and equations 12.8 and 12.9 are identities.

$$U_t^* = c_{13} + c_{14} Q_t. \tag{12.1}$$

$$C_1 = c_{11} + c_1 (U_t - U_t^*)^2 \text{ (costs of an order stock different from desired).} \tag{12.2}$$

$$LB_t^* = c_{23} + c_{24} S_t. \tag{12.3}$$

$$C_2 = c_{21} + c_2 (LB_t - LB_t^*)^2 \text{ (cost of inventories different from desired stocks).} \tag{12.4}$$

$$C_3 = c_3 (Q_t - Q_{t-1})^2 \text{ (costs of changing production).} \tag{12.5}$$

$$C_4 = c_4 (P_t - P_{t-1})^2 \text{ (costs of changing prices).} \tag{12.6}$$

$$O_t = a_O - b P_t \text{ (demand curve).} \tag{12.7}$$

$$\left. \begin{array}{l} O_t - S_t \equiv U_t - U_{t-1} \\ Q_t - S_t \equiv LB_t - LB_{t-1} \end{array} \right\} \text{ (identities).} \tag{12.8} \tag{12.9}$$

where Q_t is production; U_t, U^* is actual, desired order stock; LB_t, LB_t^* is actual, desired inventories; S is sales; P is price; O is the order stock; a_O is intercept of demand curve; and C_i, c_{ii} is costs; cost parameter.

By forming the appropriate marginal conditions for all decisions variables and all periods, application of the Z-transform technique and of the assumption that, on average, the firms predict the future correctly,

The nature of prices 141

it is possible to work out linear decision rules. This facilitates testing of the strength of reaction of inventory, orders, production and price in response to a demand surprise. Hay discovered that for the timber industry (USA, period 1953–66) a 1 per cent increase in demand evokes the cushioning response of a 0.568 output increase, 0.352 build-up of orders, 0.074 reduction of inventory stocks and a mere 0.006 price increase. Findings for the paper industry are similar, particularly in respect of the small price responses.

Since the model assumes symmetrical costs whether desired orders, goods in stock, etc., surpassed or unattained, results in the case of negative surprise would be equal in strength.

The technique described by Hay cannot be fully followed for the Austrian industry, since information on the inflow of orders (the measure of demand) is only available since 1973 and inventories are only known as annual data. Thus annual regressions are only possible since 1973, and the lags cause further degrees of freedom to be lost (cf. table 12.2).

Trials with proxies for missing variables and equations with a reduced number of variables show little change in price relative to production changes for Austria, too.[4]

Summing up the findings of the analysis we get the impression of preponderant cost determination of prices. This applies primarily to domestic prices, whereas we find proof of the price-taker role of Austrian industry in the world markets. A short-term price reaction by producers, in reaction to surprise, cannot be shown.

Table 12.2 Linear demand systems for determination of quantities, prices and inventories

1973–82	Q_t	$= 74.2$	-0.13	Q_{t-1}	-0.35	P_{t-1}	$+0.65$	IO_t	$R^2 = 0.96$
			5.26	-0.61	-2.67		5.95		
	P_t	$=$	8.23	$+0.20$	Q_{t-1}	$+0.54$	P_{t-1}	$+0.18$ IO_t	$R^2 = 0.97$
			0.49	0.83		3.52		1.42	
	LB_t	$= 46.69$	$+0.22$	Q_{t-1}	$+1.00$	P_{t-1}	$+0.27$	IO_t	$R^2 = 0.74$
			0.52	0.17		1.24		0.39	

Q = production, LB = stock of finished goods, IO = incoming orders, adjusted for price dependence of demand (see Hay 1970, footnote 6)
P = price. t-values beneath coefficients.
Interpretation: The coefficients of IO may be interpreted (see Hay 1970) as reaction of stocks, production and prices in response to a 1 per cent demand surprise. Production therefore changes by 0.65 per cent, prices by 0.02 per cent (after demand elasticity is allowed for), inventories will increase by 0.27 per cent (which is in a theoretical implausible direction). The short sample period reduces the significance of the results.

12.3 EMPIRICAL EVIDENCE OF COST BEHAVIOUR PATTERNS

In microeconomic theory under certainty the assumption of an S-shaped cost pattern predominates. This applies especially for so-called 'short-term' cost behaviour, i.e. for a time span subject to a non-variable factor (usually capital, occasionally also organization or management).

For the marginal, variable average and total average costs a U-shaped pattern devolves from the S-shaped total cost curve. The mimima are approached in the following sequence: marginal costs, variable average costs.

In the competition model, quantity determination equating marginal costs and price implies that production takes place in the ascending part of marginal costs (only in this range is quantity uniquely defined). Further it is assumed that production is in short-term equilibrium also in the ascending part of the average costs. In long-term industrial equilibrium the difference between variable and total average costs disappears and entry into the market reduces output to the average cost minimum.[5]

At this point, marginal costs, too, are already on the increase (if there is an S-shaped cost behaviour pattern). In the monopoly model under certainty, output is less than would correspond to the intersection between marginal costs and price, production can go ahead before or after the minimum of average costs.

According to the model of monopolistic competition production will proceed in a range where the minimum of average costs has not yet been reached, since production occurs at the point of tangency of the – negatively sloped – subjective demand curve and average cost curve.

Whereas microeconomic theory under certainty suggests that optimal production will take place in the range of rising average costs (especially in the short term, and in competitive markets), the authors of industrial economics rather assume an L-shaped pattern, especially for the short run. This comes about by approximately constant direct costs and an hyperbolically descending fixed cost burden per produced unit (cf. Hay & Morris 1979, p. 77).

That opinion was endorsed by Walters' (1963) summary article and by a survey poll conducted by Eitemann & Guthrie (1952) on cost-behaviour patterns among 350 firms.

Eitemann & Guthrie (1952) interviewed about 100 industrial enterprises in the USA concerning average cost patterns, specifically aiming at the firm's subjective assessment of the cost curve between production minimum and maximum (though excluding overtime), posing eight graphic and verbal response choices.

The nature of prices 143

A general rise of the unit cost curve was rebuked by the firms (be it at increasing or decreasing rate), as was a minimum of average costs in about the middle between minimal and maximal output (response 3 + 4: 1.2 per cent). U-shaped average costs with a steep rise before the capacity limit obtained only 4.2 per cent of the responses, but a slight rise elicited 33.8 per cent. The clearly dominant category was a decrease of unit costs up to capacity limit, with 60.8 per cent. According to this survey approximately constant unit costs are never experienced (0 per cent).

From their survey Eitemann and Guthrie draw the conclusion that only 5.4 per cent of the responses are compatible with the marginal theory (responses 3–5), marginal theory meaning short-term equilibrium in the competition model.

A special question within a business test was framed for Austrian industries in 1981, similarly inquiring into the cost curve under given capacities; 1100 enterprises were covered (see tables 12.3–12.4).

Unlike the Eitemann & Guthrie (1952) survey (covering firms with 500–5000 employees), firms of all size categories were covered, cost increased through overtime were not explicitly excluded, response categories regrouped, making use of the Eitemann and Guthrie experiences. The categories of continuously rising average costs were eliminated, since they are probably also insignificant for Austria, Eitemann and Guthrie's

Table 12.3 Empirical cost curves with fixed capacities

	Firms	1	2	3	4	5	6
		percentages					
Total manufacturing	1131	34.9	29.3	17.2	5.6	9.3	3.7
Basic goods	56	36.4	36.4	9.1	7.3	7.3	3.6
Investment goods	493	33.6	27.5	19.8	7.3	7.5	4.3
Consumer goods	582	35.9	30.2	15.8	3.9	11.1	3.2
Split according to employees:							
0–99	678	30.1	32.8	14.5	5.5	12.2	4.9
100–499	334	41.7	24.5	19.5	6.2	5.9	2.2
500–999	65	36.5	23.8	31.7	3.2	3.2	1.6
1000 and more	59	50.0	22.4	20.71	5.2	1.2	0

Source: Special survey 1981 (1131 firms), WIFO, Austria.
Question: How do unit costs develop between minimal efficient scale and capacity output?
  1 Unit costs decrease up to capacity output?
  2 Unit costs decrease and then remain constant (approximately from average utilization)?
  3 Unit costs decrease first and then increase slightly before capacity output?
  4 Unit costs decrease and then start to increase sharply before capacity output is reached?
  5 Unit costs are roughly constant?
  6 Other curves not mentioned?

Table 12.4 Survey results on unit cost curve in the USA (Eitemann & Guthrie 1952) and Austria (1981)

Number of firms in USA: 334	Percentages	Number of firms in Austria: 1131	Percentages
1 Unit costs minimum lies at minimum efficient scale, then unit costs increase with decreasing rate	0		
2 Unit costs minimum lies at minimum efficient scale, then unit costs increase with increasing rate	0		
3 U-shaped unit cost curve, declines sharply up to the minimum, then unit costs increase	0.3	A U-shaped with sharp increase before capacity output	5.6
4 U-shaped with minimum in the middle between minimum and maximum	0.9	B U-shaped with slight increase before capacity output	17.2
5 U-shaped curve with slow decline and sharp increase after minimum	4.2	C unit costs decline up to capacity output	34.9
6 U-shaped with minimum near capacity output (increasing slightly before capacity is reached)	33.8	D unit costs decline first and then are constant	29.2
7 Unit costs decline up to capacity output	60.8	E unit costs are roughly constant	9.3
8 Unit costs are roughly constant	0		
Conforming with 'marginal theory'[1] 3–5	5.4	A	5.6
Conflicting with 'marginal theory' 1,2,6–8	94.6	B, C, D, E	90.6
Decreasing unit costs at capacity output 7	60.8	C	34.9
Constant unit costs at capacity output 8	0	D, E	38.5
Increasing unit costs at capacity output 1–6	39.8	A, B	22.8

[1] According to Eitemann & Guthrie (1952).

Table 12.5 Response to a demand shock

	All firms			Employees											
				0–99			100–499			500–999			1000 and more		
	posi-tive	nega-tive	φ	posi-tive	nega-tive	φ	posi-tive	nega-tive	φ	posi-tive	nega-tive	φ	posi-tive	nega-tive	φ
Price reaction															
first reaction	20	20	20	12	18	15	15	20	18	31	20	26	39	21	30
for large shocks	37	48	43	41	49	45	42	50	46	12	46	27	17	36	27
seldom	43	32	37	47	33	40	43	30	36	57	34	45	44	43	43
Inventory reaction															
first reaction	60	36	48	41	26	33	66	40	53	78	55	66	81	58	69
for large shocks	17	33	25	31	39	35	13	30	22	13	34	24	7	30	19
seldom	23	31	27	28	35	32	21	30	25	9	11	10	12	12	12
Output reaction															
first reaction	56	56	56	47	46	47	65	61	63	77	74	75	55	63	59
for large shocks	27	31	29	31	39	35	24	28	26	19	16	18	45	57	41
seldom	17	13	15	32	15	18	11	11	11	4	10	7	0	0	0
Capacity change															
first reaction	16	15	16	23	18	21	19	17	18	18	14	16	0	9	5
for large shocks	50	34	42	48	48	48	52	38	45	34	23	29	57	13	35
seldom	34	51	42	29	34	31	29	45	37	48	63	55	43	78	60

Source: Special survey 1981, WIFO, Austria.
Question: In case your planned sales prove to have been too cautious (positive shock) or too favourable (negative shock) which reaction will you take within the planning period?

146   Empirical information

main group that had received 60.8 per cent of the replies was subdivided into two: response D stipulated initially declining, then constant average costs, and response C declining average costs up to the capacity limit.

A U-shaped curve with sharply rising average costs was cited by 5.6 per cent of firms (comparable with the sum of responses to categories 4 and 5 in the Eitemann and Guthrie test, *viz.* 5.1 per cent). Declining average costs with slight rise were reported by 17.2 per cent of firms, this being a little more than half of similar responses in the American survey. Initially declining, then constant unit costs were reported by 29.2 per cent, declining unit costs up to capacity limit by 34.9 per cent of firms; 9.3 per cent of Austrian businessmen – mainly smaller firms – reported largely constant unit costs.

The similarity of responses in geographically and chronologically widely separated surveys is quite startling. A rise of unit costs is rejected in both enquiries. Possibly a more distinctly declining tendency might be discovered in US replies, whereas the Austrian firms rather expect constant unit costs at capacity limit. Though it must be said that this category was made more attractive by the addition of a supplementary response category, by inclusion of possible overtime pay, and by virtue of a stronger representation of small enterprises. At any rate we find the response of decreasing unit costs (34.9 per cent) surpassing the sum of the two categories, *viz.* light and substantial resurgence combined (22.8 per cent), also in the Austrian poll; in large corporations' responses, the ratio is 50.0 to 25.9 per cent.

What proposition concerning marginal costs (in uncertainty theory terminology: concerning convexity or concavity of costs) may one deduce from the responses? The two first reply categories imply rising marginal costs: convex costs should then be typical for 22.8 per cent of industry.

The third reply category (declining, thereafter constant average costs) probably represents constant marginal costs. Strictly speaking, marginal costs may possibly rise (mirror-inverted to the declining constant cost burden) at a decreasing rate, but this effect is likely to be already exhausted when the kink of the average cost curve (which it also serves to explain) is reached. Theoretically, declining average costs up to the capacity limit (reply category C) are not incompatible with any marginal cost curve, but the space for rising marginal costs is pretty limited (the rise must be less than the constantly diminishing effect of the decline of average costs due to smaller fixed costs per output). If the two above-named categories C and D represent constant marginal costs, then constant marginal costs would be typical for about 73 per cent of industry. (If category C is interpreted as decreasing marginal costs, then constant marginal costs would be typical for 38.5 per cent and diminishing ones for 35 per cent. Such an interpretation must surely be the upper limit for the possibility of a concave cost curve.)

Generally speaking, these surveys present us with a healthy shock in face of the matter-of-course assumption of convex costs, by proving concave costs to be at least as likely. At the same time this also poses the question of how an upward limit of the output volume is to be arrived at in the competition model, given such a cost pattern. A market division, such as was assumed in the demand uncertainty model, would be one possibility. Another may be that the costs of management (the manager-owner's or his senior executives' time limits) generate convex elements that do not show up in (cost) accountants' reckonings.

12.4 THE FEASIBILITY OF SHORT-TERM PRICE AND QUANTITY REACTIONS TO DEMAND SHOCKS

12.4.1 The Question to be Answered

Macroeconomic price equations have shown that prices are determined by supply rather than by demand factors, but this applies mainly to price reactions over the longer term, not to short-term reactions to shock. Hay's (1970) decision model in section 12.2 makes allowance for the impact of inventory and order costs from the appropriate desired values and for the costs of price and quantity changes, but the results require substantial simplifying assumptions (cost symmetry in positive and negative demand shocks).

As an alternative to econometric calculations we may, again, turn to a survey among Austrian industrial enterprises (1979, 483 responses). Here the firms were explicitly asked how they would react within the planning period to contingent positive or negative surprises concerning the sales volume. A survey has the advantage that questions can be framed to enquire explicitly into reactions to shock (as distinct from reactions to expected developments), that the subjective evaluation of flexibility can be expressed and that each firm is free to interpret the concept 'planning period' to its own practice of quarterly or annual planning. The snag, as with all questionnaires, is that all such responses are non-committal.[6]

Real-world variations in actual capacity utilization is another indicator, which tells us implicitly about price flexibility. If prices were completely flexible and competition with price uncertainty the relevant real-world model, then actual capacity utilization would be relatively constant (actual capacity utilization should be near maximum capacity).

12.4.2 Subjective Assessment of the Reactions

The questionnaire envisaged four possible reactions within the planning period: variation of price, output, inventory or investments.[7] Three reply categories were possible for each of these reactions. A measure could be labelled a primary reaction to shock, one used in case of large variation only, or one only rarely used. When not otherwise stated, in the following the

148 *Empirical information*

frequencies of replies as 'primary reaction' are reported, and meanwhile we do not differentiate by the direction of the shock.

The predominant reaction of the firms is the quantity reaction, i.e. the increase or reduction of output within the planning period. This is the primary reaction of 56 per cent of the firms, 29 per cent use quantity variation for large shocks, and 15 per cent 'rarely'.

Second in frequency is the inventory variation: 48 per cent of enterprises name it as primary reaction, 25 per cent for large variation and 27 per cent for rarely.

Only 20 per cent name price reaction as their primary reaction, 43 per cent name this as usual in response to large shocks, and as many as 38 per cent name price change even then as unusual.

Variation of investment still within the planning period is named as primary reaction by 16 per cent, 43 per cent call it unusual.

If the dismissal of a variable as 'primary' reaction would indicate that it is no *ex post* control, then prices are no *ex post* control for four of every five industrial enterprises. Production on the other hand is an *ex post* control for more than half of the firms (or at least *ex post* flexibility of production exists). Slightly less than half do not close the disequilibrium brought about by shock or permit inventories at least to vary from their desired level. Corresponding to the argument in chapter 11, the order book is also likely to vary from its desired level.

12.4.3 Differences of Reactions by Size and Market Power

In monopoly, the theory of the firm under uncertainty assumes *ex post* control by either price or quantity (under *q*-mode or *p*-mode) and even holds that disequilibria (*p-q*-mode) compatible with optimization, in oligopoly price rigidities are a well-documented phenomenon. In the standard competition model (with price uncertainty), the price closes the disequilibrium. Quick price changes and the absence of any (involuntary) inventory variation are predicted.[8] An evaluation of the responses by firm-size category and surmised closeness to the competition model was used to check this forecast. The indicators chosen for competitive status were (similar to Nowotny *et al.* 1978) average enterprise and plant size, share of the four largest enterprises in value added and import and export intensity. Ten branches of industry were indicated as 'more competitive'.

The smaller an enterprise the more rarely is mention made of the possibilities of any *ex post* reaction whatsoever. At first sight this is in contrast to the empirical fact that planning errors in the smaller firms' annual sales and investment planning are usually bigger, and that, particularly, they disclose a systematic (downwards) bias (Aiginger 1977), but this may most likely be due to the fact that some of the smaller firms have *no* planning (cf. Aiginger 1980b), or at least a much shorter 'planning period'. Somehwat overstating our interpretation, in terms of uncertainty

Table 12.6 Volatility of prices and quantities in the Austrian manufacturing industry

	Mean	Standard deviation	R^2 in autoregression[1]
Prices			
R4			
II/63–IV/82	4.34	4.10	0.71
II/63–IV/73	2.77	3.25	0.54
I/74–IV/82	6.21	4.26	0.72
R1			
II/63–IV/82	1.08	1.81	0.00
II/63–IV/73	0.74	1.90	0.07
I/74–IV/82	1.49	1.64	0.05
Quantity			
R4			
II/63–IV/82	4.39	5.05	0.61
II/63–IV/73	6.38	3.62	0.42
I/74–IV/82	2.02	5.52	0.78
R1			
II/63–IV/82	1.04	2.12	0.01
II/63–IV/73	1.59	2.04	0.09
I/74–IV/82	0.37	2.05	0.13
Selling-price expectations (net balances)			
II/63–IV/82	18.92	17.23	0.43
II/63–IV/73	15.93	16.23	0.37
I/74–IV/82	22.50	17.93	0.44
Production expectations (net balances)			
II/63–IV/82	6.41	12.01	0.54
II/63–IV/73	13.51	8.62	0.35
I/74–IV/82	−2.08	9.79	0.23

[1] $x_t = f(x_{t-1})$.
*R*1, quarterly change; *R*4, annual change

theory we may say that the smaller firms need no *ex ante* control variable but can wait for actual developments to arise. This is, of course, not fully valid (unless no reaction was needed and there were no unintended inventory variations), but very likely there is greater *ex post* flexibility. Production planning can be postponed and thus more information may be obtained concerning demand.

The biggest difference by enterprise size is in the assessment of inventory reaction. Only 34 per cent of firms with a staff of less than 100 (subsequently called small) cite it, but 70 per cent of firms with more than 1000 staff (large) do; for them it is the most important reaction.

Table 12.7 Forecasting performance for prices and production in industrial sectors in West Germany 1965–83 (coefficients of correlation)

	Prices	Production
Paper and paper processing	0.86	0.49
Glass	0.69	0.31
Stone and clay	0.63	0.34
Chemicals	0.93	0.65
Machinery	0.79	0.83
Electrical appliances	0.72	0.81
Optical industry	0.75	0.68
Vehicles	0.78	0.05
Clothing	0.75	0.70
Shoes	0.60	0.45

Changes of production plan is cited by 47 per cent of small firms (this being their most important response); in large firms – though named by 59 per cent as primary response – it falls into second place.

Even in smaller firms there is no thought of determining output and afterwards accepting the market price – as assumed by the competition model under price uncertainty.

Also, a division of branches according to supposed 'competitiveness' confirms the competition model under demand uncertainty rather than that under price uncertainty. Among the 'competitive' branches 18 per cent name price variation as the most important response, 64 per cent vary output and 44 per cent allow the inventory level to vary. The responses restrict the sphere of possible validity of the competition model under price uncertainty considerably and point to models that accept unintended variation of inventory, and also to models that tolerate *ex post* flexibility of output.

12.4.4 Symmetry of the Reactions

One of the questions often asked in economics is whether shocks in different directions are reacted to asymmetrically. This is also apparent from the extensive literature concerning various price flexibilities upwards or down, which are referred to in this section for possible explanations of price rigidity.

Price – theoretically the prime suspect for asymmetries – is employed by firms to about the same extent for overcoming positive and negative shocks. They are used by 20 per cent of firms as first reaction to both positive and to negative shocks. A minimal asymmetry exists in this: that a larger percentage excludes a price rise completely when there is high demand, than a price reduction, given low demand. Within the generally fewer namings of price reactions, smaller firms report a certain overhang of price reductions (18 against 12 per cent), whereas large firms, in their more frequent mentions of price reactions, think twice as often (39 against 21 per cent) of price increases.

Output variation is mentioned as often concerning positive shock as to negative shock. Capacity increases are easier in the positive direction – as might be expected.

The greatest asymmetry is found in inventory reaction. Whereas 60 per cent of firms want to reduce their stocks as a primary reaction to positive demand shocks, only 35 per cent are willing to increase inventory holdings in response to negative shock. That asymmetry holds, independent of enterprise size and competitiveness. This points to high implicit and explicit inventory costs and low goodwill costs. The asymmetry runs counter to the conjectured limits supposedly set on stock reductions (namely to the extent of actual stock held), or to that asymmetry described by Winckler (1977, p. 20), that it is possible to store goods today for tomorrow but impossible to use tomorrow's production for demand today. For net inventories no such absolute limits exist.

12.4.5 Summing up the Evidence

Generally, the survey indicates relatively extensive *ex post* flexibility. True, an *ex post* control of prices appears more or less excluded, even for smaller and more 'competitive' firms. The larger corporations, too, seem rather inclined to use *ex post* quantity control and secondly (this to a greater extent than small firms) inventory disequilibrium. Furthermore firms seem rather to accept an inventory disequilibrium under positive shock than in negative shock. That is consistent with high inventory costs and toleration of negative net inventories.

12.5 MEASURES FOR PRICE RIGIDITY *EX POST* AND *EX ANTE*

12.5.1 Price Rigidities and their Possible Causes

The last section has shown that firms are reluctant to change prices following demand shocks.

Whether price rigidity is an empirical phenomenon, whether it is symmetrical, and what may be its causes has been discussed with some intensity: a survey may be found, for example, in recent studies by Gordon (1981) and Amihud & Mendelson (1983). Here we shall only give a brief overview of the problems of empirical measurement of the relative responsiveness of price and quantities.

152 Empirical information

Table 12.8 Differences in the responses to demand shocks for differences in the degree of competition – (A = sector with strong competition, B = sector with low competition)

(a) Mean (AM) and standard deviation of prices ($R4$) and production ($R4$), Austria 1954–82

	Prices		Production	
	AM	SD	AM	SD
Sector A	3.24	3.66	5.87	5.93
Sector B	3.91	4.36	3.90	5.10
Total	3.56	3.76	3.51	5.31

(b) Inventory sales ratio, its standard deviation (SD) and its assessment as 'voluntary'

	Inventory/sales ratio		Assessment	
Sector A	7.86	0.53	+14.62	18.67
Sector B	6.55	1.06	+16.90	14.90
Total	7.05	0.70	+15.65	13.50

(c) Forecasting performance of price and production expectations, Austria 1963–82

	Prices R^2		Production R^2	
	$V0^1$	V1	V0	V1
Sector A	0.29	0.41	0.48	0.42
Sector B	0.25	0.34	0.55	0.51
Total	0.33	0.38	0.57	0.52

(d) Reaction in cases of positive or negative surprise (difference between expected sales and actual sales)

	Sector A			Sector B		
	1^2	2	3	1	2	3
Price reaction	18	35	47	19	43	38
Inventory reaction	45	27	28	48	21	31
Quantity reaction	64	27	9	56	25	19

(e) Differences in variations of capacity utilization and assessment (as too large) in the business survey (Austria 1963–82)

	Capacity utilization		Assessment	
	AM	SD	AM	SD
Sector A	85.48	2.03	51.95	16.41
Sector B	84.03	2.97	62.57	17.93
Total	84.32	2.93	58.93	18.80

[1] V0 = forecast for current quarter, V1 = forecast for next quarter.
[2] 1, as first reaction; 2, in case of large deviations; 3, usually not.

The nature of prices

The rigidity of industrial prices was brought up for discussion in the studies of Means (1935, *Thesis of Administered Prices*), the extent, at least, of the phenomenon was doubted by Stigler & Kindahl (1973) who showed that the data used for proving price rigidity disregard empirically greatly fluctuating price discounts and that therefore the measured prices do not in fact represent *de facto* transaction prices. Blair (1972), Weiss (1977) and Lustgarten & Mendelowitz (1979) follow up, discussing the empirical multiplicity of various price rigidities.

An asymmetry in price rigidity is suspected, on the one hand, in the responsiveness of wage fluctuations (rising prices following upon cost increases, but no reduction when costs decline), and alleged on the other hand, for demand, where a more pronounced rigidity is often assumed downwards, though Qualls (1978) supposes it upwards. In a model of demand uncertainty Amihud & Mendelson (1983) present an explanation for price rigidity in general (prices being only one of the possible reaction parameters, beside inventories and order backlog), and for differing asymmetries in the direction of shock: if inventory costs are relatively higher than goodwill costs, then prices will be more flexible downwards; if goodwill costs are high, then prices will be more flexible upwards.

Among the numerous causes of price rigidity, the following – oligopoly-conditioned uncertainty (Rothschild 1952, Sweezy 1939), price-fixing as a deterrent from market entry (Bain 1956, Sylos-Labini 1962), cost of price changes (Barro 1972, Sheshinksi & Weiss 1977, Mussa 1980), consumers' search costs (Wu 1979), utilization of prices in advertising campaigns, existence of long-term contracts (Carlton 1978, 1979), and risk aversion (Schramm & Sherman 1977, Wu 1979) – can be quoted.[9]

12.5.2 The Relative Flexibility of Quantities v. Prices

Were the actual prices absolutely unchanged, this would contradict the model of prices as *ex post* control. Contrariwise, not every empirical fluctuation is an indication of the use of price as an *ex post* control, since it may have come about following planned price changes. Besides, the optimal variation of prices depends on many factors, demand elasticity among others. Therefore actual rigidity can only be taken to be a first indication for the plausibility of price and quantity as *ex post* controls.

Price development in industry is shown by all parameters to be 'smoother' than quantity development.[10] The standard deviation of price increase (quarterly data, annual increases) is shown to be 4.10 for prices in industry, against 5.05 for quantity changes, the coefficient of variation is 0.94 as against 1.15.[11] The greater output variance persists if previous quarterly changes are used, and has grown more pronounced since 1974 (see table 12.6).

Of the fluctuations shown up, a greater part is 'trend-determined' than among production fluctuations. The exponential trend by itself can explain

154   Empirical information

83 per cent of price fluctuations, but only 61 per cent of output fluctuations. The autoregressive component is larger in price than in quantity fluctuations.[12] All results are in agreement with the price functions, which have shown a strong influence of the relatively smooth labour-cost developments. This may indicate that prices are used more seldom than quantities as *ex post* controls.

12.5.3 Findings on the *ex ante* Control Variables according to Reported Expectations

We may obtain certain information on whether prices and quantities are intentionally varied or whether their fluctuations are used to bridge disequilibria by comparing expectations as reported in entrepreneurial surveys with actual quantities and/or prices.

If the prices are an *ex ante* control then they must vary according to the expected shifts of the supply and demand curves, the actual variations would have to be well forecast (high predictive validity). If they are an *ex post* control, then price expectations should be smooth and its predictive power should be poor. If output quantity is an *ex ante* control, then output expectation must have high predictive ability; if an *ex post* control, it will be smooth and unreliable.

Comparison of the expectation data with the *ex post* data is made difficult because they derive from different sources[13] and display different dimensions. To determine the 'predictive value' by linear regression (price increase in per cent) gives only a very rough approximation. Rather we might compare the price expectations and production expectations mutually, and the price dynamics and production dynamics among themselves. Although actual production increased between 1963 and 1982 at about the same rate – also average actual production and *price* increases are at about 4.4 per cent and 4.3 per cent annually – a price increase is expected much more often on average (total on average + 19 per cent) than an increase in output (total + 6 per cent). This points to a much smaller part of output increases having been planned than price increases. This causes no surprise, if prices are determined by long-term laws, and output is flexible *ex post*.

The relative predictive value of the output expectations is somewhat higher than that of the price expectations, (but) the difference was largely lost in the 1970s (a period of more vigorous price increases).

The relatively good predictive value of output expectations despite their probable bias towards tendential underrating of the output dynamism may be interpreted thus: the entrepreneurs want to plan merely the direction of future developments in the first place, but thereafter they determine the necessary extent of changes within the framework of possible *ex post* flexibility (partial *ex post* control).

In West Germany, where *ex ante* and *ex post* data are qualitatively surveyed, price expectations correlate more highly with the *ex post* data

The nature of prices 155

than do the output expectations in eight out of ten branches (exceptions being the branches of the electrical engineering and machine-building industries where production to order dominates).

12.6 COMPETITION AND PRICE FLEXIBILITY

Variance, trend dependence and cost determination were used as indications pointing to the relative rigidity of the prices at the level of total industry, and so were the survey responses about reactions to demand shock. The indicators refuted the competition model under price uncertainty, but in an oligopolistically structured industry they would not be surprising.

In the following we shall compare the relative price rigidity in branches that should be closer to the competition model (sector A: competitive sector) with price rigidity in the presumed oligopolistic sector (sector B). Beside price and quantity flexibility we examine other implications of the competition model under price uncertainty, separate by sectors:

- absence of involuntary inventory fluctuations;
- absence of fluctuations in capacity utilization;
- *ex ante* control of output; and
- use of price for market clearance.

The stronger price reaction in the competitive sector is not borne out by the empirical material. The variance of the prices in the competitive sector is even less, if anything, in the competitive sector (3.66–4.36), the variance of output growth over time is – counter to hypothesis – larger (5.93–4.10).

The relative level of finished-good inventories is higher (7.86, 6.55 per cent, respectively, of revenue) in the competitive sector, though the inventory–sales ratio shows significantly stronger fluctuations (standard deviation 1.06–0.53) in the non-competitive sector. This would correspond to the purported absence of inventories as buffers in competitive branches. Conversely, no significant difference (and even slightly greater fluctuation in the non-competitive sector) is disclosed in the assessments concerning inventories (which may be taken as a measure of the non-optimizing character of the fluctuations) expressed in the business surveys.

Average capacity utilization is 85.48 per cent in the competitive sector, in the non-competitive sector it is 84.03 per cent. The variance and its assessment[14] as involuntary is larger in the non-competitive sector.

Price expectation should possess less predictive value in the competitive sector because prices are under *ex post* control, whereas output expectations should forecast the actual developments accurately since production is determined *ex ante*. In actual fact we find the predictive value of price expectations (measured by the determination coefficient of a linear

156 Empirical information

regression) insignificantly better in the competitive sector, while that of output expectations is insignificantly worse.[15]

If we assume the chosen parameters (enterprise size, foreign-trade intensity, number of firms in the branch) to be good indicators of competitiveness, then we must evaluate the empirical evidence to be tendentially – though not in the sense of complete empirical proof – contradictory to the competition model under price uncertainty. Only the lesser inventory fluctuations and also, to a limited extent, the capacity-utilization fluctuations are not disproved by its implications. These indicators, too, cannot unreservedly be considered to be confirmatory, since they, too, may be explained by greater *ex post* flexibility (due to the smaller size of firms). The greater output fluctuations in the competition model point in that direction too. It is the competition model under demand uncertainty (with partial *ex post* flexibility) – rather than the competitive model with price uncertainty – that is most likely to be characteristic for the competitive sector of Austrian industry.

12.7 SUMMING UP THE EVIDENCE ON THE ROLE OF PRICES IN INDUSTRIES

By various methods we have examined the question of whether prices in industry are an *ex post* control for balancing disequilibria following a demand shock, whether they can be regarded as action parameters in profit optimization under uncertainty (*ex ante* control), or as relatively constant exogenous conditions in the decision-making process.

Econometric methods disclose a relatively large influence of cost factors (and of external influences, i.e. from the world market), but little impact of actual, most recent demand (shocks), and they show that quantity reactions, together with inventory reactions (and order backlogs) absorb the lion's share of shocks. In field surveys, too, there is a slight preponderance in citing cost factors over demand factors, and the responses to a further question support the view that prices are largely dictated by market trends and are only to a small degree considered action parameters.

The price variance is generally lower than that of output. This is especially valid for the irregular component (quarterly fluctuations), which ought to be volatile if price is used as an *ex post* control. Yet price expectations are higher on average in the business survey than production expectations, a tendency that may be interpreted in the sense that the bulk of price increases is being anticipated. In reply to the explicit question about reaction to shock, only one-fifth of firms name price reaction as primary.

After the division of industry by branches supposedly close to the competition model (large number of firms with high foreign trade involvement) evidence reveals that the competition model with price uncertainty must be discarded even for the sector with supposed high competitiveness. Though in this case the finished goods' inventory fluctuates rather less – conforming to theory – but the assessment of such inventories fluctates as alternatively too high and too low, varying to the same extent as in the non-competitive sector, leading to the supposition that the absence of involuntary inventories – conjectured by the model – is not likely to be real. The predictive value of price expectations – is greater than in the less competitive sector, the output expectations which, being an *ex post* control should be exact, have a lower predictive power than in the rest of the sector. The use of price as a primary reaction to demand shock is equally rare in the competitive sector, reaction by inventory shock is less often named, in conformity with hypothesis, reaction by production changes more often.

From the results it would appear that the use of prices as a promptly reacting *ex post* control – and thus the competition model with price uncertainty – is less likely for real industrial behaviour than for normative models. Little information is available that would point to the use of prices as *ex ante* control either, it is more likely that price plays the role as a comparatively fixed exogenous condition, predetermined through cost developments and long-term components or by foreign market leaders. Consequently, demand uncertainty models seem not improbable also in the 'competitive' sectors, keeping in mind that considerable *ex post* flexibility may still be feasible after the first decision has been taken. This *ex post* flexibility cannot completely bridge the gap, as is borne out by the inventory reactions (and especially their involuntary components).

NOTES

1 The willingness to reduce the price in case of sluggish demand is greater than the willingness to increase it (deviating from the full cost principle in the upward direction) in case of excess demand.
2 Simple aggregation of the shares of these categories would yield 74 per cent, but remember that firms could report more than one model as realistic.
3 See also Pollan (1977), Marin (1980), however, criticizes the view that foreign prices are used as a proxy for price leadership. They could, as Marin purports, also be a proxy for input prices.
4 The results of one model indicated that a one per cent change in demand would lead to 0.65 per cent change in production volume, a 0.02 per cent change in prices and a 0.60 per cent change in orders. The regression coefficient of inventories however has the wrong sign, therefore, the results should not be overemphasized.
5 Recall the idea of Hall and Hitch (1939), that firms may empirically operate at some point of their cost curve without attempting to do so.
6 See Machlup (1966) or the discussion of implicit *v.* explicit expectations in Pyle (1962), Pesando (1962). Appendix 2 discusses advantages and disadvantages of survey results.

Empirical information

7   The last category makes sense only in conjunction with output variation. The survey attempted to get information whether investment plans could be revised easier in the upward direction than downward.
8   On the other hand the outsider model of competition with demand uncertainty implies involuntary changes in the inventories and in capacity utilization.
9   Despite the progress which has been made in explaining the rationality of price stickiness, the point made by Wood (1938) is still relevant '. . . these factors may help to explain why price policies are what they are, but they do not explain how in a competitive industry a seller can have a price policy . . .'.
10 We used an implicit price index which may incorporate some quality changes.
11 The use of an explicit price index (which may be unable to reflect a changing degree of discounts) and an implicit price (by confronting nominal and real transactions) yielded similar results. The last one should reflect 'transaction prices' as proposed in the literature.
12 In a linear equation using lagged quarterly changes as independent variable 71 per cent to 61 per cent of the variations were 'explained'.
13 *Ex post* data are published by the Austrian Statistical Office, *ex ante* data by the Austrian Institute of Economic research (these data are categorical).
14 The difference of the means is not statistically significant, that of the variance only at the 90 per cent level.
15 Competitiveness and price variations are – contrary to theoretical implications – not positively linked.

13 Towards a Realistic Description of the Decision Process in Modern Industrial Society

13.1 OVERVIEW OF THE CHAPTER

In the last two chapters we have gathered important empirical information about the decision process. We have got the impression that quantities seem to be more variable than prices, in general as well as in response to demand shocks. We have found evidence that inventories fluctuate considerably and firms reported in surveys that at least a part of these fluctuations were considered as involuntary. The same is true for capacity utilization. We have furthermore seen that backlogs are an important fact in developed economies, usually being larger than inventories for finished goods. Profit shares are far from being equal to unit costs.

We want to gather more information in this chapter on the question of whether the *ex post* flexibility of production and investment is symmetric or easier in the upward direction (13.2), then try to find out something about the risk attitude of entrepreneurs (13.3). We report on a survey in which firms were asked to assess their own situation as far as market structure, mode and random variables were concerned (13.4). Finally we try to combine all the information to assess which models will be best able to represent actual behaviour.

13.2 ASYMMETRIES IN THE FLEXIBILITY OF THE PRODUCTION FACTORS

Econometric calculations as well as the results of the business opinion surveys have indicated relatively extensive *ex post* flexibility - especially of output, less of prices (chapter 12). Asymmetry in the reaction, depending on the direction of the shock, was rather small in these variables, but it was more noticeable in the inventories (an increase of the inventory level is considered less feasible and more unfavourable than a reduction in case of strong demand. Capacity increase was cited more often than capacity reduction. It is our interpretation that the smaller enterprises quite often revise upwards but do not stress this in their verbal reports, since they often interpret this procedure as a rounding-off of their plans, not a plan revision.

The asymmetry of plan revisions can be shown for Austrian industry in the aggregate and for the firms' reports. On average the aggregated investment plans of Austrian industry in the years 1965–82 were revised upwards between planning in the preceding year's October (first plan) and the definite outcome (fifth plan) by 12.3 per cent. The extent of the revision fluctuates cyclically, which means that it is really a matter of *ex post* flexibility, not of errors, incomplete reports, unforeseen machinery breakdowns, etc. During the period of higher growth up to 1975 the revision lay near 16 per cent, since then it has become less (7 per cent) but is still high (positive in five out of six years). In all the eighteen years the aggregate investment was revised upwards in sixteen years and down only twice (1975 and 1982). The large extent of *ex post* flexibility may be gauged by considering how late in the year plan revisions – especially increases – can still be made.

Between the October survey of the current year (third plan) and the final result, plans are still increased on average by 5.5 per cent. Also this component of the end-of-year revision (Aiginger 1977, p. 42) discloses cyclical differences. The revisions vary greatly by size of enterprise. For firms with above 1000 staff they are below 10 per cent; for firms with up to 100 staff they amount to roughly one-third (Aiginger 1977, p. 32).

The extent of flexibility as seen at the aggregated level gives an incomplete picture of actual plan changes at the micro level. In 1974 showing an approximately average pattern for total industry, there were the following revisions on the single firm level: ninety-four firms reduced their plans in plan implementation by more than half, seventy-eight firms by more than a quarter (but less than half), 108 firms by up to a quarter of original intentions. On the other hand, 102 firms increased their plans up to a quarter, fifty-eight firms between one-quarter and half, and finally, 258 firms – this being more than a third of the sample – raised plans by over half. The figures are an ample demonstration of the variability of investment plans in the light of unforeseen events and they document the asymmetry (280 downward revisions, 418 upwards).

At the level of the firm, too, flexibility varies by firm size. Nearly one in two firms employing less than 100 staff raised the plans in the course of the year by more than 50 per cent, the average increase since 1974 amounts to +250 per cent in this subgroup, thus plans are more than tripled. Of the firms with more than 1000 employees over one-sixth increased the original plans by more than 50 per cent, but almost half of the large firms reduce plans. The plan cuts in the large firms are, it seems, less deliberate reactions to new information concerning demand but rather involuntary delays occurring in the implementation of large investment programmes.

The empirical flexibility of the investments, and its asymmetry, is of particular importance. Capital stock was considered an *ex ante* control (in contrast to the more flexible labour input) in the theoretical models. The empirical asymmetry is important since theoretical models dealing with the optimal choice of production factors under uncertainty tended to imply a large (as long as *ex post* control of prices are assumed) capital stock. But the tendency to retain one's options in case of favourable demand is clearly more than compensated (especially for the smaller firms, but also in the aggregate) by the nearly unlimited large and upwards *ex post* flexibiltiy. For large firms, *ex ante* control of investments may more likely be a reality.

The *ex post* flexibility may also be asymmetric for labour. In the first place, overtime can only be reduced to the extent that it exists; in the second place, it is largely considered by the working force as part of their fixed income, earmarked for example, for the repayment of loans. Abrupt reductions may therefore provoke resistance. A third reaction might be the increase or reduction of staff. Organizational limits are set for an increase, firms have to anticipate a broad wage increase (possibly a wage increase for the total labour force) as well as search and training costs; yet an increase is easier (cheaper) than a staff reduction. The latter is limited by social/labour legislation (notice terms, early warning requirements, etc.) by self-imposed or implicit employer behaviour (which may be interpreted as goodwill investment) and labour relations.

Especially in these latter respects there are very considerable differences between Austria and other countries, where lay-offs are customary. For a discussion of lay-offs and their partial surrogates in Austria see Gutierrez *et al.* (1981).

An overall evaluation of cost differences depending on the direction of shock may be found in a business survey conducted by WIFO in 1979.

Table 13.1 The asymmetry of plan revisions

	5th plan/ 1st plan (average over years)	5th plan/ 3rd plan	Number of years			
			upward revision 5th plan/1st plan	downward revision 5th plan/1st plan	upward revision 5th plan/3rd plan	downward revision 5th plan/3rd plan
ϕ 1965/82	+12.3	+5.6	16	2	18	0
ϕ 1965/75	+15.8	+7.1	10	1	11	0
ϕ 1976/82	+ 6.8	+3.4	6	1	7	0

1st plan surveyed in October $t-1$.
3rd plan surveyed in October t.
5th plan = actual result.
Source: Investment surveys 1965–82, WIFO, Austria.

162 Empirical information

To the question of whether revenue shocks are symmetrical or if revenue is more (often) underestimated or overestimated, 62 per cent replied that it is dearer to overestimate revenue, only 17 per cent declared that underestimates are more expensive, and 21 per cent described the costs as symmetrical.

The asymmetry increases with enterprise size. In firms with up to 100 staff the ratio was only two to one; in large firms the ratio was ten to one, 64 per cent of large firms thought optimism more expensive, 6 per cent called pessimism dearer. This reflects the growing inflexibility of large enterprises in the reduction, among other things, of production factors.

Table 13.2 Number and average of revisions of investment plans on the firm level

	5th plan/1st plan		5th plan/3rd plan	
	Number	%[1]	Number	%[1]
Downward revisions				
more than 50%	94	−58.3	31	−61.4
−50−25	78	−35.0	64	−35.1
−25−0	108	−12.6	158	−10.4
Upward revisions				
0−25	102	13.1	259	9.0
25−50	58	37.8	82	39.6
more than 50%	258	146.0	128	108.7
All firms	698		722	
down	280		253	
up	418		469	

Source: Investment survey 1974, WIFO, Austria.
[1] Average of revision in subgroup.

Table 13.3 Cost differences by errors of same size and different sign (1100 firms, Austria)

	All firms	Small firms	Large firms
Costs are about the same	21%	18%	30%
Larger for optimistic sales forecast	62%	58%	64%
Larger for pessimistic sales forecast	17%	24%	61%

Question: Despite the fact that higher sales are usually better than lower, do you think that:
– errors in planning in both directions involve approximately the same costs?
– it is more expensive if sales have been anticipated 5 per cent higher than they actually prove to be?
– it is more expensive if sales are anticipated 5 per cent lower than they prove to be?
Source: Special survey 1979, WIFO, Austria.

13.3 ARE ENTREPRENEURS RISK-AVERSE?

Many experimental studies have investigated this topic. We chose another way and asked entrepreneurs whether they based their decisions on the expected return of investment projects alone, or whether they preferred, between two investment projects, one with high risks and considerable chances, or one where they might forego some mean expected profits for the certainty of the return.

We defined as small projects those which amount to approximately one-half of an annual investment programme, and as large those exceeding an annual programme considerably. For small risks, risk averters (36.82 per cent of the firms) and risk lovers (33.66 per cent) balanced each other out, less than one third being risk-neutral. Risk aversion and risk-loving increased for small firms, and risk neutrality is predominant for firms with more than 1000 employees (60.78 per cent).

For large projects, risk aversion outperforms risk-loving (53.15 : 12.37). Approximately one-third are risk-neutral for large decisions. Again risk aversion and risk-loving decreased with the size of the firm. Only 3.92 per cent of the large firms are risk lovers (14 per cent of the firms with less than 100 employees).

We may be critical of the method of obtaining information about risk behaviour by the means of surveys. However, the resulting difference in risk attitude between small repeated decisions and large one-shot decisions seems highly plausible (see appendix 5 for the exact results).

13.4 ON THE TYPE AND MODE OF UNCERTAINTY

It is difficult to define the difference between risk and uncertainty proper in a way to make it assessable in an empirical survey. We tried to capture the notion of risk and uncertainty, respectively in the following way.

Which of the following descriptions fits the present situation better?

- The economic situation is characterized by imponderabilities. The analysis of past developments and market forecasts enable us, however, to estimate a '*mean expected demand*' as well as a rather *pessimistic* variant for which we can access an estimated probability and an *optimistic* variant which again will occur with a certain probability.
- Uncertainty is so strong that past developments do not offer any clues as to future sales' possibilities, market forecasts are not really useful. The important thing is to be *prepared for anything*, to remain *flexible* and to *act quickly* on opportunities and risks.
- None of the above applies.

164   Empirical information

A majority of 57 per cent: 41 per cent of the firms chose the first against the second alternative, only somewhat less than 2 per cent reported that neither of the alternatives applied. Again we cannot rule out that different wordings of the alternatives yielded different results. Maybe the nearly equal spread of the answers shows that the truth may be somewhere in the middle, maybe as proposed in chapter 9, rough assessments of probabilities are possible, but a large degree of uncertainty leads to sticky prices and preferences for flexible techniques.

Another survey question was intended to find out whether firms behaved as if they followed the behaviour described in one of the competitive models or more like oligopolists or monopolists. We asked firms to assess their market share and report the number of competitors. The answers to these questions are highly subjective, they cannot be objectively inferred from firm size or from statistical analysis, since they depend on the definition of 'the relevant market'. Twenty-one per cent of the respondents reported a domestic market share in Austria of 5 per cent or less, the remaining 80 per cent split into 30 per cent reporting a share between 20 and 50 per cent and 17.5 per cent as possessing a market share larger than 50 per cent. The results are pretty consistent with the results about the number of the competitors. (Only 22 per cent reported themselves as having many competitors hence assessing themselves in a competitive environment.) Five per cent were the only domestic producers, 40 per cent had up to five competitors, remaining in the oligopolistic range. One-third had a few large and many small competitors. The same question concerning the position on the world market showed, as expected, a somewhat more competitive picture, but still one-third of the firms reported possessing a market share of more than 5 per cent. Since we know from another investigation that less than one-half of the firms export at all, the majority of exporters regard themselves as having a non-negligible world market share. We conclude from this survey that firms tend to define their relevant market in a rather narrow way. They try to serve a very specialized market in which they have a considerable market share. It would not be surprising then, that they do not behave according to the competitive model (setting the output and waiting for the market-clearing price). To get more information we asked which variables had to be set *ex ante* and which *ex post*.

Setting the price *ex ante* and the quantity to be produced *ex post* was chosen by 28 per cent as the relevant model. Setting the quantity *ex ante* and then optimally adjusting their own (monopoly) price was chosen by 16 per cent. These descriptions should indicate the relevance of the two monopoly models in which an *ex post* control exists (and involuntary inventories are absent).

The *p-q* model in which firms have to choose both quantity and prices *ex ante* (and face equilibria *ex post*) was assessed as realistic by 22.5 per cent. A model in which a preliminary quantity had to be chosen *ex ante*, where prices

The decision process   165

were fixed and some *ex post* adjustment of quantity is feasible got the highest share of the answers (31.1 per cent). The competitive model, where quantity had to be chosen and market price adjusted got a minority vote of 7 per cent. This is surprising if we start from theoretical considerations, but consistent with empirical price rigidity as well as with the firm's contention to be in a rather monopolistic or oligopolistic situation in a very narrow specialized market.

The fixed-price competitive model was not listed among the feasible answers, in order to oblige the firms to stay within the framework of normatively appealing models. We posit that part of the *p-q-ex ante* model and the *ex post* flexibility (totalling more than 50 per cent of the vote) would have switched to this category.

13.5 INDUSTRIAL BEHAVIOUR UNDER UNCERTAINTY

Before trying to start on the daring task of finally assessing the empirical relevance of the models, we want to stress the limitations of our attempt. We tried to gather evidence, wherever we could, mostly on the aggregate level, using *ex post* data. The methods ranged from econometric evidence, using statistical indicators, to survey methods. We used data which are clouded with errors, which cover only a restricted time period, and often refer only to the Austrian economy. And above all the data do not give information on normative behaviour but only on empirical behaviour, sometimes not even on actual behaviour but on subjective assessments.

If nevertheless we try to assess the relevance of the models offered in the theoretical part, we arrive at the following tentative conclusions:

1   The mainstream competitive model with output decided *ex ante* and prices adjusting *ex post* describes only a very small part of real behaviour. This is documented by the following results:

- in the direct survey only 7 per cent label the textbook competitive model as characteristic for their own situation;
- firms report behaviour as if they have considerable market shares and very few competitors (at least at home);
- prices seem to react much more to wage variations than to demand conditions (or demand shocks);
- involuntary variations in inventories and in capacity utilization are well documented; and
- the quantity of production planned and actual production (as well as investment) differs quite a lot indicating that quantity need not be fixed *ex ante*.

2   The outsider-competitive model (which can also be interpreted as fixed price model under stochastic demand or as an attempt to characterize some

166 Empirical information

features of monopolistic or oligopolistic behaviour) cannot be dismissed as easily as it should from the normative viewpoint:

- price rigidity (at least in the sense of reluctance of prices to follow demand shocks in the very short run) seems to be a 'stylized fact';
- inventories fluctuate in response to demand shocks;
- a preliminary decision over quantity and some fine-tuning seems feasible; and
- quantities (instead of prices) are reported to be the main reaction according to the answers of entrepreneurs in the survey.

3 Among the three monopoly models we cannot rank according to their importance:

- the answers in the questionnaire seem to favour the p-mode over the q-mode, but the p-q-mode appears as the absolute winner. Maybe the firms had difficulties distinguishing between price setting and stickiness of prices, and between quantity-setting and adjusting quantities; and
- it looks as if something between competition and monopoly is the dominant feature of industrial production. Two-thirds of the firms have market shares between 5 and 50 per cent. No elegant model is offered for this market position under uncertainty by theory.

4 Quantities seem to be rather flexible (at least as compared to prices):

- the standard deviation of output is larger than that of prices;
- output follows more rapidly on demand shocks (this is demonstrated econometrically as well as in surveys); and
- fine-tuning of quantities seems to be feasible *ex post*.

5 *Ex post* adjustments are feasible but asymmetric:

- it seems easier to revise the production upwards than downwards as documented by the underestimation tendency of sales and export forecasts; and
- this is especially true for investment decisions.

6 The empirical parameters relevant for the production and inventory decision seem to favour starting stock lower than expected demand:

- the profit share is much smaller than the share of value added which has to be used for costs;
- backlogging is feasible and backlogs are usually larger than finished stock inventories;
- inventory-holding costs do not seem much lower than goodwill costs; and
- price speculation does not seem very important as a determinant for inventory fluctuations.

7 Though we do not want to follow literature in over-emphasizing the importance of risk attitude, we have found preliminary evidence that people:

- behave on average risk-neutral for small and repeated decisions; but
- risk-averse in one-shot and all-important decisions.

If these are the correct conclusions for the 'reality' of modern industrial production, it looks as if the results stemming from operationalizations 3 and 4 are at least as relevant for the evaluation of the impact of uncertainty as the dominant proposition 1 or the elegant proposition 2. If price stickiness exists and the asymmetric *ex post* flexibility is a fact, it is very likely that production will be biased downwards under uncertainty. Concave utility functions or a negative third cross-derivative of the profit function would yield the same results, but cannot be tested easily by empirical methods.

Part IV
Conclusions

14 The Main Findings of the Book

1   Uncertainty theory offers the possibility, that 'cautious' decisions can be considered as rational under a number of circumstances and that real economies are probably working under conditions where these circumstances will hold. We have formally derived under which conditions the optimal value of the decision variable chosen under uncertainty has to be smaller than under certainty – or if the latter is not available under which condition the optimal value will lie below expected demand. If there exists some *ex post* flexibility we can derive from these also the conclusion that optimal anticipations (plans, expectations) can lie below realizations even in the long run (on average). Downward-biased reported expectations can be – and under realistic empirical circumstance are – economically rational.

2   Following the mainstream theory we model behaviour under 'risk' and not under 'uncertainty proper', under which (according to the old dichotomization of Knight) no probabilities can be assessed for the different states of nature. We furthermore assume that the axioms of the Neumann–Morgenstern Utility Theory apply. We made these two assumptions, not because we believe that they are more realistic than alternatives either proposed by Keynesian macroeconomists or by critics of expected utility maximization, but because we believe that these methods constitute the stricter test for the casual notion of the businessman 'that we should behave cautiously under uncertainty'. Nevertheless we try to bridge the gap between standard mathematical theory and (Post) Keynesian economists since we allow maintained arguments of Post-Keynesians (for example, that prices tend to be rigid under uncertainty or that flexibility and liquidity gain importance), to influence the model selection. And if these stylized facts are accepted we can show that Keynesian results can be derived from models even with expected utility maximization. The conciliation will remain incomplete, however, since neoclassical economists will question the rationality of price stickiness and at least defy its importance for normative questions, while Keynesians will think that too much of the assertion of 'totally different' behaviour under uncertainty is lost if they accept the Procrustean bed of expected utility maximization.

172 Conclusions

3 Within the risk models we arrive at the conclusion that the role uncertainty exerts seems to differ qualitatively depending on some *a priori* assumptions. In models where we did not allow an *ex post* control to bridge differences between supply and demand, in which prices do not adjust, and in which unused capacity cannot be disposed of, uncertainty exerts a more substantive effect on the decision, and the direction of the influence could be easily assessed. The same holds true for large one-shot decisions in contrast to repeated small decisions. In models with *ex post* controls the impact of uncertainty depends on facts difficult to evaluate empirically (like third cross-derivatives). We used this finding tentatively to propose a new *dichotomization* of uncertainty models into those with 'severe' uncertainty and those with 'petty' uncertainty. These dichotomizations show some resemblance to the old 'uncertainty–risk' dichotomy and may be used to describe the controversy between Keynesians and neoclassical economists. The decisive criterion, however, is not whether a probability function can be assessed, but whether there are *ex post* controls whose *ex post* adjustment can reduce the imbalancing effects of decision errors.

4 Four sources for the rationality of 'cautious' decisions have been identified:

- risk aversion implies a lower optimal value under uncertainty. The two preconditions – a linear technology and a positive relation between the optimal decision value under certainty and the random variable (dY^*/dX) – are sometimes forgotten in the literature, but overall this effect is well documented. We repeat this as a sort of reminder, we did not follow this path in detail, since it is the very preoccupation of literature with risk attitude which prevented the literature from investigating more objective (technical) reasons for the influence of uncertainty;
- technological concavity proper: given linear utility function, whether Z_Y (the certainty optimum) is concave, linear or convex in the random variable, decides in which direction optimal decision under uncertainty differs from certainty. Technological concavity (Z_{YXX} smaller than zero) may stem from the cost function, production functions characteristics, demand curve, etc. Though this rather general condition can be derived quite easily, it is not elaborated in literature;
- marginal cost of uncertainty: if there is no *ex post* control which closes a difference between supply and demand, the expected costs of these imbalances have to be incorporated. Here a cost component enters the calculation which had not been present under certainty. The results deriving from such models are much more robust (they do not need an evaluation of a third cross-derivative), but, on the other hand, the question of the rationale for this lack of *ex post* control arises. Prices have to be assumed not only to be sticky but also to be identical under certainty and uncertainty; and

The main findings of the book   173

- asymmetrical *ex post* flexibility: if it is feasible to revise a decision during the planning period and if this revision is easier (less costly) in the upward direction, this leads to a cautious first plan for the decision variable. Any of the three reasons mentioned before plus an easier upward revision of preliminary decisions may result in 'cautious' first plans, repeatedly lower than the *ex post* realizations.

5   Perfect neoclassical models with rapid price adjustments, no imbalances, perfect future markets, and total reversibilities tend to produce results with no (or arbitrary) effects of uncertainty. For example, risk aversion may create a downward bias in the competition model under price uncertainty. This can be partly reduced by the introduction of future markets. Models with rigidities (competition with demand uncertainty, *p-q* monopoly, irreversibility of investment, *a priori* fixed capacity) result more often in optimal decisions *lower* under uncertainty.

6   The strongest theoretical pressure for *higher* optimal values under uncertainty operates for input factors. Here technological convexity results from possible higher expected profits in the case of possible positive realizations of uncertain demand. The optimality of 'large' investment programmes in case of uncertainty is grossly at variance with the well-documented tendency that investment plans are on average revised upwards and not downwards.

7   The operationalization of the notion of rational expectations as the conditional expected value implicitly assumes a linear objective function. If the only reason for non-linearity were the risk attitude, this would not seem to be overly restrictive. Since we purport that the main elements of non-linearity may be technological *in the wider sense,* we should try to derive more general concepts of rationality. We derive the concept of economically rational expectations, which incorporate the consequences of errors into the formation of expectations. *Economically rational expectations* are decisions (actions) in the terminology of decision theory. We think that sales' anticipations formed by firms, and forecasts made by macroeconomists are approximations of this concept of economically rational expectations since they are not formed without explicitly or implicitly considering errors. Reported expectation in surveys may now deviate from realizations not due to psychological factors, planning errors, or sampling biases, but due to very economic reasons (one of the four sources as mentioned in chapter 4). Annex 3 demonstrates that non-linearities destroy the main outcome, derived by the application of mainstream rational expectation to economic policy, namely the impotence result.

8   In the standard model of competition under price uncertainty only risk aversion (loving) can distort the decision from its equivalent under

174 Conclusions

certainty. With risk neutrality, uncertainty is unimportant. In the outsider model of competition under demand uncertainty, uncertainty unambiguously biases the decision downward due to the additional cost component of potentially unsold production. This model may comprehend elements of oligopolistic behaviour or may capture behaviour in regulated markets. The price stickiness however – albeit necessary only in the very short run – may be considered to be at variance with the spirit of competition.

9 Following Leland, the literature informs us that in the monopoly model with price as an *ex post* control, optimal quantity is independent of uncertainty. This is not true for a type of multiplicative uncertainty (type B in section 5.3) where price uncertainty decreases with higher price. Here optimal production is lower under uncertainty under quite general conditions (linear or quadratic demand).

In the monopoly model without *ex post* control (p-q-mode), multiplicative uncertainty tends to induce a higher price and a lower optimal output; in models with additive uncertainty empirical parameters decide about the outcome. We argued in the empirical part that these parameters will lie in a range yielding a lower output under uncertainty in this model too.

10 Inventory theory yields a fruitful complement to the one-period models since it takes the value of the imbalances at the end of the (first) period into account. Usually inventory models start with fixed prices, in this case the comparison may be done only with expected demand. The optimal stock on hand (inventory after production and before demand) will lie below or above expected demand depending on the relative importance of costs to profits, of goodwill to holding cost, and of backlogging feasibility *v.* durability.

The results of this part of the book contradict prevailing literature in the following ways:

- we show that the asymmetry of profits to cost (the first are much lower per unit than the latter) creates a strong tendency for small stocks on hand (and also for small production). In the newsboy model this asymmetry decides alone; in a dynamic model it is still a decisive force (together with the other parameters mentioned above);
- we insist that at least in all theoretical models the feasibility of backlogs should be incorporated, its *a priori* neglect biases the results in a very serious way; and
- we show how the implicit prejudice of inventory theory – that uncertainty increases inventories – is far from evident. Most probably the contrary is true. We correct formulae presented in articles and textbooks on the forgotten revenues from backlogged sales.

11 In general – this duplicates a lot of parallel findings in the literature – the results of static and dynamic models do not differ too much. Dynamic

The main findings of the book   175

models bring some additional insights, the results tending to lie between that of the certainty model and the static model under uncertainty (the costs of uncertainty can be partly recovered by repetition). The intuitive notion, that production in a dynamic model must be higher (e.g. Mills 1962) since inventories have a value, is misleading, since on the other hand backlogged demand has a value too.

12   One of the critical facts theory points out and which has to be evaluated empirically is the degree of price stickiness in modern industrial production. Uncertainty will yield different decisions as compared with certainty if prices are sticky, albeit this has to be only a short-term stickiness and partial stickiness. Only if prices are flexible in the sense of immediately offsetting demand shocks do no disequilibrium costs have to be incorporated. We have demonstrated empirically by econometric and by survey methods that:

- industrial prices tend to reflect cost conditions and may be some price signals stemming from international markets, but do not react rapidly to demand shocks;
- prices seem to be less variable than quantities, especially the short-run fluctuations;
- price expectations are not less inaccurate as compared with production expectations (as they should be if the prices were an *ex post* control);
- price rigidities are at least as dominant in that sector of manufacturing for which a large number of enterprises, their small average size, etc., would suggest more competitive behaviour than for the rest; and
- asked about their response to a demand shock only 20 per cent of the firms in a survey cited price change as primary response.

13   On the other hand, quantities seem to be more flexible than assumed in most models, be it that production is an *ex post* control or be it that a preliminary production can be decided upon. Then, after demand is revealed, the decision variable can be partially adjusted (*ex post* flexibility); as indicators for a partial adjustment of quantities with a remaining part of disequilibria we found:

- the capacity utilization of industry as well as the inventory sales ratio fluctuates to a considerable extent, and surveys tell us that firms do consider these fluctuations as involuntary;
- output volume follows demand shocks closer than prices; and
- asked about reaction to demand shocks, 56 per cent of the firms labelled quantity changes a primary response, and 48 per cent reported changes in inventories (part of the disequilibrium is maintained).

14   In general, *ex post* flexibility seems to be greater than suggested in standard models. The distinction between *ex ante* variables, which have to be decided before the veil of uncertainty is lifted and *ex post* variables, which have to be decided (or which adjust) thereafter is not watertight.

176 *Conclusions*

However, *ex post* flexibility of quantities seems easier than that of prices (in contradiction to theoretical assumptions).

15   *Ex post* flexibility seems easier upwards than downwards. This seems especially true for input decisions, where this tendency for reported investment anticipations can easily be demonstrated on the micro and macro level. This asymmetry overcomes the theoretical tendency of uncertainty to increase optimal investment. From the theoretical viewpoint this source of bias is not very attractive. To model an asymmetry sounds *ad hoc*, if it is empirically true, the theoretical implications are trivial.

16   The mainstream model of competition with price uncertainty is exposed as an outsider in a real economy. Only 7 per cent of the firms consider it as relevant to their situation; a monopoly model with price as *ex post* control is chosen by 16 per cent. The remaining majority reported that prices are not an *ex post* control; quantity-setting and a partial *ex post* adjustment of the quantity set are considered as the most realistic models.

17   If we should draw a picture of a standard 'representative firm' in modern industry we would do so in the following way: industrial firms have to decide on a preliminary production, they set up a cost price (or accept a market price). In case of demand shocks, output is partly adjusted, partly backlogs and/or inventories are changed, prices change slowly and in response to large stocks. Adjusting quantities upwards is easier/less costly than adjusting them downwards. At least sources three and four (marginal cost of uncertainty and asymmetric *ex post* flexibility) usually tend to bias (preliminary) decision under uncertainty downwards, technological concavity may add some other source of asymmetry.

18   Risk attitude is the most popular channel in the literature but most difficult to assess. If the results of entrepreneurs in a survey may be considered reliable, it looks as if entrepreneurs behaved as if they were risk-neutral for small, repeated decisions and risk-averse for large, one-shot decisions.

19   Optimal starting stocks depend positively on the profits, goodwill costs and the durability of stocks, and negatively on production costs, holding costs, backlogging facility and the discounting factor. In the empirical part we showed that:

- profits are much lower than production costs;
- firms allow their inventories more frequently to go down than to pile up; and
- backlogged demand – as measured by order stock – is much higher than finished-good inventories.

These empirical facts would indicate that optimal stocks on hand should decrease with uncertainty and lie on average below expected demand.

20   Inventory fluctuations are shown to conform with the main features of the models presented. Profits are shown to be an important determinant, price speculation not (hinting that inventories' fluctuation does not result from optimizing activity, rather they are a disequilibrium phenomenon). Inventories declined, in a period of presumed greater uncertainty and backlogs increased.

21   We arrive at the conclusion that the dominant dichotomization of uncertainty literature into 'risk' and 'uncertainty proper' (according to the criterion whether probability functions about the uncertainty variable can be formed or not) is not very fruitful, since in the latter case only very crude rules of behaviour can be derived in a coherent and consistent way. The Keynesian view, that economic decisions are done in an environment much more complex than in an optimization problem where one certain variable is substituted by one for which a probability function is known, is nevertheless a useful warning. That no probability function can be assessed (or used implicitly) is an extreme alternative however, and precludes the economic analysis of a large area of economic problems.

We believe that it is important how the decision model is constructed, whether the importance of uncertainty will be considerable or minor, not whether we assume that probabilities can be assessed. If we construct models in which disequilibria exist and are not instantaneously closed by some *ex post* control, if we model the decision process as choosing between alternative techniques and degrees of flexibility, then we can use Neumann–Morgenstern's expected utility theory in general and probability functions and nevertheless describe a situation in which people behave 'qualitatively differently' under certainty and uncertainty.

We tentatively propose that the real divide between uncertainty that matters and uncertainty with less consequences is whether there are chances to correct a decision (or at least to make errors in some way unimportant). This correction can either be a two-stage optimization process (short-run optimization for a given long-term optimization, e.g. for labour and capital), or it can be that the market price adjusts automatically yielding equilibrium for any quantity decision or that goods are durable so that unsold production can be used in the next period. We propose to label situations in which such adjustments are feasible as *'petty' uncertainty,* since the importance of uncertainty is mitigated to a large extent by these strategies. Models in which there are less strategies for *ex post* adjustments are labelled as *'severe' uncertainty,* since they usually result in disequilibria with important medium- or long-run consequences.

178   Conclusions

22   We want to stress some limitations of our book:

- we assumed expected utility maximization (EUM). Assuming other models may lead to divergent results, we still think that EUM is a strong test for our findings;
- in the theoretical part a whole variety of models had to be presented, many could have been added;
- we were concerned only with the optimization for the individual firm and did not derive consequences for industry or total economy;
- especially modelling *ex post* flexibility showed a large discrepancy between models available and their presumed empirical importance. Work has to be done, especially in simultaneously deciding the optimal degree of flexibility and the optimal decision;
- out of inventory models we had to make some rather restrictive assumptions like infinite horizon, i.i.d. demand, fixed prices, (sometimes) linear cost, and the absence of delivery lags;
- in the empirical part we had to concentrate on some crucial issues, among them price stickiness and inventory behaviour, empirical importance of disequilibria;
- as sources of information we had to rely on econometric analysis of aggregate data, on surveys and market results. Problems of aggregation of differences between individual optimization market results have to be assumed as not dramatically changing our result; and
- sometimes information was restricted to Austrian data; but wherever possible we used information from the USA, Japan and countries of the European Community.

23   If we want to sum up the results of this book in one paragraph – bearing in mind the limitations presented – we think that the theoretical feasibility of cautious production under uncertainty may for realistic conditions of industrial production come into effect due to price stickiness, disequilibria, backlogs and *ex post* flexibility. Production will most probably be *lower* under *uncertainty* than under certainty, this will be true *a fortiori* for optimal preliminary plans in a world of easier upward revision. *Economically* rational expectations may well persistently lie below actual outcomes.

Appendix 1 Schedule of Repeatedly Used Symbols

π	profit
U	utility
Z	argument of utility function (e.g. profit)
X	random variable; $EX = X_0$ (value of variable(s) under uncertainty)
Y	action variable
$\hat{Y}, Y^*$	optimal decision under uncertainty or certainty, respectively
U_{YXX}, Z_{YXX}	suffixes signify partial derivatives
p	price ($\tilde{p} = p + g$: extended opportunity costs = price + goodwill costs); $p \geq c$; $p \geq c'(q)$
$c(q)$	production costs (c' = marginal costs, c'' = 2nd derivation with respect to q; c = constant unit costs)
c_1, c_2	costs of lowering and increasing output *ex post*
x, q, s	demanded, produced, sold quantity
$y = q + I$	starting stock (inventory after production and ordering, before demand)
I	initial stock (= inventory before production or order. Calculated from the flow maintenance equation ($y_{t-1} - x_{t-1} = I_t$) in case of complete order backlog and durability of goods
E	expectation operator
$f(\cdot)$	density function (symmetrical, smoothly differentiable); if $f(\cdot)$ is used in demand function (e.g. section 5.3), then $\varrho(\cdot)$ is used as density function
$F(\cdot)$	distribution function of $f(\cdot)$, values between 0 and 1
u	random variable (additive and multiplicative) if multiplicative: $E(u) = 1$, $0 \leq u \leq 2$
h, g	inventory-holding and goodwill unit costs respectively
$\alpha = \dfrac{1}{1+r}$	discounting factor (r = discount rate)
$r(x), r(q)$	revenue function in dependence on demanded, on produced quantity

Appendix 1

a, b	durability parameter ($a=1$ for durable goods, $a=0$ for perishable goods) or loyalty parameter $b=1$ if demand can be backlogged in full, $b=0$ if it is completely lost = lost sales case). In chapter 8, a and b show the technical possibility of *ex post* revision of production plans downwards or upwards
w, i	wages, investment costs (per unit)
MR,EMR,MC	marginal revenue, expected marginal revenue, marginal costs (with respect to action variables)
N, EN, En_Y	net revenue, expected net revenue, expected net marginal revenue
ϵ	price elasticity of demand
$K, \hat{K}, K^*$	capital stock, optimal capital stock under uncertainty, optimal capital stock under certainty
$L, \hat{L}, \tilde{L}$	labour input, optimal labour input under uncertainty, optimal utilization in short-term profit function
σ, μ, θ	elasticity of substitution, scale parameter, capacity utilization (θ optimal for maximization of short-term profit function)
$F(K,L)$	production function
AM, S	arithmetic mean, standard deviation
R, R^2, DW	correlation coefficient, determination coefficient, Durbin-Watson
$R1, R4, R$	relative difference of 1st order, 4th order (i.e. given quarterly data, previous year's rate of change), $R=R4$ if quarterly data used, $R=R1$ if annual data used
LI, LB	inventory investment, inventory level
*,**	significant at 95, 99 per cent (in the context of statistical tests)
(. . .)	values in brackets under regression coefficient are *t*-values

Where symbols are used in one part of the text only, explanations are given there.

Appendix 2 Business Surveys as Sources of Information

A2.1 INTRODUCTION

In this study we have made very intensive use of business surveys to gain information about economic (business) operations. The literature on surveys, their advantages and disadvantages and on the various surveying and evaluation techniques is extensive; we neither intend to repeat nor to summarize it here. We merely want to give a brief description and assessment of this relatively new source of economic information, which has now spread over most industrialized countries.

A2.2 TYPES OF SURVEY

Business surveys have been collected for decades by various agencies in various countries. Usually they are not conducted by the central statistical agency but by some private or semi-private institution (research institute, interest group, business association). One of the oldest, has been conducted by a railroad shippers agency in the midwest of the USA, and was used to discuss the matter of regressive expectation in economic literature. Today maybe the most oft-cited one in academic journals, is Livingston's price forecast (conducted by a journalist in Philadelphia, USA).
  The most widely spread method of investigation today is the so-called 'qualitative business test' which originated from the IFO institute in Munich and which has spread over forty countries in the world, partly through the help of biannual international conferences (CIRET Conferences, named after the Centre for International Research on Business Tendencies in Munich). These surveys usually ask firms for an evaluation of orders, inventories and capacity as well as expectation on prices and production volume. The question are categorical, that means three categories of answers are supplied (high/normal/low or rising/about the same/ declining). The success of this type is due to its relative low costs, the rapid availability of the results and the predictive power of the series,

especially for turning points. The OECD has recently incorporated these qualitative data into its set of short-term cyclical indicators. The qualitative information is complemented by quantitative surveys (sometimes labelled investment tests) in which data on investment, sales, and inventories are collected. In contrast to publications by central statistical offices, anticipations can be asked also for quick evaluations before final balance-sheet data are available.

Occasional special surveys elicit information concerning specific subjects: for example, behaviour under uncertainty. In these special surveys the decision framework can be more specifically modelled than in standard surveys. This source of data comes near to the experiments used in decision theory, though the number of respondents is usually far greater here and the questions more general than in experiments.

A2.3 ASSESSMENT OF RESULTS OF BUSINESS SURVEYS

From the statistical point of view some misgivings may be roused concerning the information value of surveys, first, about the choice of firms (determination of the reporting units, weighting) and, second, about the utilization of the results (problems of aggregation, balancing, assignment of a linear relation between response percentage shares and percentage changes in, for example, output). Conversely, there exists plain evidence that survey results are able to signal cyclical trends sooner than official data and than econometric functions, but at any rate explain, in conjunction with 'objective' variables, the economic development more completely. This may have something to do with the fact that the econometric methods also miss out on some of the model specific requirement conditions (coverage of all-important variables, structural constancy, behaviour of the error term, etc.).

Beside the statistical considerations, two more arguments militate against surveys, and they cannot be set aside even given perfect surveying procedures and the most complicated techniques of evaluation. The first is the problem that the businessman, in answering surveys, might not detail his actual motivations but may give rationalizations of his actions. This objection was most succinctly formulated by Machlup (1966, p. 57) when defending the marginal theory against the objections arising in the wake of the Hall & Hitch (1939) survey: 'Matters of business policy are extraordinarily difficult to investigate, because the businessman will usually be very much concerned to prove by his answers that he is intelligent, well informed and fair.'

A further objection related to this argument of *ex post* rationalization is the rejection of polls by many followers of REH for the reason that answers to questionnaires have no consequences (in contrast to transactions in the stockmarket).

Appendix 2   183

In the study presented here the method was followed – roughly parallel to Nowotny *et al.* (1978) – of utilizing surveys to augment econometric analyses or statistical analyses of 'official' data, under the working assumption that all these sources would supplement each other in their information value. To gain background information and for ascertaining the subjective assessments of entrepreneurs, for arriving at hypotheses and in particular also concerning problems of possible asymmetries, information may be acquired from published surveys that cannot be obtained from official data.

Appendix 3 Rational Expectations and Policy Ineffectiveness

One of the main 'innovations' in the literature on macroeconomic policy in the 1970s had been the 'rational expectations' revolution' (see Begg 1982, Mishkin 1983, Carter & Maddock 1984, Klamer 1983).

This literature shows that (a) given a type of supply function where deviation of actual output y_t from the natural output $\bar{y}$ is proportionate to differences of a policy instrument x_t and a somehow formed expectation $\hat{x}$ (equation A3.1), and (b) given the assumption that these expectations are formed according to the mainstream rational expectations' hypothesis (equation A3.2), a systematic variation of a policy instrument x cannot create deviations of output from the natural level (equation A3.3):

$$y_t - \bar{y} = \alpha(x_t - \hat{x}_t) - \beta u_t. \tag{A3.1}$$

$$\hat{x}_t = \int_{-\infty}^{+\infty} x_t f(x_t | I_{t-1}) dx_t = Ex_t | I_{t-1}. \tag{A3.2}$$

Inserting equation A3.2 into A3.1 gives (omitting the information set, I_t, Ex is conditioned upon):

$$y_t - \bar{y} = \alpha(x_t - Ex_t) - \beta u_t. \tag{A3.3}$$

It is well known in statistics that only in the case of linear models is the concept of the expected value a good one-point approximation of the distribution function. We have derived a concept of economically rational expectation for non-linear models in chapter 2 of the book. We supplied a great deal of evidence that - on the firm level - linearity will not *a priori* be the all-dominating case, and here we maintain that this will not be the case on the macro level. But though it was early discovered by Shiller (1978) that the policy-impotence result only holds for linear models, the following literature did not stress upon what heroic assumption this popular 'outcome' of the theory of economic policy had been built.

Examples for articles using non-linear, rational expectation models on a very high technical level are Fair & Taylor (1983) and Dickinson *et al.* (1982), but I have not found a single textbook in which the linearity assumption is mentioned as restricting the relevance of the ineffectiveness hypothesis.

How non-linearity affects the impotence result is easily seen in equation A3.1. If x and the 'appropriate' one-point estimator of x, say $\hat{x}$, differs from $E(x)$, then the use of the instrument x, (even if people guess it on average correctly) does not lead to policy ineffectiveness. y_t deviates from $\bar{y}$ in response to x_t.

$$\hat{x} = \min_{x^e} \int_{-\infty}^{\infty} L(x,x^e) f(x) | I_{t-1}) dx = \min_{x^e} E(x,x^e). \quad (A3.4)$$

$$L(|x-x^e|) \neq L(|x^e-x|). \quad (A3.4a)$$

This is the case if the loss function $L(x,x^e)$ is asymmetric as in equation A3.4a.

This way of introducing 'economically rational expectations' is terribly *ad hoc* and has been used only for demonstration and to show the connection between the macroeconomic policy literature and the matter presented in chapter 2 of this book. For a more thorough investigation we must look at how the supply function (equation A3.3) comes about. Equations A3.5–A3.7 give a supply function, a demand function and a price-formation equation:

$$y_t - \bar{y} = a(p_t - \hat{p}_t) + u_t, \quad \text{supply (when } \hat{p} \text{ is a price expectation} \quad (A3.5)$$
$$\text{whose formation has to be specified).}$$

$$y_t = -bp_t + x_t, \quad \text{demand.} \quad (A3.6)$$

$$\hat{p}_t = E p_t | I_{t-1}, \quad \text{price formation.} \quad (A3.7)$$

Equating demand and supply (forming the solution with exogenous expectations) gives equation A3.8:

$$p_t = \frac{1}{a+b}(a\hat{p}_t + x_t - \bar{y} - u_t), \quad (A3.8)$$

and using the REH, A3.7 gives A3.9:

$$\hat{p}_t = E[p_t | I_{t-1}] = E\left[\frac{1}{a+b}(a\hat{p}_t + x_t - \bar{y} - u_t)\right]. \quad (A3.9)$$

Appendix 3

But

$$E\hat{p}_t = \hat{p}_t, \quad E\bar{y} = \bar{y}, \quad Eu_t = 0, \qquad (A3.10)$$

so

$$\hat{p}_t = \frac{1}{a+b}(a\hat{p}_t + Ex_t - \bar{y}). \qquad (A3.11)$$

Substituting A3.11 and A3.8 in A3.5 gives:

$$y_t - \bar{y} = \frac{a}{a+b}\left[(x_t - Ex_t) - u_t\right] + u_t. \qquad (A3.12)$$

Equation A3.12 is identical, after the appropriate transformation of the parameters with A3.3 ($a/a+b = \alpha; \frac{a}{a+b} - 1 = \beta$).

Where do we have to insert the asymmetry (the non-linearity)? the best way to insert the asymmetry is the demand function (A3.6). The policy instrument influences demand in a way not exactly known (there fore we add an error term v), this random variable is asymmetric. If the policy is expansionary, the positive effect on demand is less than if it is restrictive. That downward sensibility is greater may be due to certain arguments in this book (technological concavity, marginal costs of uncertainty, asymmetric *ex post* flexibility), maybe to some Keynesian arguments or maybe due to the possibility of bankruptcy.

$$y_t = -bp_t + x_t + v_t \quad Ev = -\epsilon \neq 0 \text{ cov }(x,v) \neq 0. \qquad (A3.6a)$$

Equating demand (equation A3.6a) and supply (equation A3.5) gives:

$$p_t = \frac{a\hat{p}_t + x_t - u_t + v_t - \bar{y}}{a+b}. \qquad (A3.8a)$$

$$\hat{p}_t = E[p_t | I_{t-1}] = E\left[\frac{a\hat{p} + x_t - u_t + v_t - \bar{y}}{a+b}\right].$$

But $E\hat{p}_t = \hat{p}_t, \quad E\bar{y} = \bar{y}, \quad Eu_t = 0, \quad Ev_t = -\epsilon.$ \qquad (A3.10a)

$$\hat{p}_t = \frac{1}{a+b}(a\hat{p}_t + Ex_t - \bar{y} - \epsilon). \qquad (A3.11a)$$

$$y_t - \bar{y} = \frac{a}{a+b}[x_t - Ex_t - u_t + \epsilon + v_t] + u_t. \qquad (A3.12a)$$

Since ϵ is not independent of x (remember cov $(x,v) \neq 0$), the deviation of actual output from the natural depends on a variation of policy. While the policy parameter is well perceived by people ($x_t = \mathrm{E}x_t$), its effects may be asymmetric and economically rational agents will know this. However evident the result is for anybody familiar with statistical concepts, the demonstration seemed necessary since textbooks forgot to mention the restrictive assumption of linearity.

Appendix 4 Categorization of the Literature with Regard to Backlogging

A tiny but hopefully representative part of the immense literature on optimal inventory stock is surveyed in table A4.1. We tried to classify the articles and books into four groups depending on their treatment of backlogs.

1 The first group wants to study the LS case and explicitly assumes that backlogging is not possible (e.g. Karlin 1958, Zabel 1972). This may create unrealistic models from the empirical point of view, but is a methodologically correct procedure.

2 The second group – which seems the largest – implicitly assumes the LS case. This is an omission and even a serious omission if the authors authoritatively pronounce their formula as an 'important' and 'well-known' result of inventory theory, without confessing that it simply depends on the implicit LS assumption. The result, that uncertainty 'naturally' increases the optimal inventory level or that a high service level is an unambiguous economic target, depends crucially on the implicit non-backlogging assumption (see chapter 6).

Examples for such 'serious omissions' are De Groot (1970), Hey (1979, 1981), and Benassy (1982) who presents the conclusion that nearly all of potential demand should be provided for.[1] The omission of making the LS assumption explicit is less serious in papers which try to develop solutions to complicated problems, where backlogging could easily be incorporated. Sometimes, the informed reader can at least guess that the LS case is treated, since the mathematical formulae contain a small remark, that the initial stock (before ordering), x, is assumed to be positive (Dvoretzky 1952, Arrow et al. 1951, Zabel 1967).[2]

3 The third group explicitly refers to the backlogging case and accomplishes this task in a correct way. In table A4.1 we classify only four papers

Table A4.1 Survey on inventory models with special regard to the BL case

Author	Treatment of backlogs; references to earlier papers	Result for $F(y)$ to determine y^* in linear model	Main purpose of the analysis; interpretation of results on the impact of uncertainty on y^*
Arrow et al. 1951, p. 259	EP interpretation with penalty assumed to be 100 times higher than $c+h$ Fry 1928, Eisenhart 1951	—	seminal paper on inventory theory 'The penalty for depleted stocks may be very high: "A horse, a horse, my kingdom for a horse, cried defeated Richard III"' (p. 259)
Dvoretzky et al. 1952, pp. 188, 198	implicit LS (see eq. 3.3) Massé 1946, Arrow et al. 1951	—	a 'general theory' of inventory behaviour (p. 187)
Bellman et al. 1956, pp. 83, 85	EP interpretation: g is a cost (p. 85) Arrow et al. 1951, Dvoretzky et al. 1952	—	application of functional equations to inventory problems
Karlin 1958, p. 136	explicit LS model, Arrow et al. 1951	—	dynamic inventory problem: in an example optimal stocks equal 331 cans while expected demand is 192
Karlin & Scarf 1958, p. 156f. Mills 1959	LS (=EP) and BL, correct treatment of BL implicit LS	—	order–delivery time lags
			effect of uncertainty on optimal price $y<x$ yields a cost (goodwill loss) but $y>x$ yields a positive value of inventories
Karlin 1960, p. 232	explicit BL forgetting ERBS	LS: $\dfrac{p+g+c}{p+g-\alpha c+h}$ BL: $\dfrac{p+g-c(1-\alpha)}{p+g+h}$	demand distribution may change from time to time $Y^*_{\text{BL}} > Y_{\text{LS}}$

(continued)

Table A4.1 Survey on inventory models with special regard to the BL case *(continued)*

Author	Treatment of backlogs; references to earlier papers	Result for F(y) to determine y* in linear model	Main purpose of the analysis; interpretation of results on the impact of uncertainty on y*
Iglehart & Karlin 1962, pp. 128–37	LS and BL, correct treatment of BL	—	optimal policy for correlated demand distributions
Karlin & Carr 1962, p. 162	implicit LS	—	joint optimization of prices and quantities
Mills 1962, p. 117ff.	purports that shortage function allows alternatively LS, EP or BL interpretation (p. 108, 118); if BL is used then ERBS is forgotten	$\dfrac{p+g-c}{p+g+h-c}$	the interpretation of the results concentrates on prices (under multiplicative v. additive uncertainty) multiperiod price and output decision for constant probability of shortage lower than in one-period model (on p. 119, 1:25); shortage is a cost, inventories a source of revenue
Scarf 1963, p. 199	explicit BL, L(y) not specified to see if ERBS is forgotten or not (p. 199); Arrow *et al.* 1951, 1958	—	survey
Veinott 1963, pp. 90–112	explicit BL and LS cases forgetting ERBS for BL case Karlin 1960	—	an inventory policy that permits large shortages to occur persistently will generally be of little value (p. 189) critical quantities for BL and LS
Veinott 1966, pp. 753–5	explicit BL forgetting ERBS	$\dfrac{p+g+\alpha bc-c}{p+g+\alpha bc+h-\alpha ac}$	survey on inventory literature; no interpretation, but formula 3.8 yields optimal stock increasing with the feasibility of backlogging (*b*)

Zabel 1967, p. 196	implicit LS Mills 1962	—	price behaviour of competitive firms
De Groot 1970, p. 409f.	implicit LS Arrow et al. 1951 Dvoretzky et al. 1952	$\dfrac{p-c}{p-\alpha c}$	infinite stages inventory problem no great loss by having stocks unsold even for a long period; implicitly for $\alpha \to 1$, $y^* \to \infty$
Zabel 1970, p. 205	implicit LS (I = non-negative)	—	price behaviour of monopolies
Morton 1971, pp. 1708–12	explicit BL and LS forgetting ERBS	BL: $\dfrac{p-c(1-\alpha)}{p+h}$ LS: $\dfrac{p-c}{p+h-\alpha c}$	myopic rules as approximations to costly calculations $y^*_{BL} > y^*_{LS}$; in the text on the mixed case Morton distinguishes between p and P (p. 1715), which would allow a correct solution, but no P is to be found in the respective formula
Zabel 1971, p. 122	implicit LS Zabel 1967	—	impact of risk attitude on competitive firm
Zabel 1972, p. 524	explicit LS	—	optimal policy with multiplicative v. additive uncertainty

(continued)

Table A4.1 Survey on inventory models with special regard to the BL case (continued)

Author	Treatment of backlogs; references to earlier papers	Result for $F(y)$ to determine y^* in linear model	Main purpose of the analysis; interpretation of results on the impact of uncertainty on y^*
Johnson & Montgomery 1974, p. 53	explicit BL forgetting ERBS	$\dfrac{p-c+\alpha c}{p+h}$	quantitatively oriented textbook in an example $y^* > E(x)$
Hey 1979, p. 160ff.	implicit LS De Groot 1970	$\dfrac{p-c}{p-\alpha c}$	textbook on uncertainty for $\alpha \to 1$, y^* approaches the maximum value that x may take (p. 161)
Nahmias 1979, p. 917	explicit (partial) BL Morton 1971, Karlin & Scarf 1958	—	defines different shortage costs for LS and BL (p. 917), so that the second one may be interpreted to incorporate ERBS
Hillier & Liebermann 1980, p. 529	explicit BL forgetting ERBS	$\dfrac{p-c(1-\alpha)}{p+h}$	textbook since α near to unity (p. 531, 0.995) a very high proportion of potential demand (92.7%) should be provided for
Archibald 1981, pp. 1171–7	explicit BL forgetting ERBS Hadley & Whitin 1963 Morton 1971	—	costs of approximations optimal inventory in BL larger than in LS (e.g. 20% on p.1176)
Hey 1981, p.135	implicit LS	$\dfrac{p-c}{p-\alpha c + \alpha h}$	textbook
Arran & Moses 1982, 190A	implicit LS Arrow et al. 1958/1962 Dvoretzky et al. 1952 Hadley & Whitin 1963	—	joint determination of prices and inventories
Benassy 1982	implicit LS Arrow et al. 1958 Bellman 1956	$\dfrac{p-c}{p-\alpha\alpha c}$	'dynamic strategy may lead to an overprovision' (p. 192) optimal policy under uncertainty

LS, lost-sales model; BL, backlog model; EP, emergency procurement; ERBS, expected revenue of backlogged sales.

Table A4.2 Overall record of twenty-seven inventory models

LS models			BL models		
explicit LS	implicit LS[1]	correct incorporation of ERBS[2]	forgetting ERBS		emergency procurement models[3]
Karlin 1958	Dvoretzky et al. 1952	Karlin & Scarf 1958	Karlin 1960		Arrow et al. 1951
Zabel 1972	Mills 1959	Iglehart & Karlin 1962	Mills 1962		Bellman 1956
	Karlin & Carr 1962	Scarf et al. 1963	Veinott 1963		
	Zabel 1970	Nahmias 1979	Veinott 1966		
	De Groot 1970		Johnson &		
	Hey 1979		Montgomery 1974		
	Hey 1981		Hillier & Lieberman 1980		
	Benassy 1982		Archibald 1981		
	Arran & Moses 1982				
	Zabel 1967				
	Zabel 1971				
2	11	4	8		2

[1]Including the cases where the non-negativity constraint on the initial inventory is given in the mathematical part.
[2]Including the cases where different shortage functions are defined for the BL and LS case, which are not specified so that they could incorporate the ERBS (Nahmias 1979).
[3]Including the cases where emergency procurement costs are defined to be positive unambiguously.

Appendix 4

in this group: Karlin & Scarf (1958), Iglehart & Karlin (1962), Scarf (1963) and Nahmias (1979). Unfortunately these authors were not interested in the special influence of backlogged orders on the actual order quantity (none of them calculated a 'newsboy-type' formula for the linear case with and without backlogging). These papers concentrate mainly on the conceptual problems the backlogging or the lost-sales case implies for the optimality or uniqueness of the solution. Therefore the third column of table A4.1, which aims to present an operational result for the linear case, is empty as far as correct results are concerned.

4 The fourth group explicitly includes the feasibility of backlogging, but forgets about the revenues from backlogging. Backlogging has a cost, namely that the backlogged excess demand has to be produced in the next period, thus that part of the function which incorporates the expected future effects of an initial inventory is not truncated at the point $x=0$ in the BL case, as it is in the LS case: if excess demand is backlogged, it has to be produced in the next period. This is the cost of backlogging. On the other hand, it also creates revenues, namely the properly discounted revenues from selling the goods after the orders (production) are carried out. These revenues should best be incorporated in that part of the function which is usually called the L $(\cdot)$ or G $(\cdot)$ function, which represents the one-period expected losses (gains) from a certain order (production), while the f_{t-1} - or $V(\cdot)$ - term contains the future consequences of an item stocked or backlogged. Iglehart & Karlin (1962), for example, used this way to incorporate revenues from backlogs. Out of the twelve papers and textbooks which purport to treat the BL case, the revenues of backlogs are forgotten in eight.

The crucial consequence of forgetting revenues from backlogs is that backlogging seems to be an unfavourable event and optimal production is increased in order to avert this cost component. On the other hand, if backlogging results in revenues higher than costs ($p>c$), backlogging opens the opportunity to delay the order or production process up to the time where uncertainty has lifted. This decreases the cost of a low inventory, and optimal post-order (post-production) inventory stock should be lower in the BL case than in the LS case.

Examples of papers where the feasibility of backlogging increases optimal post-order (post-production) stocks are Veinott (1966, p. 753ff.), Morton (1971, p. 1708ff.) and Archibald (1981, p. 175ff.).

NOTES

1 Formulae and conclusion: see columns 3 and 4 in table A4.1.
2 There are papers which can be classified neither as BL nor as LS cases since there are neither shortages to be backlogged nor sales lost. These papers assume that

Appendix 4 195

eventually unsatisfied demand is met by emergency procurement. In that case, shortage is met by the individual maximizer (and not by his competitors), but is not carried over into the next period. Authors who allow their shortage function – usually labelled $g(\cdot)$ – to be interpreted in this way and disregard the possibility of future costs stemming from a negative initial stock do not make an error, but they cannot be considered as modelling the backlog case. Whenever there is a feasibility of emergency procurement, we have two order (or production) quantities to consider (the initial optimal quantity and the *ex post* quantity ordered or produced). Here we want to differentiate between shortage costs which cannot be recovered in the next periods (this is the goodwill loss incurred since the firm could not meet demand immediately, even if the consumer finally gets an item during the next period), and the revenues and costs of shortage which accrue from the later delivery (in our model, these depend on the price, production cost, time discount and on the feasibility of backlogging).

Appendix 5 Survey on Firms' Strategies Under Uncertainty (conducted among Austrian entrepreneurs in January 1984, 1000 firms)

Changes in the world economy, changes in the structure of demand, larger price fluctuations and the reactions of economic policy are all often subsumed under the heading 'increased uncertainty'. This questionnaire is designed to supplement the theoretical discussion with practical criteria (*numbers on the left are percentages of firms*).

1 Characterization of uncertainty: '*Uncertainty*' *can have many different faces. Please check which of the following planning situations applies most closely to your firm. If possible check only one* answer:

27.6 In our planning we determine the *price* at which we want to sell and adjust quantity produced depending on demand. Unintended stock fluctuations are rather unusual.

7.0 We plan *quantity* to be produced during the next month or quarter. Market prices fluctuate in a way that we normally sell everything we produce. Unintended stock fluctuations are rather unusual.

15.9 We plan *quantity* produced during the next month or quarter. There is no single market price, but we adjust *our own* price in such a way that we can sell our production. Unintended stock fluctuations are rather unusual.

22.5 We have to plan *quantity as well as price* (or the price is sticky in the short run). Higher or lower demand is reflected in lower or higher stocks of finished goods.

31.1 We plan an *ex ante* (preliminary) production *quantity*, in the short run the price is fixed. When demand is higher we can *adjust production* upwards (or downwards in the reverse case).

Appendix 5 197

2 When comparing two investment projects which amount to around half of your usual annual investment-budget you can easily calculate the rate of return for project A. Project B has high chances of success but also considerable risks.
 The same alternative exists for strategic decisions, i.e. an investment programme that amounts to a multiple of a usual annual investment programme:

for 'small' decisions   for 'large' decisions
36.1 We prefer the project with known rate of return.   53.2
33.7 We prefer the project with *higher chances* but also *higher risks.* 12.4
29.5 *We decide according to the higher rate of return* which the   34.5
      alternatives have, assuming 'normal' economic conditions.

3 Which of the following decriptions fits the present situation better?

57.1 The economic situation is characterized by imponderabilities. The analysis of past developments and market forecasts enable us, however, to estimate a *'mean expected demand'* as well as a rather *pessimistic* variant for which we can assess an estimated probability and an *optimistic* variant which again will occur with a certain probability.
41.0 Uncertainty is so strong that past developments do not offer any clues as to future sales' possibilities, market forecasts are not really useful. The important thing is to be *prepared for anything*, to remain *flexible* and to *act quickly* on opportunities and risks.
  1.9 None of the above applies.

4 Assuming that a firm notices that stocks of unsold products accumulate considerably, and given that slack demand is likely to persist for a while, why does such a firm not lower its price in such a situation?

39.5 because demand would not increase with the lower price
23.3 because competitors would also cut prices
27.1 short-term price cuts spoil the market
  4.4 short-term price cuts are technically unfeasible
13.9 price cuts confuse the purchaser
  6.5 to cut prices according to market conditions inhibits the production planning process
  8.1 our firm normally adjusts prices so rapidly that stocks rarely accumulate
35.9 we produce only on order
30.8 we adjust quantity rapidly so that stocks do not accumulate
  4.9 other . . .

Appendix 5

5 Which of the strategies mentioned do you think is able to overcome the uncertain economic situation?

69.1 opening up of new markets
16.2 concentration on few markets
 1.4 increase in finished-good stocks
 0.6 increase in raw-material stocks
 9.6 switch to production on order
11.4 longer-term production planning
27.6 more flexible production techniques
29.6 improved market information
49.5 higher marketing efforts
15.6 wider product variety
 9.6 decrease in finished-good stocks
 6.8 lower raw-material stocks
21.5 speciality production
 8.2 increase in desired profit margin
11.9 stricter selection of investment projects
13.0 rapid investment plan adjustments
27.8 more research and development

6 Frequently it is difficult to estimate the size of a product's market. If this should be possible for your major product. . . .

How large is your market share?

	domestic	foreign
less than 5%	20.7	65.8
5–20%	30.3	16.1
20–50%	31.6	10.3
more than 50%	17.5	7.8

How many competitors do you have?

	domestic	foreign
only producer	4.8	1.1
up to 5 competitors	39.8	14.9
few large, many small ones	33.0	25.6
many competitors	22.5	58.5

References

AER	American Economic Review
AESM	Annals of Economic and Social Measurement
BJEMS	Bell Journal of Economic and Management Science
BPEA	Brookings Papers on Economic Activity
EJ	Economic Journal
Em	Econometrica
Jb. f. NÖ u. Stat	Jahrbücher für Nationalökonomie und Statistik
IER	International Economic Review
JASA	Journal of American Statistical Association
JB	Journal of Business
JEL	Journal of Economic Literature
JET	Journal of Economic Theory
JF	Journal of Finance
JIE	Journal of Industrial Economics
JM	Journal of Marketing
JMathE	Journal of Mathematical Economics
JMCB	Journal of Money, Credit and Banking
JME	Journal of Monetary Economics
JORS	Journal of the Operations Research Society?
JPE	Journal of Political Economy
JRSS	Journal of the Royal Statistical Society
MS	Management Science
NBER	National Bureau of Economic Research
OEP	Oxford Economic Papers
OR	Operations Research
QJE	Quarterly Journal of Economics
QREB	Quarterly Review of Economics and Business
REStat	Review of Economics and Statistics
REStud	Review of Economic Studies
SEJ	Southern Economic Journal
SJE	Scandinavian Journal of Economics
WEJ	Western Economic Journal
WIFO-MB	Monatsberichte des österreichischen Instituts für Wirtschaftsforschung
WIPO-BI	Wirtschaftspolitische Blätter
WWA	Weltwirtschaftliches Archiv
ZfN	Zeitschrift für Nationalökonomie

200 References

Abel, A. B., *Optimal Investment under Uncertainty*, AER, Vol. 73(1), 1983, pp. 228-33.

Abele, H., Nowotny, E., Schleicher, St. & Winckler, G.: *Handbuch der österreichischen Wirtschaftspolitik.* Wien, Manz, 1982.

Abramovitz, M.: *The Role of Inventories in Business Cycles.* NBER. 1948, New York.

Aiginger, K.: *The Use of Survey Data for the Analysis of Business Cycles.* CIRET-Studies 24, München, 1977.

Aiginger, K.: Mean, Variance and Skewness of Reported Expectations and their Difference to the Respective Moments of Realizations. *Empirica* 2/1979, pp. 217-65.

Aiginger, K.: *Wirtschaftliche Mobilität in Österreich.* Wien, Signum Verlag, 1980 (1980a).

Aiginger, K.: Unternehmensplanung in der österreichischen Industrie. *WIFO-MB*, August 1980, Vol. 53(8) (1980b), S. 403-16.

Aiginger, K.: *Empirical Surveyed Expectational Data and Decision Theory.* CIRET-Conference, Athens, 1981 (1981a).

Aiginger, K.: Empirical Evidence on the Rational Expectations Hypothesis. *Empirica* 1/1981, pp. 25-72 (1981b).

Aiginger, K.: *Die Wirkung von asymmetrischen Verlusten auf die Bildung von rationalen ökonomischen Erwartungen.* IFO-Studien, 1983, Vol. 29(3).

Aiginger, K.: Alternative Empirical Measures for the Degree of Uncertainty. In: Oppenländer, K. H. & Poser, G. (eds): *Business Cycle Surveys in the Assessment of Economic Activity.* Gower, Aldershot, 1986, pp. 125-74.

Aiginger, K., Musil, K. & Sladky, R.: Ergebnisse des Investitionstestes vom Frühjahr 1973. *WIFO-MB*, July 1974, Vol. 46(7), pp. 322-38.

Aiginger, K. & Tichy, G.: *Die Größe der Kleinen.* Wien, Signum Verlag, 1984.

Alfred, A. M.: Company Pricing Policy. *JIE*, November 1972, Vol. 21(1), pp. 1-16.

Allais, M. & Hagen, O.: *Expected Utility Hypotheses and the Allais Paradoxon. Contemporary Discussions of Decisions under Uncertainty with Allais' Rejoinder.* Dordrecht, Reidel, 1979.

Amihud, Y. & Mendelson, H.: Price Smoothing and Inventory. *REStud*, 1983(1), Vol. 50, 1983, pp. 87-98.

Andrews, P. W. S.: *Manufacturing Business.* London, Macmillan, 1949.

Appelbaum, E. & Kohli, R.: Canada-United States Trade. Tests for the Small-Open-Economy Hypothesis. *Canadian Journal of Economics*, 1979, Vol. 12(1), pp. 4-14.

Archibald, B. C.: Continuous Review (s. S) Policies with Lost Sales. *MS*, 1981, Vol. 27(10), pp. 1171-7.

Arran, L. & Moses, L. N.: Inventory Investment and the Theory of the Firm. *AER*, March 1982, Vol. 72(1), pp. 186-93.

Arrow, K. J.: The Future and the Present in Economic Life. *Economic Inquiry*, April 1978, Vol. 16, pp. 157-69.

Arrow, K. J. & Fischer, A. C.: Environmental Preservation, Uncertainty and Irreversibility. *QJE*, May 1974, Vol. 88(2), pp. 312-20.

Arrow, K. J., Harris, T. & Marschak, J.: Optimal Inventory Policy. *Em*, 1951, Vol. 19, pp. 250-72.

Arrow, K. J. & Intriligator, M. D.: *Handbook of Mathematical Economics*, Vol. (1) 1981, Vol. (2) 1982. Amsterdam, North Holland.

Arrow, K. J., Karlin, S. & Scarf, H.: *Studies in the Mathematical Theory of Inventory and Production.* Stanford, Stanford University Press, 1958.

Arrow, K. J., Karlin, S. & Scarf, H.: *Studies in Applied Probability and Management Science.* Stanford, Stanford University Press, 1962.

References

Arzac, E. R.: Profits and Safety in the Theory of Firm under Price Uncertainty. *IER*, February 1976, Vol. 17(1), pp. 163–71.
Bain. J.: *Barriers to New Competition*. Cambridge, Harvard University Press, 1956.
Baron, D. P.: Price Uncertainty, Utility, and Industry Equilibrium in Pure Competition. *IER*, October 1970, Vol. 11, pp. 463–80.
Barro, R. J.: A Theory of Monopolistic Price Adjustment. *REStud*, January 1972, Vol. 39(1), pp. 17–20.
Barro, R. J.: Rational Expectations and the Role of Monetary Policy. *JME*, January 1976, Vol. 2(1), pp. 1–32.
Batchelor, R. A. & Sherrif, T. D.: Unemployment and Unanticipated Inflation in Postwar Britain. *Economica*, 1980, Vol. 47, pp. 179–92.
Batra, R. N. & Ullah, A.: Competitive Firm and the Theory of Input Demand under Price Uncertainty. *JPE*, May–June 1974, Vol. 82(3), pp. 537–48.
Bayer, K.: Die Struktur der Kapitalrenditen in der österreichischen Industrie. *WIFO-MB*, November 1977, Vol. 50(11), pp. 533–44.
Bayer, K.: Charakteristika der österreichischen Industriestruktur–Ein Vergleich mit der BRD. *WIFO-MB*, August 1978, Vol. 51, pp. 297–409.
Beckmann, M. J. & Muth, R. F.: On the Two-Bin Inventory Policy: An Application of the Arrow-Harris-Marshak Model. In: Arrow *et al.* 1958, pp. 210–19.
Begg, D. K. H.: *The Rational Expectations Revolution in Macroeconomics*. Oxford, Philip Allan, 1982.
Bell, S.: *Quantitative Methods for Administration*. Homewood, Irwin, 1983.
Bellman, R., Glicksberg, I. & Gross, O.: On the Optimal Inventory Equation. *MS*, 1956, Vol. 2(1), pp. 83–104.
Belsley, D. A.: *Industry Production Behavior: The Order Stock Distinction*. North Holland, Amsterdam 1969.
Benassy, J. P.: *The Economics of Market Disequilibrium*. New York, Academic Press, 1982.
Bernanke, B. S.: Irreversibility, Uncertainty and Cyclical Investment. *QJE*, February 1983, Vol. 97(1), pp. 85–106.
Blair, J. M.: *Economic Concentration*. New York, Harcourt Brace Jovanovich, 1972.
Blinder, A. S.: Inventories and Sticky Prices: More on the Microfoundation of Macroeconomics. *AER*, June 1982, Vol. 72(3), pp. 334–48.
Blinder, A. S. & Fischer, S.: Inventories, Rational Expectations and the Business Cycle. 1981, *JME*, Vol. 8, pp. 277–304.
Breuss, F. & Wüger, M.: Consumer Sentiments as an Indicator for Consumption Behaviour. In: Oppenländer, K. H. & Poser, G. (eds): *Business Cycle Surveys in the Assessment of Economic Activity*. Aldershot, Gower, 1986, pp. 125–74.
Browne, F. X., Price Setting for Traded Goods – The Irish Case, in Applied Economics, April 1983, pp. 153–63.
Buchan, J. & Königsberg, E.: *Scientific Inventory Management*. Englewood Cliffs. Prentice Hall, 1963.
Carlson, J. A.: A Study of Price Forecasts. *AESM*, March 1977.
Carlton, D. W.: Market Behavior with Demand Uncertainty and Price Inflexibility. *AER*, September 1978, Vol. 68(4), pp. 571–87.
Carlton, D. W.: Contracts, Price Rigidity and Market Equilibrium. *JPE*, October 1979, Vol. 87(5), Part 1, pp. 1034–62.
Carter, M. & Maddock, R.: *Rational Expectations: Macroeconomics for the 1980s?* London, Macmillan, 1984.

References

Christ, C. F.: Judging the Predictive Power of Econometric Models of the US Economy. *IER*, February 1975, Vol. 16(1), pp. 54-74.

Clark, J. M.: Business Acceleration and the Law of Demand: A Technical Factor in Economic Cycles. *JPE*, March 1917, Vol. 25(2), pp. 217-35.

Costrell, R. M.: Profitability and Aggregate Investment under Demand Uncertainty. *EJ*, March 1983, Vol. 93(1).pp. 166-81.

Cyert, R. & March, J.: *Behavioral Theory of the Firm.* Englewood Cliffs. Prentice Hall, 1963.

Daboni, L. et al. (eds): *Recent Developments in the Foundations of Utility and Risk Theory.* Reidel, Dordrecht 1986.

Darling, P. G. & Lovell, M. C.: Factors Influencing Investment in Inventories. In: Duesenberry et al. (eds): *Brookings Quarterly Model of the United States*; Chicago, North Holland, 1965.

De Finetti, B.: Foresight: Its Logical Laws, its Subjective Sources. In Kyburg, H. E., Smokler, H. E., (eds) *Studies in Subjective Probability*, New York, John Wiley & Son, 1937, pp. 99-158.

De Groot, M.: *Optimal Statistical Decisions.* New York. McGraw Hill, 1970.

Diamond, P. A. & Stiglitz, J. E.: Increases in Risk and in Risk Aversion. *JET*, July 1974, Vol. 8(3), pp. 337-60.

Dickinson, D. G., Driscoll, M. J. & Ford, J. L.: Rational Expectations, Random Parameters and the Non-Neutrality of Money. *Economica*, August 1982, Vol. 49, pp. 241-8.

Drazen, A.: Recent Developments in Macroeconomic Disequilibrium Theory. *Em*, March 1980, Vol. 48(3), pp. 283-313.

Dvoretzky, A., Kiefer, J. & Wolfowitz, J.: The Inventory Problem. I. Case of Known Distributions of Demand, *Em*, April 1952, Vol. 20(2), pp. 187-222.

Dvoretzky, A., Kiefer, J. & Wolfowitz, J.: The Inventory Problem. I. Case of Known Distributions of Demand. *Em*, October 1953, Vol. 21(4), pp. 586-96.

Dvoretzky, A. Kiefer, J. & Wolfowitz, J.: The Inventory Problem. II. Case of Unknown Distributions of Demand, *Em*, Vol. 20(3), pp. 450-466.

Dvoretzky, A., Kiefer, J. & Wolfowitz, J.: On the Optimal Character of the (s. S) Policy in Inventory Theory. *Em*, 1953, Vol. 21, pp. 586-96.

Earley, J. S.: Marginal Policies of Excellently Managed Companies. *AER*, March 1946, Vol. 46(1), pp. 44-70.

Eckstein, O. & Fromm, G.: The Price Equation. *AER*, December 1968, Vol. 58(5), pp. 1158-83.

Economic Report of the President. Washington, The Council of Economic Advisers, US Government Printing Office, 1983.

Edgeworth, F. Y.: The Mathematical Theory of Banking. *JRSS*, 1978, Vol. 51, pp. 113-27.

Eitemann, W. J.: Price Determination in Oligopolistic and Monopolistic Situations. *Michigan Business Report 33.* University of Michigan, 1960.

Eitemann, W. J. & Guthrie, G. E.: The Shape of the Average Cost Curve. *AER*, December 1952, Vol. 42(6), pp. 832-8.

Evans, M. K.: *Macroeconomic Activity.* New York, Harper Row, 1969.

Fahrnleitner, J.: *Die Paritätische Kommission. Institution und Verfahren.* Prugg Verlag, Eisenstadt, 1974.

Fair, R. C.: *A Short Run Forecasting Model of the United States Economy.* Lexington, Massachusetts, Heath Lexington Books, 1971.

Fair, R. C. & Taylor, J. B.: Solution and Maximum Likelihood Estimation of Dynamic Non Linear Rational Expectations Models. *Em*, 1983, Vol. 51, pp. 1169-86.
Falkinger, J.: Modellierung der Unsicherheit – Keynes'sche Position. Vortrag für die Tagung der Nationalökonomischen Gesellschaft in Wien 1983. Erscheint in: *Quartalshefte der Girozentrale*. Wien.
Falkinger, J.: Investment under Uncertainty and the State of Confidence. *Empirica*, 1986, Vol. 13, pp. 97-104.
Feldstein, M.: Production with Uncertain Technology. *IER*, 1971, Vol. 12(1), pp. 27-38.
Feldstein, M. & Auerbach, A.: Inventory Behavior in Durable Goods Manufacturing: The Target Adjustment Model. *BPEA* 2/1976, pp. 351-96.
Figlewski, St. & Wachtel, P.: The Formation of Inflationary Expectations. *REStat*, February 1981, Vol. 62(1), pp. 1-10.
Fishburn, P. C.: Mean – Risk Analysis with Risk Associated with Below-Target Returns. *AER*, March 1977, Vol. 67(1), pp. 116-24.
Fitzpatrick, A.: *Pricing Methods of Industry*. Colorado, Pruett Press, 1964.
Fog, B.: *Industrial Pricing Policies*. Amsterdam, North Holland, 1960.
Friedman, M. & Savage, L. J.: The Utility Analysis of Chances Involving Risk. *JPE*, August 1948, Vol. 56(4), pp. 279-304.
Friend, I. & Taubmann, P.: A Short Term Forecasting Model. *REStat*, August 1964, Vol. 46(3).
Friend, I. & Thomas, W.: A Re-evaluation of the Predictive Ability of Plant and Equipment Anticipations. *JASA*, June 1970, Vol. 65(2), pp. 510-19.
Fry, T. C.: *Probability and its Engineering Use*, 1928, pp. 229-232.
Gordon, R. J.: Output Fluctuations and Gradual Price Adjustment. *JEL*, June 1981, Vol. 19(2), pp. 493-530.
Guger, A.: Markstruktur und Stabilisierungspolitik. In: Nowotny, E. *et al.* 1978, pp. 264-310.
Gutierrez-Rieger, H. & Podczek, K.: On the Nonexistence of Temporary Layoff Unemployment in Austria, *Empirica* 2/1981, pp. 277-90.
Hadley, G.: *Nonlinear and Dynamic Programming*. Palo Alto, Addison Wesley, 1964.
Hague, D.: Economic Theory and Business Behavior. *REStud*, May 1949, Vol. 15, pp. 144-57.
Hahn, F.: Die Entwicklung des industriellen Cash Flows 1981. *WIFO-MB*, November 1981, Vol. 54(11), pp. 644-8.
Hall, R. & Hitch, C.: Price Theory and Business Behavior. *OEP*, May 1939, Vol. 2, pp. 12-45.
Hart, A. G.: Risk, Uncertainty and the Unprofitability of Compounding Probabilities. In: Lange, O. & McIntyre, F. (eds): *Studies in Mathematical Economics and Econometrics*. Chicago University Press, 1942.
Hart, A. G.: Anticipation, Uncertainty, Dynamic Planning, *JB*, (Supplement) 1950.
Hartman, R.: The Effects of Price and Cost Uncertainty on Investment. *JET*, October 1972, Vol. 5(2), pp. 258-66.
Hartman, R.: Adjustment Cost, Price and Wage Uncertainty, and Investment. *REStud*, April 1973, Vol. 40(2), pp. 259-67.
Hartman, R.: Competitive Firm and the Theory of Input Demand under Price Uncertainty: Comment. *JPE*, December 1975, Vol. 83, pp. 1289-90.
Hartman, R.: Factor Demand with Output Price Uncertainty. *AER*, September 1976, Vol. 66(4), pp. 675-81.

204 References

Hay, D. A. Morris & D. J.: *Industrial Economics*. Oxford, Oxford University Press, 1979.
Hay, G. A.: Production, Price and Inventory Theory. *AER*, September 1970, Vol. 60, pp. 531-45.
Hay, G. A.: The Dynamics of Firm Behavior under Alternative Cost Structures. *AER*, June 1972, Vol. 62(3), pp. 403-14.
Heiner, R. A.: The Origin of Predictive Behavior. *AER*, 1983, Vol. 73(4), pp. 560-95.
Henderson, J. M. & Quandt, R. E.: *Mikroökonomische Theorie*. (3. Auflage), München, Franz Vahlen, 1973.
Henry, C.: Investment Decisions Under Uncertainty: The 'Irreversibility Effect'. *AER*, December 1974, Vol. 64(5), pp. 1006-12.
Hey, J. D.: *Statistics in Economics*. London, Martin Robertson, 1974.
Hey, J. D.: *Uncertainty in Microeconomics*. Oxford, Martin Robertson, 1979.
Hey, J. D.: Measuring Risk and Measuring Risk Aversion. In: Currie, D. A. & Peters, W. (eds): *Contemporary Economic Analysis, Vol. 2*. Croom Helm, London, 1980.
Hey, J. D.: *Economics in Disequilibrium*, Oxford, Martin Robertson, 1981.
Hey, J. D.: Goodwill-Investment in the Intangible. *University of York Discussion Paper* 46, 1982.
Hey, J. D.: Experimental Investigations into Economic Behavior under Uncertainty. Paper presented to the 3rd Conference on the Foundations of Risk and Utility, Aix en Provence, 1986.
Hillier, F. D. & Lieberman, G. J.: *Introduction into Operations Research*. San Francisco, Holden-Day, 1980.
Hirsch, A. A. & Lovell, M. C.: *Sales Anticipations and Inventory Behavior*. New York, John Wiley, 1969.
Hoffman, A. & Jacobs, W.: Smooth Patterns of Production. *MS*, 1954, Vol. 1(1), pp. 86-94.
Holt, C. C., Modigliani, F., Muth, J. & Simon, H.: *Planning Production, Inventories and Work Force*. Englewood Cliffs, Prentice Hall, 1960.
Holthausen, D. M.: Hedging and the Competitive Firm under Price Uncertainty. *AER*, December 1979, Vol. 69(5), pp. 989-95.
Howard, R. A.: Dynamic Programming. *MS*, 1966, Vol. 12(5), pp. 317-48.
Hymans, S. H.: The Price Taker: Uncertainty, Utility, and the Supply Functions. *IER*, September 1966, Vol. 7(3), pp. 346-56.
Igelhart, D. & Karlin, S.: Optimal Policy for Dynamic Inventory Process with Non-Stationary - Stochastic Demands. In: Arrow *et al.* 1962, pp. 127-47.
Iwai, K.: The Firm in Uncertain Markets and its Price, Wage and Employment. *REStud*, April 1974, Vol. 41(2), pp. 257-76.
Johnson, L. A. & Montgomery, D. C.: *Operations Research and Production Planning, Scheduling and Inventory Control*. New York, John Wiley, 1974.
Jöhr, W. A.: Zur Rolle des psychologischen Faktors in der Konjunkturtheorie. *IFO-Studien*, 1972, Vol. 18(2), pp. 157-84.
Juster, T. F. & Comment, R.: A Note on the Measurement of Price Expectation. University of Michigan Mimeo, 1978.
Kahneman, D. & Tversky, A.: Prospect Theory: An Analysis of Decision Under Risk. *Em*, March 1979, Vol. 47(2), pp. 263-91.
Karlin, S.: Optimal Inventory Policy for the Arrow-Harris-Marshak Dynamik Model. In Arrow *et al.* 1958, pp. 135-54.

Karlin, S. & Scarf, H.: Inventory Models of the Arrow-Harris-Marshak Type with Time Lag. In: Arrow et al. 1958, pp. 155-78.
Karlin, S.: Dynamic Inventory Policy with Varying Stochastic Demands. In: Arrow et al. 1960, pp. 321-58.
Karlin, S. & Carr, S.: Prices and Optimal Inventory Policy. In: Arrow et al. 1962, pp. 159-72.
Karni, E. & Safra, Z.: Preference Reversal and the Observability of Preferences by Experimental Methods. Paper presented to the 3rd Conference on the Foundations of Risk and Utility, Aix en Provence, 1986.
Kawasaki, S. & Zimmermann, K. F.: *Testing the Rationality of Price Expectations for Manufacturing Firms*. Institut für Volkswirtschaftslehre und Statistik, Universität Mannheim, 1984.
Keynes, J. M.: *The General Theory of Employment, Interest and Money*. London, Macmillan, 1936.
Keynes, J. M.: The General Theory of Employment. *QJE*, February 1937, Vol. 51(2), pp. 209-23.
Kirchgässner, G.: Sind die Erwartungen der Wirtschaftssubjeckte ,,rational"?: Eine empirische Untersuchung für die Bundesrepublik Deutschland. *WWA*, 1982, Vol. 18(2), pp. 215-40.
Klamer, A.: *Conversation with Economists*, Ottawa, Rowman, Alanheld, 1984.
Knight, F. H.: *Risk, Uncertainty and Profit*. Boston, Houghton Mifflin, 1933.
Kon, Y.: Capital Input Choice under Price Uncertainty: A Putty-Clay Technology Case. *IER*, February 1983, Vol. 24(1), pp. 183-97.
Koutsoyiannis, A.: *Modern Microeconomics*. London, Macmillan, 1979.
Kramer, H.: *Industrielle Strukturprobleme Österreichs*. Wien, Signum Verlag, 1980.
Kraus, M.: A Comparative Statics Theorem for Choice Under Risk. *JET*, December 1979, Vol. 21(3), pp. 510-17.
Kuhbier, P. & Sauer, A.: Die im Konjunkturtest erfaßten Einschätzungen der Wirtschafts- und Geschäftslage als Indikatoren der Investitionstätigkeit. *Jb. f. NÖu. Stat.*, 1983, Vol. 80(3), pp. 193-210.
Lachs, T.: *Wirtschaftspartnerschaft in Österreich*. Wien, Verlag des Österreichischen Gewerkschaftsbundes, 1976.
Laden, B. E.: Perfect Competition, Average Cost Pricing and the Price Equation. *REStat*, February 1972, Vol. 54(1), pp. 84-8.
Lahiri, K.: Inflationary Expectations: Their Formation and Interest Rate Effects. *AER*, March 1976, Vol. 66, pp. 124-31.
Lange, O.: *Optimal Decisions*. Oxford, Pergamon Press, 1971.
Lanzillotti, R. E.: Pricing Objectives in Large Companies. *AER*, December 1958, Vol. 48, pp. 921-40.
Laughhunn, D. J., Payne, J. W. & Crum, R.: Managerial Risk Preferences for Below-Target-Returns. In: *MS*, December 1980, Vol. 26(12), pp. 1238-49.
Leland, H. E.: Theory of the Firm Facing Uncertain Demand. *AER*, June 1972, Vol. 62(3), pp. 278-91.
Lim, C.: The Ranking of Behavioral Modes of the Firm Facing Uncertain Demand. *AER*, March 1980, Vol. 70(1), pp. 217-24.
Lippman, S. A. & McCall, J. J.: The Economics of Uncertainty: Selected Topics and Probabilistic Methods. In: Arrow, K. J. & Intriligator, M. D., 1981, Vol. 1, pp. 211-84.

Loomes, G.: Different Experimental Procedures for Obtaining Valuations of Risky Assets: Some Implications for Utility Theory. Paper presented to the 3rd Conference on the Foundations of Risk and Utility, Aix en Provence, 1986.
Loomes, G. & Sugdan, R.: Regret Theory: An Alternative Theory of Rational Choice under Uncertainty. *EJ*, December 1982, Vol. 92(4), pp. 805-24.
Lovell, M. C.: Sales Anticipations, Planned Inventory Investment, and Realizations. In: Ferber, R. (ed.): *Determinants of Investment Behavior*. New York, Columbia University Press, 1967.
Lucas, R. E.: Expectations and the Neutrality of Money. *JET*, April 1972, Vol. 4(2), pp. 103-24.
Lucas, R. E.: An Equilibrium Model of the Business Cycle. *JPE*, December 1975, Vol. 83, pp. 1113-44.
Lucas, R. E.: Understanding Business Cycles, In: Brunner, K. & Meltzer, A. H. (eds), *Stabilization and International Economy*, Amsterdam, North Holland, 1977.
Lucas, R. E.: Asset Prices in an Exchange Economy. *Em*, November 1978, Vol. 46(6), pp. 1429-45.
Luce, R. D. & Raiffa, H.: *Games and Decisions*. New York, John Wiley, 1957.
Lund, P. & Rushdy, F.: The Effect of Demand on Prices in British Manufacturing Industry. *REStud*, October 1967, Vol. 34(4), pp. 361-74.
Lustgarten, S. & Mendelowitz, A. I.: The Covariability of Industrial Concentration and Employment Fluctuations. *JB*, April 1979, Vol. 52(2), pp. 291-304.
Machina, M. J.: 'Expected Utility' Analysis Without the Independence Axiom. *Em*, March 1982, Vol. 50(2), pp. 277-323.
Machlup, F.: *Wettbewerb im Verkauf*. Göttingen, Vandenhoek & Ruprecht, 1966.
Malinvaud, E.: *Profitability and Unemployment*. Cambridge, Cambridge University Press, 1980.
Marin, B.: *Die Paritätische Kommission*. Wien, Internationale Publikationen, 1982.
Marin, D.: Wechselkurs und Industrielle Preissetzung. *IHS—Forschungsbericht* No. 188, April 1983.
Markowitz, H. M.: Portfolio Selection. *JF*, March 1952, Vol. 7(1), pp. 77-91.
Markowitz, H. M.: *Portfolio Selection*. New York, Wiley & Sons, 1959.
Maron, P. A. P.: *The Theory of Storage*. London, Macmillan, 1961.
Marshak, T. & Nelson, R.: Flexibility, Uncertainty, and Economic Theory. *Metroeconomica*, April/August, December 1962, Vol. 14, pp. 42-58.
Martirena-Mantel, A. M.: Optimal Inventory Policy and Capital Policy under Certainty. *JET*, September 1971, Vol. 3, pp. 241-53.
McCall, J. J.: Probabilistic Microeconomics. *BJEMS*, Autumn 1974, Vol. 2, pp. 403-33.
McCallum, B. T.: The Effect of Demand on Prices in British Manufacturing: Another View. *REStud*, January 1970, Vol. 37, pp. 147-56.
McCallum, B. T.: Rational Expectations and the Natural Rate Hypothesis: Some Consistent Estimates. *Em*, January 1976, Vol. 44, pp. 43-53.
McCallum, B. T.: Price-Level Stickiness and the Feasibility of Monetary Stabilisation Policy with Rational Expectations. *JPE*, June 1977, Vol. 85(3), pp. 627-34.
McCallum, B. T.: Price-Level Adjustments and the Rational Expectations Approach to Macroeconomic Stabilization Policy. *JMCB*, November 1978, Vol. 10(4), pp. 418-36.
McCallum, B. T.: Rational Expectations and Macroeconomic Stabilization Policy, *JMCB*, Vol. 12, 1980, pp. 716-46.

McFetridge, D.: The Determinants of Price Behavior: A Study of the Canadian Cotton Textile Industry. *JIE*, December 1973, Vol. 22(2), pp. 141-52.
Means, G. C.: Industrial Prices and their Relative Inflexibility. *US Senate Document 13*, 74th Congress, 1st Session, Washington, 1935.
Menezess, C., Geis, C. & Tressler, J.: Increasing Downside Risk. *AER*, December 1980, Vol. 70(5), pp. 921-32.
Metzler, L. A.: The Nature and Stability of Inventory Cycles. *REStat*, February 1941, Vol. 23(1), pp. 13-129.
Mills, E. S.: The Theory of Inventory Decision. *Em*. April 1957, Vol. 25, pp. 222-38.
Mills, E. S.: Uncertainty and Price Theory. *QJE*, February 1959, Vol. 73, pp. 116-30.
Mills, E. S.: *Price, Output and Inventory Policy*. New York, Wiley & Sons, 1962.
Mincer, J. & Zarnowitz, V.: The Evaluation of Economic Forecasts. In: Mincer, J. (ed.): *Economic Forecasts and Expectations*, New York, NBER, 1969.
Mishkin, F. S.: *A Rational Expectations Approach to Macroeconomics*. Chicago, University of Chicago Press, 1983.
Modigliani, F.: Business Reasons for Holding Inventories and their Macroeconomic Implications. In: *Problems of Capital Formation: Concepts, Measurement and Controlling Factors*. NBER, Princeton, University Press, 1957.
Morton, T. E.: The Near Myopic Nature of the Lagged-Proportional-Cost-Inventory Problem with Lost Sales. *OR*, November/December 1971, Vol. 19(7), pp. 1708-16.
Mullineaux, F. J.: Inflation Expectation and Money Growth in the United States. *AER*, Vol. 70(1), March 1980, pp. 149-61.
Müllner, R. & Richter, F.: Bilanzkennzahlen, österreichischer Industrieunternehmungen 1973-80. *Mitteilungen des Direktoriums der österreichischen Nationalbank* 10/1982, Beilage 1, pp. 1-46.
Mussa, M.: *Sticky Individual Prices and the Dynamics of the General Price Level*. Carnegie Rochester Conference, 1980.
Muth, J. F.: Rational Expectations and the Theory of Price Movements. *Em*, July 1961, Vol. 29, pp. 315-35.
Nahmias, S.: Simple Approximations for a Variety of Dynamic Leadtime Lost Sales Inventory Models. *OR*, 1979, Vol. 27(5), pp. 904-24.
Nelson, R. R.: Uncertainty, Prediction and Competitive Equilibrium. *QJE*, March 1961, Vol. 75(1), pp. 41-62.
Nerlove, M. & Zepeda, P. M.: Sales Production and Prices. In: Oppenländer, K. H. & Poser, G. (eds). *Business Cycle Surveys in the Assessment of Economic Activity*. Aldershot, Gower, 1986, pp. 499-530.
Nermuth, M.: Modellierung der Unsicherheit: Moderne Theorie und Keynes. Vortrag für die Tagung der Nationalökonomischen Gesellschaft in Wien 1983. In: *Quartalshefte der Girozentrale*, Wien.
Neumann, M. J. M. & Buscher, H. S.: Inflationsprognosen der Arbeitsgemeinschaft deutscher Wirtschaftswissenschaftlicher Forschungsinstitute: Sind sie „rational"? *WWA*, 1980, Vol. 116(3), pp. 533-50.
Nevin, A. J.: Some Effects of Uncertainty: Simulation of a Model of Price. *QJE*, 1966, Vol. 80(1), pp. 73-87.
Nickell, S. J.: *The Investment Decisions of Firms*. Cambridge Economic Handbooks. Digswell Place, Cambridge University Press, 1978.

Nowotny, E., Guger, A., Suppanz, H. & Walther, H.: *Studien zur Wettbewerbsfähigkeit in der österreichischen Wirtschaft*. Schriftenreihe des Ludwig Boltzmann-Institutes für Wachstumsforschung, Vol. 1, Wien, Orac, 1978.

Oi, W. Y.: The Desirability of Price Instability under Perfect Competition. *Em.* January 1961, Vol. 29(1), pp. 58-64.

Okun, A. M.: The Value of Anticipations Data in Forecasting National Product. In: *NBER: The Quality and Economic Significance of Anticipations Data*. Princeton, Princeton University Press, 1960.

Okun, A. M.: The Invisible Handshake and the Inflationary Process. *Challenge*, January/February 1980, pp 5-12.

Orr, D.: Production Stability and Inventory Variation. *Econometric Research Program, Memorandum No. 15*. Princeton, Princeton University, 1960.

Papadia, F.: EEC DG II Inflationary Expectations. *European Community, Internal Paper*, 1981.

Pashigan, P. B.: The Accuracy of the Commerce – SEC Sales Anticipations. *REStat*, November 1964, pp. 398-405.

Pearce, D. K.: Comparing Survey and Rational Measures of Expected Inflation. *JMCB*, November 1979, Vol. 11(4), pp. 447-56.

Person, M.: Rational Expectations in Log Linear Models. *SJE*, 1979, Vol. 81, pp. 378-86.

Pesando, J. E.: A Note on the Rationality of the Livingston Price Expectations. *JPE*, August 1975, Vol. 83(4), pp. 849-58.

Petersen, R. & Silver, E. A.: *Decision Systems for Inventory Management and Production Planning*. New York, 1979.

Pigou, A. G.: *Industrial Fluctuations*, London, Macmillan, 1927.

Pindyck, R. S.: Adjustment Costs, Uncertainty, and the Behavior of Firm. *AER*, June 1982, Vol. 72(3), pp. 415-27.

Pleeter, S. & Horowitz, I.: The Implications of Uncertainty for Firm and Market Behavior, *Metroeconomica*, December 1974, Vol. 24, pp. 181-93.

Pollan, W.: Der Einfluß des Konjunkturverlaufes und der Fremdarbeiterbeschäftigung auf die industrielle Lohnstruktur. *WIFO-MB*, 1977, Vol. 50(2), pp. 63-70.

Pollan, W.: Wage Rigidity and the Structure of Austrian Manufacturing Industry – An Econometric Analysis of Relative Wages. *WWA*, 1980, Vol. 116(4), pp. 697-728.

Pollan, W.: Einkommenspolitik. In: Abele *et al.* 1982, pp. 163-74.

Poole, W.: Rational Expectations in the Macro Model, *BPEA*, 2/1976, pp. 463-514.

Pope, R. D. & Just, R. E.: Uncertainty and the Competitive Firm: Comment, *SEJ*, 1978, pp. 669-74.

Pye, R.: A Formal Decision – Theoretical Approach to Flexibility and Robustness. *JORS*, March 1978, Vol. 29(3), pp. 215-27.

Pyle, D. H.: Observed Price Expectations and Interest Rates. *REStat*, August 1972, Vol. 54, pp. 475-80.

Qualls, D. P.: Market Structure and Price Behavior in US Manufacturing, 1967-72. *QREB*, 1978, Vol. 18(1), pp. 35-57.

Radner, R.: Statisficing. *JMathE*, 2/1975, pp. 253-62.

Radner, R.: Equilibrium Under Uncertainty. In: Arrow, K. J. & Intriligator, M. D., 1982, Vol. 2, pp. 923-1006.

Ratti, R. A. & Ullah, A.: Uncertainty in Production and the Competitive Firm. *SEJ*, April 1976, Vol. 42(4), pp. 703-10.

References 209

Reagan, P. B. & Sheehan, D. P.: The Stylized Facts about the Behavior of Manufacturers' Inventories and Backorders over the Business Cycle: 1959-80. *Working Papers No. GPB 82-10, Graduate School of Management*, University of Rochester, Rochester 1982.

Reisman, A., Dean, B. V., Salvador, M. S. & Oral, M.: *Industrial Inventory Control*. New York, Gordon, 1972.

Ripley, F. C. & Segal, L.: Price Determination in 395 Manufacturing Industries. *REStat*, August 1973, Vol. 55(3), pp. 263-71.

Roodman, G. M., The Fixed Coefficient Production Process Under Production Uncertainty, *JIE*, July 1972, pp. 273-86.

Rothschild, K. W.: Price Theory and Oligopoly. In: Stigler, G. & Boulding, K. (eds): *Readings in Price Theory*. Homewood, Irwin, 1952.

Rothschild, K. W.: Einführung in die Ungleichgewichtstheorie. *Heidelberger Taschenbücher*, Vol. 212, Berlin, Springer Verlag, 1981.

Rothschild, M. & Stiglitz, J. E.: Increasing Risk: 1. A Definition, 2. Its Economic Consequences. *JET*, September 1970, Vol. 2(3), pp. 225-43; March 1971, Vol. 3(1), pp. 66-82.

Rowley, J. C. R. & Trivedi, P. K.: *Econometrics of Investment*. London, John Wiley, 1975.

Roy, A. D.: Safety First and the Holding of Assets. *Em*, July 1952, Vol. 20(4), pp. 431-49.

Sandmo, A.: On the Theory of the Competitive Firm under Price Uncertainty. *AER*, March 1971, Vol. 61(1), pp. 65-73.

Sargent, T. J.: Rational Expectations, the Real Rate of Interest and the Natural Rate of Unemployment. *BPEA*, 3/1973, pp. 429-72.

Sargent, T. J.: A Classical Macroeconomic Model for the United States. *JPE*, 1976, Vol. 84, pp. 207-38.

Sargent, T. J. & Wallace, N.: Rational Expectations and the Theory of Economic Policy. *JME*, April 1976, Vol. 2(2), pp. 169-83.

Scarf, H., Gilford, D. & Shelly, M. (eds): *Multistage Inventory Models and Techniques*. Stanford, Stanford University Press, 1963.

Scherer, F. M.: *Industrial Pricing*. Chicago, Rand McNally, 1970.

Schneider, D.: *Investitionen und Finanzierung. 5. Auflage*. Wiesbaden, Gabler, 1980.

Schoemaker, P. J. H.: The Expected Utility Model: Its Variants, Purposes, Evidence and Limitations. *JEL*, June 1982, Vol. 20(2), pp. 529-63.

Schramm, R. & Sherman, R.: A Rationale for Administered Pricing. *SEJ*, 1977, Vol. 44(1), pp. 125-35.

Shackle, G. L. S.: *Uncertainty in Economics and other Reflections*. London, Cambridge University Press, 1955.

Sheffrin, St. M.: *Rational Expectations*. Cambridge, Cambridge University Press, 1983

Sheshinski, E. & Dreze, J. H.: Demand Fluctuations, Capacity Utilization, and Costs. *AER*, December 1976, Vol. 66(5), pp. 731-42.

Sheshinksi, E. & Weiss, Y.: Inflation and the Cost of Price Adjustment. *REStud*, April 1977, Vol. 64(2), pp. 287-303.

Shiller, R. J.: Rational Expectations and the Dynamic Structure of Macroeconomic Models. *JME*, 1978, Vol. 4, pp. 1-44.

Shipley, D. D.: Pricing Objectives in British Manufacturing Industry. *JIE*, June 1981, Vol. 29(4), pp. 429-43.

Silver, E. A.: Operations Research in Inventory Management: A Review and Critique. *OR*, July – August 1981, Vol. 29(4), pp. 630ff.

Simon, H. A.: A Formal Theory of the Employment Relationship. *Em*, July 1951, Vol. 19(3), pp. 293–305.

Simon, H. A.: A Behavioral Model of Rational Choice. *QJE*, February 1955, Vol. 69(1), pp. 99–118.

Simon, H. A.: Rationality as Process and as Product of Thought. *AER*, May 1978, Vol. 68(2), pp. 1–16.

Skinner, R. C.: The Determination of Selling Prices. *JIE*, July 1970, Vol. 18, pp. 201–17.

Smeral, E.: Gewinnspannen und Preisverhalten im österreichischen Export. *WIFO-MB*, April 1983, Vol. 56(4), pp. 250–9.

Solow, R. A.: Book Review on '*Macroeconomics after Keynes: A Reconsideration of General Theory*, by Victoria Chick'. *JPE*, 1984(4), pp. 781–4.

Stewart, M. B.: Factor Price Uncertainty with Variable Proportions. *AER*, 1982, Vol. 86, pp. 468–73.

Stigler, G.: Production and Distribution in the Short Run. *JPE*, June 1939, Vol. 47(3), pp. 305–28.

Stigler, G. & Kindahl, J.: Industrial Prices, as administered by Dr Means. *AER*, September 1973, Vol. 63(4), pp. 717–21.

Stigum, B. P. & Wenstop, F.: *Foundations of Utility and Risk Theory with Applications*, Reidel, 1983.

Streissler, E.: Die Bedeutung der Investitionen für das Wirtschaftswachstum. *WIPO-BI*, 1971, Vol. 18(1–2), pp. 5–14.

Streissler, E.: Investment Stimulation and the Hierarchy of Individual Plans. In: Schmitz, W. (ed.): *Convertibility, Multilateralism and Freedom. Essays in Honour of Reinhard Kamitz*. Wien, Springer Verlag, 1972, pp. 49–65.

Streissler, E.: Sozialpartnerschaft und Gewinne, *WIPO-BI*, 1976, Vol. 23(4), pp. 40–50.

Streissler, E.: Investitionsförderung und Wirtschaftswachstum. *Quartalshefte der Girozentrale*, 3/1981, Vol. 16(3), pp. 21–7.

Sweezy, P. M.: Demand Conditions under Oligopoly. *JPE*, 1939, Vol. 47, pp. 568–73.

Sylos-Labini, P.: *Oligopoly and Technical Progress*. Harvard University Press, 1962.

Tichy, G.: Die Bedeutung der Lager für die Konjunktur. *Empirica*, 1/1976, pp. 3–45; 2/1976, pp. 153–96.

Tichy, G.: Austro-Keynesianismus–Gibt's den? Angewandte Psychologie als Konjunkturpolitik. *WIPO-BI*, 1982, Vol. 29(3), pp. 50–64.

Tobin, J.: Liquidity Preference as Behavior towards Risk. *REStud*, February 1958, Vol. 25(1), pp. 65–86.

Turnovsky, S. J.: The Theory of Production under Conditions of Stochastic Input Supply. *Metroeconomica*, 1971, Vol. 23(1), pp. 51–68.

Turnovsky, S. J.: Production Flexibility, Price Uncertainty and the Behavior of the Competitive Firm. *IER*, June 1973, Vol. 14(2), pp. 395–413.

Überlaa, K.: *Faktorenanalyse*, 2nd ed., Berlin, Springer, 1971.

Veinott, A. F.: Optimal Stockage Policies with Non-Stationary Demands. In: Scarf, H., Gilford, D. & Shelly, M. (eds), *Multistage Inventory Models and Techniques*, Stanford, California, Stanford University Press, 1963.

Veinott, A. F.: The Status of Mathematical Inventory Theory. *MS*, July 1966, Vol. 12(11), pp. 745–77.

References

Veinott, A. F.: Lattice Programming: Substitutes and Complements in Network Flows. *Bulletin of the Operations Research Society of America*, 1975, Vol. 23.
Wachtel, P.: Survey Measures of Expected Inflation and Their Potential Usefulness. In: Popkin, J. (ed.): *Analysis of Inflation: 1965-74. Studies in Income and Wealth, Vol. 42.* Cambridge Mass., NBER, 1977, pp. 361-95.
Wagner, H.: *Statistical Management of Inventory Systems.* New York. Wiley, 1962.
Walter, G. K. & Grabner, J. R.: Stockout Cost Models: Empirical Test in a Retail Situation, *JM*, July 1975, Vol. 39(3), pp. 56-68.
Walters, A. A.: Production and Cost Functions: An Econometric Survey. *Em*, January-April 1963, Vol. 31(1-2), pp. 1-60.
Walterskirchen, W.: Die Entwicklung der Lohnunterschiede in Österreich. *WIFO-MB*, 1979, Vol. 52(1), pp. 9-22.
Weiss, L. W.: Business Pricing Policies and Inflation Reconsidered. *JPE*, April 1966, Vol. 74(2), pp. 177-87.
Weiss, L. W.: Stigler, Kindahl and Means on Administered Prices. *AER*, September 1977, Vol. 67(4), pp. 610-19.
Winckler, G.: *Walrasianische und keynesianische Aspekte der Lagerhaltungstheorie.* Wien, Österreichische Akademie der Wissenschaften, 1977.
Winckler, G.: Probleme der Zinspolitik in Österreich. *Wirtschaft und Gesellschaft* 5/1979, pp. 61ff.
Winckler, G.: Das Ende der aktiven Nominalzinspolitik in Österreich. *Die Erste, Wirtschaftsanalysen*, 4/1980, pp. 32ff.
Winckler, G.: Geld und Währung. In: Abele, H. *et al.* 1982, pp. 199-219.
Wonnacott, T. H. & Wonnacott, R. J.: *Introductory Statistics.* New York, John Wiley & Sons, 1969.
Wu, S. Y.: An Essay on Monopoly Power and Stable Price Policy. *AER*, March 1979, Vol. 69(1), pp. 60-72.
Zabel, E.: Monopoly and Uncertainty. *REStud*, April 1970, Vol. 37(2), pp. 205-19.
Zabel, E.: A Dynamic Model of the Competitive Firm, *IER*, Vol. 8, No. 2 (June), pp. 194-208.
Zabel, E.: Risk and the Competitive Firm. *JET*, 1971, Vol. 3(2), pp. 109-33.
Zabel, E.: Multiperiod Monopoly under Uncertainty. *JET*, December 1972, Vol. 5(5), pp. 524-36.
Zarnowitz, V.: Unfilled Orders, Price Changes and Business Fluctuations. *REStat*, November 1962, Vol. 44(4), pp. 294-367.
Zarnowitz, V.: Orders, Production and Investment - A Cyclical and Structural Analysis. New York, *BPEA*, 1973.
Zarnowitz, V.: Process and Performance in Economic Prediction. Paper presented to the 15th CIRET Conference, Athens, 1981.
Zarnowtiz, V.: *Rational Expectations and Macroeconomic Forecasts.* Working Papers 1070, Cambridge Mass., NBER, 1983.
Zimmerman, K. F.: *On the Rationality of Business Anticipations: A Micro Analysis of Qualitative Responses.* Institut für Volkswirtschaftslehre und Statistik der Universität Mannhein, 1984.

Index

Abel, A. B., 92
Abramovitz, M., 127
accelerator-buffer-stock model, 119-23
action variable, prices as see prices, empirical
actions see optimal decisions
additive uncertainty, 50, 51-2, 54-5, 57, 100
Aiginger, K., 12, 16, 17, 26, 96, 148, 160
Alfred, A. M., 135
Allais, M., 32
 paradox, 30
Amihud, Y., 43, 127, 133, 151, 153
Andrews, P. W. S., 135
Appelbaum, E., 140
Archibald, B. C., 192, 193, 194
Arran, L., 80, 192, 193
Arrow, K. J., 67
 backlogging, 188-93 passim
 inventory models, 70, 77-80, 117
 irreversibility, 91
 precautionary motive, 118-19
 rational expectations, 12
 stockholding, 118
Arzac, E. R., 28
assymetrical
 density function, 32
 flexibility, 97, 172
  ex post, 8, 12
  of production factors, 159-62, 166
 goodwill, 133
 inventory reaction, 151
 price rigidity, 153
 profits and costs, 125
Auerbach, A., 119-20

Austria, 178
 competitors, 164
 cost patterns, 143-6
 expected inflation, 17
 finished goods inventories, 128-30
 investment plans, 160-2
 pricing, 135, 136-41, 147, 152
 ratio of cash flow to value added, 124
 regression estimates, 121
 strategies under uncertainty, 196-8

backlogging 8, 9, 105, 107, 125, 129, 174, 175
 and inventory models, 73-5, 77-8
 literature on, 188-95
 see also order backlogs
Bain, J., 153
Barro, R. J., 153
Batra, R. N., 83
Begg, D. K. H., 184
Belgium,
 inventories assessment and capacity utilization, 122-3
Bell, S., 29, 78
Bellman, R., 70, 192, 193
'below target returns' see 'downside risk'
Belsley, D. A., 127
Benassy, J. P., 43, 78, 81, 188, 192, 193
Bernanke, B. S., 91
bias, downward 3, 6, 24, 103
 see also optimal decisions
BL see backlogging
Blair, J. M., 153
Blinder, A. S., 127
Breuss, F., 17

Index 213

Browne, F. X., 140
buffers, inventories as, 118, 119–23
Buscher, H. S., 17
business surveys as sources of
  information, 7, 122–3, 181–3
  results, assessment of, 182–3
  types of, 181–2
  see also individual countries

capacity
  utilization and inventory
    assessment, 122–3
  see also optimal capacity
capital and labour, substitutability
  between, 84–7
  see also investment
Carlton, D. W., 153
Carr, S., 50, 59–60, 65, 80, 100,
  190, 193
Carter, M., 19, 110, 184
cash flow, ratio to value added, 124
'cautious' decision, rationality of,
  172–3
Centre for International Research on
  Business Tendencies (CIRET), 181
certainty, 3, 175
  concept, 11
  'effect', 29
  inventory theories under, 117–18
  models, 37
choice see optimal choice
'choiceless utility', 29
Clark, J. M., 133
cognitive limits of agents, 30
competition under uncertainty, 4, 7,
  38, 41–9, 98, 105, 115, 164–6,
  173, 176
  conceptual problems, 42–4
  non-linear objective function,
    45–6
  non-linear utility function, 48–9
  and demand uncertainty, 46–8
  and prices 134, 136–7, 142, 148,
    156–7, 165
  flexibility, 155–6
  uncertainty, q-mode, 9, 44–5,
    84–7, 98
control see ex ante; ex post
Costrell, R. M., 43
costs
  assymetrical, 125
  behaviour patterns, 142–7

of future periods see inventory
  theory
goodwill, 69–70
holding, 69–70
  inventory-holding v, 123–5, 133
  marginal 10, 97, 142
  and pricing, 135–40, 142–7
  of production changes, 118
  and profits, 26, 123–5
  of revision of decision see flexibility
  of shortages, 125
  stable see inventory models
  storing see backlogging
Cyert, R., 42

Daboni, L., 33
De Finetti, B., 30
De Groot, M., 30, 77, 188, 191, 192,
  193
decision
  process in modern industrial
    society, towards realistic
    description of, 159–67
  assymetries in flexibility of
    production factors, 159–62, 166
  risk-averse entrepreneurs, 163
  uncertainty, individual behaviour
    under, 165–7
  uncertainty, type and mode of,
    163–5
  theory and empirical evidence,
    108–11
  see also optimal decisions;
    uncertainty
  variable concept, 11
delivery lags excluded see inventory
  models
demand
  function in competition and
    monopoly, 42–3, 47, 48, 51–3
  identically and independently
    distributed see inventory
  mean expected, 163
  military, 79
  and prices, 136–9
  shocks, 117, 175
    price and quantity reaction to,
      147–52, 156
  uncertainty, 46–8, 98–100
  without irreversibility, 89–90
  unexpected, 127, 128

demand *(continued)*
  see also shocks
density function, 20, 32, 51
Diamond, P. A., 34
dichotomization, alternative, 6, 8, 103-7, 177
Dickinson, D. G., 185
disequilibrium models, 10, 11, 36-7, 103, 105
  costs, 12
  of monopoly, 59-61
'downside risk aversion', 29-30, 32
downward
  bias, 3, 6, 24, 103
  irreversibility, 90-1
Drazen, A., 27
Dreze, J. H., 12, 27
durability, 8
Dvoretzky, A., 70, 188-9, 191, 192, 193
dynamic
  effects resulting from goodwill and holding costs, 69-70
  investment models, 88-91, 174-5
    demand uncertainty without irreversibility, 89-90
    downward irreversibility, 90-1
  programming, 70-2

Eckstein, O., 137
econometrics and pricing, 135-41, 156
economically rational expectations, 15, 20, 24, 178
  see also optimal decisions
Edgeworth, F. Y., 119
Eisenhart, G., 189
Eitemann, W. J., 142-6
empirical
  evidence
    and decision theory, 108-11
    on relevance of models and range of critical parameters *see* decision process; prices, empirical; inventory
  implications of models, 98-102
  phenomenon of biased reported expectations, 17-18
equilibrium models, 9-10, 103
  of monopoly, 56-9
EUM *see* expected utility maximization

European Economic Community, 178
  inventories assessment and capacity utilization, 122-3
ex ante
  control, 26, 27, 161
  defined, 11
  inputs in static models as, 83-4
  decision towards market equilibrium, 4
  measures for price rigidity, 151-2
  price setting, 42, 164
ex post
  control, 8, 26-7, 31-2, 164-5
  optimal capacity with labour as, 84-7
  flexibility 12, 25, 102, 173, 175-6, 178
  defined, 11
  of production decisions, 4-5, 8-9, 93-7, 159, 161, 165, 167
  reasons for price rigidity, 151-5
  revisions of decision variables, 25
  variable prices, 8
exogenous variable, prices as *see* prices, empirical
expectations, 3, 15
  and actions *see* reported expectations
  expected utility maximization, 28-33, 34, 45, 178
  irrational, 20
  rational, 20, 173, 184-7
  Rational Expectations Hypothesis, 3, 6, 10, 12, 18-21, 23, 31, 182
  see also Neumann-Morgenstern; reported expectations
expected utility maximization (EUM), 28-33, 34, 45, 178
  alternatives, 28-33
exports *see* international trade

factor demand models, 101-2
  see also optimal choice of inputs
Fair, R. C., 185
fair prices, 136
Falkinger, J., 33, 105
Feldstein, M., 63
Feldstein, N., 119-20
Figlewski, S., 17
finished-good inventories, 128-32
firm
  theory and inventory theory, 67-8

Index 215

under uncertainty *see* optimal
   output
Fishburn, P. C., 33
Fitzpatrick, A., 135
fix-price model under stochastic
   rationing, 4, 43
flexibility, 33, 87, 163
   assymetrical, 97, 172
   ex post, 8, 12
   of production factors, 159–62,
      166
   investment, 160–3
   price, 153–6
   quantity, 166, 175–6
   v prices, 153–4
   symmetrical, 97
   see also ex post
Fog, B., 135
forecasts, optimal, interpreting
   reported expectations as, 21–5
France
   inventories assessment and capacity
      utilization, 122
   ratio of cash flow to value added,
      124
Friend, I., 27
Fromm, G., 137
Fry, T. C., 189
future
   markets, 12
   revenues and costs *see* inventory
      theory

gains, value assigned to, 29
Germany, West
   finished goods inventories in,
      129–31
   inventories assessment and capacity
      utilization, 122–3
   pricing in, 140, 150, 154–5
   ratio of cash flow to value added,
      124
goodwill
   assymetrical, 133
   costs, 133
      dynamic effects from, 69–70
      v inventory-holding costs, 123–5
Gordon, R. J., 151
Grabner, J. R., 125
Guger, A., 137
Guthrie, G. E., 142–6
Gutierrez-Rieger, H., 161

Hadley, G., 192
Hagen, O., 32
Hague, D., 135
Hall, R., 135, 157, 182
Hart, A. G., 95
Hartman, R., 83, 84–5, 87, 91,
   101–2, 103
Hartmann-Nickell model, 85, 87
Hay, D. A., 136, 142
Hay, G. A., 135, 140–1, 147
Henderson, J. M., 80
Henry, C., 91
Hey, J. D., 12, 27–8, 32, 39–40, 54,
   74, 77, 83
   dynamic programming, 70
   factor demand models, 101
   fees to participants in experiments,
      111
   inventory model, 126
   lost-sales case, 74
   non-linear objective function, 45
   quantity, 42, 65
   uncertainty, 35, 39, 42
Hillier, F. D., 68, 74, 78, 80, 192, 193
Hitch, C., 135, 157, 182
holding costs, dynamic effects from,
   69–70
Holt, C. C., 19, 124, 140
Holthausen, D. M., 4, 46, 107
Horowitz, I., 27
Howard, R. A., 70
Hurwicz rule, 28
Hymans, S. H., 12, 42–3, 48, 98

Igelhart, D., 70, 190, 193–4
ineffectiveness of policy and rational
   expectations, 184–7
inflation *see* prices
inputs
   as *ex ante* control, 83–4
   inventories, 79
   models of investment, 82–91
   passim, 97
   see also optimal choice
international prices and trade, 18,
   137, 138–40, 156
interpretation of reported
   expectations *see* optimal decisions
inventory/inventories under
   uncertainty
   empirical evidence on function of
      8, 115–33

inventory/inventories under
 uncertainty *(continued)*
 and backlogs, 126-8
 evidence required, 115-16
 finished-goods, test for, 128-32
 macroeconomic inventory
  functions, 119-23
 accelerator-buffer stock model,
  119-23
 assessment and capacity utilization,
  122-3
 profits *v* costs and goodwill *v*
  inventory-holding costs, 123-5,
  133
 reaction to demand shocks, 147,
  149, 151
 reasons for carrying, 116-19
  under certainty, 117-18
  under uncertainty, 118-19
 role of, survey information on,
  123
 models, 6, 25, 67-81, 100, 107,
  134, 174, 177
 backlogging, crucial role of, 73-5
 dynamic effects from goodwill and
  holding costs approximation,
  69-70
 dynamic programming methods
  used in 70-2
 limitations of models, 79-80
 newsboy model, 68-9, 98, 107
 non-linear models, extension to,
  75-7
 prejudices of traditional
  mainstream literature, 77-9
 testable implications of, 125-6
 theory and theory of firm, 67-8
inventory-holding *v* goodwill costs,
 123-5, 133
investment
 decision, 8
 expectations, 18
 flexibility, 160-3
 input models of, 82-91 *passim*, 97
 and prices, 136
 reaction to demand shocks, 147
 risk-averse, 163
 see also dynamic
irrational expectations, 20
irreversibility
 demand uncertainty without,
  89-90

downward, 90-1
isolation effect, 29
Italy: inventories assessment and
 capacity utilization, 122

Japan, 178
 expectations, 17-18
 ratio of cash flow to value added,
  124
Jensen's inequality, 35
Johnson, L. A., 68, 74, 78, 192, 193
Jöhr, W. A., 23
Just, R. E., 63, 66

Kahneman, D., 4, 29, 30, 32
Karlin, S., 40, 50, 59-60, 65, 79, 80
 backlogging, 188-90, 192-4
 demand elasticity, 80
 feasibility excluded, 65
 monopoly, 59-60, 100
Kawasaki, S., 17
Keynes, J. M./Keynesianism, 171-2,
 177
 expected utility maximization,
  30-2, 33
 inventory-holding models, 107,
  115, 117
 investment, 23
 Post-Keynesians, 31, 171
 uncertainty, 10, 105
Kindahl, J., 153
Kirchgässner, G., 17
Klamer, A., 184
Knight, F. H., 6, 10, 28, 33, 171
Kohli, R., 140
Kon, Y., 84, 86 7, 102, 103, 105
Koutsoyiannis, A., 80
Kraus, M., 35
Kuhbier, P., 27

labour
 and capital, substitutability
  between, 84-7
 optimal capacity with, 84-7
Laden, B. E., 135
Lahiri, K., 21, 110
Lange, O., 78, 81
Lanzillotti, R. E., 136
Laughhunn, D. J., 30
Leland, H. E., 40
 monopoly, 12, 97, 99
 models, 51-2, 54-6, 174

Index 217

uncertainty, 7, 65
LEREH (Less-Evaluating Rational Expectations), 21, 22
Lieberman, G. J., 68, 74, 78, 80, 192, 193
Lim, C., 26, 49, 50, 59, 134
limitational production function, 84
linear
  cost-curve behavior patterns *see* inventory models
  technology, 35, 39
  see also non-linear
Lippman, S. A., 9, 12, 39, 83, 126
'Livingston survey', 17, 18
long-term profits, 85, 86
Loomes, G., 29, 33
losses
  minimization *see* safety first
  risk-aversion and, 30
  value assigned to, 29
  see also lost-sales
Loss-Evaluating Rational Expectations, 21, 22
lost-sales case, 7, 73, 74–5, 188, 194
  see also losses
Lovell, M. C., 120
LS *see* lost-sales
Lucas, R. E., 19, 33
Luce, R. D., 32
Lund, P., 137
Lustgarten, S., 153

McCall, J. J., 9, 12, 39, 83, 126
McCallum, B. T., 19, 21, 27, 110, 137
McFetridge, D., 137
Machina, M. J., 6, 30, 33
Machlup, F., 136, 157, 182
macroeconomic
  forecasting, 17
  inventory functions, 119–23
  thought, 117
Maddock, R., 19, 110, 184
Mainstream Rational Expectations Hypothesis, 20, 21–2, 27
Malinvaud, E., 43
March, J., 42
MAREH *see* Mainstream Rational etc
marginal costs of uncertainty, 142
  in competition with demand uncertainty, 97
  in disequilibrium models, 10
  in newsboy model, 97
  recovered, 97
marginal principle, 136
Marin, D., 157
market
  equilibrium, 4, 26, 27
  future, neglected, 12
  power and prices, 148–50
  share, short-term fixed, 4
Markowitz, H. M., 32
Maron, P. A. P., 78
Marshak, T., 95
Martirena-Mantel, A. M., 118
Masse, P., 189
mathematical expectations, 20
  see also Mainstream etc
maximization
  profit *see* competition; monopoly
  utility *see* expected
mean expected demand, 163
mean variance criteria, 28
Means, G. C., 153
Mendelowitz, A. I., 153
Mendelson, H., 43, 127, 133, 151, 153
Menezess, C., 29
Metzler, L. A., 133
military demand, 79
Mills, E. S., 59, 133, 175, 189–91, 193
  inventory model, 67, 69
Mincer, J., 26
minimax rules, 28
Mishkin, F. S., 19, 184
mode concept, 11
Modigliani, F., 119
monopoly under uncertainty, 5, 7, 31, 41, 49–61, 88, 97, 99–100, 105, 166, 174
  conceptual problems, 49–50
  evaluation of outcome of equilibrium models, 56–9
  p-mode, quantity taker, 53–6, 58
  additive uncertainty, 54–5
  Leland's model, 54
  multiplicative uncertainty, 55–6
  p-q, 164–5, 174
  -mode disequilibrium model, 59–61
  and prices, 134, 155
  see also p-mode; q-mode

monopoly under uncertainty
(continued)
  productivity uncertainty, 61-4
  q-mode, 44-8
  price taker, 50-3, 58
    additive uncertainty, 51-2
    Leland's model, 51
    multiplicative uncertainty, 52-3
Montgomery, D. C., 68, 74, 78, 192, 193
Morgenstern *see* Neumann-Morgenstern
Morris, D. J., 136, 142
Morton, T. E., 191, 192, 194
Moses, L. N., 80, 192, 193
multiplicative uncertainty, 50, 52-3, 55-6, 57, 100, 174
Mussa, M., 153
Muth, J. F., 3, 6, 10, 18-19, 23, 26

Nahmias, S., 192, 193-4
negative
  inventories, 125-6, 128, 129
  orders and backlogs, 126-8
Nelson, R., 27, 95
neoclassical economics, 30, 172, 173
Nerlove, M., 17
Nermuth, M., 33, 39
net inventory position, 125, 126, 129
Netherlands: inventories assessment and capacity utilization, 122
Neumann, M. J. M., 17, 33
Neumann-Morgenstern Utility-Maximizers, 6, 10, 30, 33, 34, 171
see also expectations
Nevin, A. J., 61
newsboy model, 68-9, 98, 107, 174, 194
Nickell, S. J., 12, 107
  dynamic investment models, 83, 87, 97
  static, 84-5
  under uncertainty, 88-90
  factor demand models, 101, 102, 105
  multiplicative uncertainty, 52-3, 99
  risk-aversion, 40
  non-linear, 184-5
    equilibrium models, 38
    inventory models, 75-7
    objective function, 45-6

technology, 39
utility function, 46, 48-9
Norway: ratio of cash flow to value added, 124
Nowotny, E., 136, 137, 148, 183

objective
  factors, 39
  function, non-linear, 45-6
OECD, 182
Oi, W. Y., 27
Okun, A. M., 27, 43
oligopoly, 4, 41
  see also monopoly
one-period models *see* optimal output
one-step decision process, 24
optimal
  capacity
    with labour as *ex post* control, 84-7
    under wage uncertainty, 88
  choice of inputs, impact of uncertainty on, 82-92
    see also dynamic models; static models decisions (actions)
  output decreased, 4
    and uncertainty, influence of, 9, 34-40
    see also reported expectations
  output or price decisions, 41-66
    see also competition; monopoly; production
optimism, 163
order backlogs, determination of, 126-8
  see also inventory
output *see* optimal output; production

p-mode quantity taker *see* prices; monopoly
partial
  analysis, 5
  decision models concept, 11-12
  passive situation concept, 12
patterns of behavior costs, 142-7
pay *see* wage
Pesando, J. E., 27
pessimism, 163
Petersburg paradox, 30
Petersen, R., 78

'petty uncertainty', 31, 32, 103–7, 171
Pigou, A. G., 23
Pindyck, R. S., 92
Pleeter, S., 27
policy ineffectiveness and rational expectations, 184–7
'Policy Inefficiency Theorem', 19, 25
Pollan, W., 157
Poole, W., 21, 27
Pope, R. D., 63, 66
portfolio theory, 28
p-q-mode, 164–5, 174
  disequilibrium model, 59–61
precautionary motive, 117, 118–19
prices
  constant see inventory models
  decisions see optimal output and demand, 156–9
  see also empirical
  empirical evidence on, 134–58
    competition and price flexibility, 155–6
    and costs, 135–40, 142–7
    demand shocks, short-term quantity and price reactions to, 147–52, 156
    rigidity, ex post and ex ante, measures for, 151–5
    surveys and econometrics, 135–41
  ex ante, 42, 164
    rigidity, 151–5
  ex post
    rigidity, 151–5
    variable/control, 8, 27, 174
  exogenous, 48
    inflation unexpected, 17–18
    and quantity, 5, 153–4
  rigidity, 43, 100, 155, 175
    measures for, 151–5
    as rational strategy, 31
    short-term, 4, 8
  setting, 5
  stickiness, see rigidity
  -taker, 137, 140–1
  q-mode, 50–3
  uncertainty, 4
    and competition, 9, 42, 44–5, 84–7, 98
    static models, 84–5
  see also fix-price; p-mode; competition; monopoly
probability, 20, 32
production/productivity
  assymetrical flexibility, 159–62, 166
  costs of changing, 118
  decision, 8
    ex post flexibility of, 4, 8, 9, 93–6
    see also optimal decision
  estimation, 18
    as ex post control, 27
  input models of, 82–91 passim
  limitational functions, 84
  reaction to demand shock, 147, 150, 151, 156
  uncertainty, 9, 61–4
  see also empirical evidence; theories
profits, 176
  assymetric, 125
  and costs, 26, 123–5
  long-term, 85, 86
  margins, 136
  maximization see competition; monopoly
Prospect Theory, 6, 29, 32
psychological expectations, 20
putty-clay assumptions, 82, 85, 86
Pye, R., 30

q-mode competition
  and price uncertainty, 44–5
  and quantity uncertainty, 46–8
  see also quantity; monopoly
'qualitative business test', 181
  see also business surveys
Qualls, D. P., 153
Quandt, R. E., 80
quantity, 12
  flexibility, 166, 175–6
  reaction to demand shocks, 147–52, 156
  setting, 5
  -taker, p-mode, 53–6
  uncertainty, 4
    and competition, 46–8
  v prices, relative flexibility of, 153–4
  see also q-mode; competition; monopoly

Index

Radner, R., 27, 30
Raiffa, H., 32
random variable concept, 11
  prices as see prices, empirical
rational expectations, 173
  and policy ineffectiveness, 184-7
  see also optimal decisions
Rational Expectations Hypothesis, 3, 6, 10, 12, 18-21, 23, 182
  strategy, price rigidity as, 31
rationality of 'cautious' decision, 172-3
rationing, stochastic fix-price model under, 4, 43
Ratti, R. A., 63, 84
Reagan, P. B., 127
'reflection effect', 29
Regret Theory, 6, 29, 32
REH see Rational Expectations Hypothesis
Reisman, A., 125
reported expectations as optimal decisions, 15-27, 154-5
  bias, 17-21, 24
  business surveys as sources of information, 7, 122-3, 181-3
  optimal forecasts, 21-5
  results of theoretical models, 8, 97-107
  evaluation of, 97-103
  inventory model, 107
  'petty' v 'severe' uncertainty, 6, 8, 103-7
revenues of future periods see inventory theory
rigidity see price
Ripley, F. C., 137
risk, 6, 163, 171-2, 176-7
  -aversion, 4, 9, 28-30, 32, 35, 40, 163, 167, 172, 173
    competition and monopoly, 45-6, 49, 64
    and linear technology, 6
  -loving/seeking, 30, 35, 39
    competition and monopoly, 45-6, 49
  -neutrality, 6-7, 9, 28, 35, 167, 174
    assumed see inventory models
    competition and monopoly, 44, 46

v uncertainty, 28, 179
utilization effect, 86-7
Roodman, G. M., 63
Rothschild, K. W., 6, 12, 30-1, 34, 43, 153
Rothschild-Stiglitz condition, 9, 36, 42
Rowley, J. C. R., 117, 119
Roy, A. D., 33
Rushdy, F., 137

'safety-first' principles, 6, 28, 29
sales expectations, 18, 119
  see also losses; lost-sales
Sandmo, A., 44-5, 98
Sargent, T. J., 19
Sauer, A., 27
Scarf, H., 80, 189, 190, 192, 193-4
Scherer, F. M., 43
Schoemaker, P. J. H., 32
Schramm, R., 153
Segal, L., 137
'severe' uncertainty, 31
  v 'petty', 6, 8, 32, 103-7, 171
Shackle, G. L. S., 30
Sheffrin, S. M., 19
Sherman, R., 153
Sheshinski, E., 12, 27, 153
Shiller, R. J., 19, 184
Shipley, D. D., 136
shocks see demand
short-term
  fixed market share, 4
  price quantity reaction to demand shocks, 147-51
  price rigidity, 4, 8
Silver, E. A., 78, 125
Simon, H. A., 30, 79, 81, 126
size of firm, 148-50, 161
Skinner, R. C., 135
Solow, R. A., 33
speculative motive, 117, 118, 120, 121
'stable' exogenous variable, prices as
  see prices, empirical
static models of optimal choice of inputs, 83-8, 175
  ex ante control, both inputs as, 83-4
  optimal capacity with labour as ex post control

limitational production functions, 84
substitutability between labour and capital, 84–7
optimal capacity under wage uncertainty, 88
Stigler, G., 95, 153
Stiglitz, J. E., 9, 12, 34, 36, 42
Stigum, B. P., 33
stochastic rationing, fix-price model under, 4, 43
stock
 -adjustment models, 121
 on hand, optimal, 7
 see also inventory models
substitutability between labour and capital, 84–7
Sugdan, R., 29, 33
Sweezy, P. M., 152
Sylos-Labini, P., 152
symbols, schedule of, 179–80
symmetrical
 density formation, 32
 flexibility, 97
 reactions to demand shocks, 150–1

Taubmann, P., 27
Taylor, J. B., 185
technological/technology
 concavity, 11, 12, 36, 38–9, 64, 97, 105, 172
 fact, 127
 in the wider sense, 173
 non-linear, 39
 reasons/causes, 39, 82, 103
 theories *see* decision theory; *ex post* flexibility; inventory models; optimal choice; optimal decisions; optimal output; results; utility maximization
Thomas, W., 27
Tichy, G., 78, 96, 120, 125
trade *see* international
Tobin, J., 32
transaction motive, 117–18
Trivedi, P. K., 117, 119
'true' uncertainty, 10
Turnovsky, S. J., 38, 63, 84, 96
Tversky, A., 4, 29, 30, 32
two-step decision process, 24

Ullah, A., 63, 83, 84
uncertainty, 11
 about demand, 46–8, 89–90, 98–100
 Keynesian, 10, 105
 about price, 4, 9, 42, 44–5, 84–7, 98
 'petty', 31, 32, 103–7, 179
 about productivity, 9, 61–4
 about risk, 28, 179
 about wages, 82, 83, 88
 underestimation of growth and inflation, 17–18
United Kingdom: inventories assessment and capacity utilization, 122
United States, 178
 backlogging, 127
 cost patterns in, 142–6
 expectations, 17–18
 finished goods inventories in, 128–30
 pricing in, 141
 ratio of cash flow to value added, 124
utility
 'choiceless', 29
 function, 34
 non-linear, 46, 48–9
 maximization *see* expectations
utilization risk effect, 86–7

value/s
 assigned to gains and losses, 29
 for decision variables, 17–18
Veinott, A. F., 119
 backlogging, 74–5, 78, 190, 193–4
 inventory models, 70, 74–5, 78, 80, 100

Wachtel, P., 17
wage uncertainty, optimal capacity under, 82, 83, 88
Wagner, H., 70
Wallace, N., 19
Walter, G. K., 125
Walters, A., 142
Weiss, L. W., 153
Weiss, Y., 153
Wenstop, F., 33
West Germany *see* Germany

Whitin, T. M., 192
Winckler, G., 107, 115, 117, 120, 133, 151
Wood, R. C., 158
Wu, S. Y., 153
Wüger, M., 17

Zabel, E., 67, 191, 193
backlogging, 77, 188, 191, 193
inventory models, 77, 80
monopoly under uncertainty, 50
multiplicative uncertainty, 61, 65
Zarnowitz, V., 17, 26, 79, 127
Zimmerman, K. F., 17